D1342903

OH JOY!
OH RAPTURE!

∼

THE ENDURING PHENOMENON
OF GILBERT AND SULLIVAN

IAN BRADLEY

OXFORD
UNIVERSITY PRESS

OXFORD
UNIVERSITY PRESS

Oxford University Press, Inc., publishes works that further
Oxford University's objective of excellence
in research, scholarship, and education.

Oxford   New York
Auckland   Cape Town   Dar es Salaam   Hong Kong   Karachi
Kuala Lumpur   Madrid   Melbourne   Mexico City   Nairobi
New Delhi   Shanghai   Taipei   Toronto

With offices in
Argentina   Austria   Brazil   Chile   Czech Republic   France   Greece
Guatemala   Hungary   Italy   Japan   Poland   Portugal   Singapore
South Korea   Switzerland   Thailand   Turkey   Ukraine   Vietnam

Published by Oxford University Press, Inc.
198 Madison Avenue, New York, New York 10016

www.oup.com

First issued as an Oxford University Press paperback, 2007.

Oxford is a registered trademark of Oxford University Press

Library of Congress Cataloging-in-Publication Data
Bradley, Ian C.
Oh joy! oh rapture! : the enduring phenomenon of
Gilbert and Sullivan / Ian Bradley.
p.   cm.
Includes bibliographical references and index.
ISBN 978-0-19-516700-9; 978-0-19-532894-3 (pbk.)
1. Sullivan, Arthur, Sir, 1842–1900. Operas.
2. Gilbert, W. S. (William Schwenck), 1836–1911.
3. Opera—Great Britain—20th century.   I. Title.
ML410.S95B73 2004
782.1′2′0922—dc22   2004030003

3   5   7   9   8   6   4   2
Printed in the United States of America
on acid-free paper

This book is dedicated to all Savoyards, especially those who have shared their enthusiasm and knowledge so generously with me. More particularly, it is for the student members of the St. Andrews University Gilbert and Sullivan Society, who have made me their president and allowed me to play some of my favourite roles with them. I hope that they go on to derive as much pleasure from G & S as I have over the last forty-plus years. I also dedicate it to the memory of the late, great Kenneth Sandford, whose interpretation of the bass-baritone roles in the Savoy operas was a constant delight and inspiration to me and many others.

PREFACE TO THE PAPERBACK EDITION

The appearance of this paperback edition allows me to present a brief update on developments since the hardback appeared in 2005.

The D'Oyly Carte Opera Company has still not resumed productions but otherwise professional performances of Gilbert and Sullivan are booming. Following the success of Elijah Moshinsky's production of *Pirates* over the winter of 2005–6, English National Opera has brought *Gondoliers* into its repertoire with a production by Martin Duncan, which opened in November 2006 and was reprised in March 2007.

Opera Della Luna continues to delight with its scaled-down and up-dated productions. In September 2005 it added *The Burglar's Opera*, an adaptation of Gilbert's short story *The Burglar's Story*, with songs set to tunes from Sullivan's orchestral output. The Carl Rosa Opera Company goes from strength to strength. It has established a regular annual pattern of a spring tour of the United States and Canada, with *Pirates* as the featured show in 2007 and *Mikado* and *Pinafore* in 2008, summer performances at Buxton, with *Iolanthe* and *Yeomen* in 2007, followed by a UK tour in the autumn. Peter Mulloy hopes soon to add *Trial, Patience,* and *Sorcerer* to the repertoire.

The 2006 Buxton G & S Festival included a performance of *Mikado* in Japanese by the Tokyo Theatre Company and a non-stop performance of the entire G & S canon in thirteen different locations, including a pub, a church, a London bus, a stately home, and the municipal swimming pool. It took twenty-eight hours and eight minutes, creating a new world record which some group of terrified amateurs will doubtless attempt to break ere long. The 2007 Festival programme includes performances from societies in England, Scotland, Ireland, Canada, South Africa, and the United States, testifying to the vibrant state of amateur performance across the English-speaking world.

The current strength and versatility of the amateur scene is also shown by the number of G & S productions emanating from both sides of the Atlantic at the Edinburgh Festival fringe. The 2005 fringe offerings included a *Hot Mikado*, a straight production of *Pirates* from the American High School Theatre Festival, Texas, an up-dated *Gondoliers* about the efforts of George Bush to import democracy to the Middle East, a whistle-stop tour through every G & S role by four performers in eighty minutes and a *Singalong Trial by Jury* with the principal roles sung by members of four British university G & S societies. In 2006 St Andrews University students had great success at the Festival fringe with a *Starship Pinafore* featuring Captain Kirkoran and Little Robocup.

Despite these and many other signs of its vitality and continuing appeal, the work of Gilbert and Sullivan continues to be sniped at by critics and pundits who claim that it is long past its sell-by date. In November 2006 I was invited onto BBC Radio 3's *Music Matters* programme to do battle against two such scoffers, the author A. N. Wilson and the *Guardian* music critic, Philip Henshall, who maintained that the audience for G & S consisted only of those in their dotage. My defence was aided by the infectious enthusiasm of students from King's College, London, speaking about their production of *Gondoliers,* but I fear we will always have to contend with the anti–G & S brigade. As King Gama reflected, isn't your life extremely flat with nothing whatever to grumble at?

On a more positive note, I have become aware of several more examples of Gilbert and Sullivan references and quotations in popular television programmes. An early episode of *Inspector Morse* had the Oxford detective falling in love with a student member of the University G & S Society. An episode of *Kavanagh QC*, entitled 'Briefs Trooping Gaily' featured the Pinner and Hatch End Amateur Operatic Society. A 2005 storyline in *Joey*, the *Friends* offshoot, involved Joey's girlfriend's grandmother playing Mabel in a performance of *Pirates* in her retirement home. Further splendid examples of G & S–inspired eccentricity continue to be reported. I was delighted to learn that Canon Brian Andrews, mentioned on page 123, finished his final service after 26 years as vicar of Abbots Langley by cycling down the aisle of his church dressed as Dr Daly and singing 'Time was when love and I were well acquainted'.

The most moving of the many testimonies to the liberating and therapeutic powers of G & S that I have encountered since writing *Oh Joy, Oh Rapture* is in Kathleen Karr's book *Gilbert and Sullivan Set Me Free* (New York: Hyperion, 2003). It tells the true story of a chaplain in a women's prison in Boston, Massachusetts, in 1914 who transformed the lives of the prisoners by staging a performance of *Pirates.* Libby, who plays Mabel, says that Gilbert and Sullivan have set her free through the experience of working together with others, making decisions, and thinking for herself. The chaplain tells another prisoner who is bemused by the topsy-turvy plot, 'sometimes in life you just have to open your arms wide to the ridiculous. Such is the great gift Gilbert and Sullivan have given us'. To which I can only respond, as Arac, Scynthius, and Guron do as they are about to be thrust into prison, 'Hear! Hear!'

APOLOGIA AND ACKNOWLEDGEMENTS

This is not yet another book about Gilbert and Sullivan, their stormy collaboration, the genesis of the Savoy operas, and their early performance history. Rather it is about their continuing appeal today and the extraordinary enduring phenomenon that they have become.

The pages that follow will be peppered with allusions to and quotations from the Savoy operas and I may as well begin with one because it perfectly expresses the book's theme. In act 2 of *The Pirates of Penzance*, the policemen keep announcing that they are about to go off and do battle with the pirates but they seem very reluctant actually to do so, provoking the major general's somewhat testy remark 'Yes, but you don't go'. Something very similar has happened to the works of Gilbert and Sullivan over the last fifty years or so. Despite being periodically written off as anachronisms by their detractors, they have not just survived but positively thrived into the twenty-first century.

The starting point for this book is not 1871, the date of Gilbert and Sullivan's first collaboration, *Thespis*, where most studies of their work begin, but rather 1961, the last year of copyright on Gilbert's works and the D'Oyly Carte Opera Company's monopoly on their professional performance in Britain. Although I will occasionally venture back earlier to trace a particularly important theme, influence, or personality, my main focus is on the last forty years or so. This is generally regarded as a period during which the appeal and performance of Gilbert and Sullivan's works has been in steady decline. The heyday of their popularity is often taken to be the 1940s and 1950s. The Savoy operas certainly helped to keep morale going during the Second World War—a hospital gramophone playing selections from *The Mikado* and *Ruddigore* was said to be 'worth a double medical staff' in treating wounded soldiers. There are moving stories of productions in prisoner-of-war camps. The book *Women Beyond Wire* describes an Anglo-Dutch choir in a camp in Sumatra whose repertoire included 'Ring Forth Ye Bells' from *The Sorcerer* and 'I Stole the Prince' from *The Gondo-*

liers. Trevor Hills, who sang with the D'Oyly Carte company from 1951 to 1956, cut his G & S teeth performing *HMS Pinafore, Mikado, The Gondoliers,* and *The Yeomen of the Guard* while a PoW in Stalag 383, Hohenfels, Bavaria, between 1942 and 1945. The novelist J. G. Ballard recalls performances of *Pirates of Penzance* and *Trial by Jury* in the camp in Lunghua where he was interned as a child:

> The music was probably played on a piano—I can't remember any kind of orchestra. There was a stage at the end of the dining hall where productions were held. Everything was in full costume. Prisoners of War and civilian internees had vast amounts of idle time and a great deal of ingenuity so it would not have been difficult to assemble scenery and costumes. Gilbert and Sullivan was very popular—I have never seen a G & S production since leaving the camp but can still recite large sections of the libretti—partly or largely because they are so English. My impression is that they were quite elaborate productions. They certainly held me mesmerised. Most of the British internees, nearly 2000 in all, were professionals (doctors, teachers, managers, architects, etc.) and at that time, the 1940s, would have been extremely familiar with G&S, unlike today.[1]

Gilbert and Sullivan remained very popular through the 1950s, that decade that now seems so far-off in its innocence, security, and formality. Their survival through the ensuing decades covered by this book is in many ways remarkable. The swinging sixties and seventies, the yuppified and brutalist eighties and nineties, the fraught and pessimistic 2000s have all challenged their gentlemanly, understated, middle-brow, lighthearted ethos. Yet like the policemen, they have resolutely refused to exit stage left, as they might, on any rational grounds, have been expected to do long ago. Indeed, in many ways, their position today is stronger than it has ever been—certainly in terms of recordings and professional productions of their work. To give just three examples, there are at present nineteen complete versions of *The Mikado* available on CD, around twenty-five opera companies in the United States currently have G & S in their repertoire, and on one Saturday in London in May 2001 there were a total of nine professional performances of four different operas. Two further recent pointers to the renaissance that they are enjoying come from unconnected decisions made by prestigious professional companies on either side of the Atlantic in 2004. In London English National Opera introduced a new production of *The Pirates of Penzance* to go alongside its highly successful long-standing *Mikado* and in Minneapolis the Guthrie Theater chose the same work for its first venture into opera in its forty-year history.

I also have a personal reason for starting this book in 1961. It was the year that my own love affair with Gilbert and Sullivan began—when I first appeared on stage and saw my first Savoy opera (*Iolanthe* performed by the D'Oyly Carte Company at the Savoy Theatre in London). Over the years since then I can honestly say that Gilbert and Sullivan has consistently given more pleasure than anything else. It thrilled me as a teenager in the 1960s much more than the Beatlemania that gripped most of my contemporaries and it enriched my time at university in the 1970s. The annotation of the Savoy operas for publication proved one of my main and most enjoyable extracurricular activities through the 1980s and 1990s, and the 2000s have brought me back on stage as a performer. My wife and I held our eve-of-wedding party in the *Pinafore* room of the Savoy Hotel and I celebrated my fiftieth birthday by taking my family to a charity gala performance of *Trial by Jury* in the same venue. Whether it was such a treat for them as it was for me, I am not sure but they have been wonderfully supportive of, if slightly bemused by, this obsessive in their midst.

Gilbert and Sullivan is for me, as I know it is for many others, a balm, a tonic, and a stimulant. When I am down, it picks me up. When I am tired, it restores me. When I am feeling on top of the world, it lets me express my joy in song. It has, indeed, to quote from the sacred texts again, provided 'joy and rapture' in overflowing measure and also been 'the divine emollient' serenaded in that most hymnlike of all songs from the Savoy operas, 'Hail, Poetry'. It is with a profound sense of gratitude for all that it has done to soften, relax, and uplift me that I offer this book as a small tribute to its remarkable staying and sustaining powers.

One of the many joys of the world of Gilbert and Sullivan enthusiasts is that it is populated with such delightful, kind, and generous-spirited people. I have had huge help from many individuals during the researching and writing of this book. Stephen and Rosie Shipley have given me generous hospitality and warm friendship during my annual visits to the Buxton G & S Festival. The festival organizers, Ian and Neil Smith, have also been very helpful and supportive. Arthur Barrett kindly lent me complete runs of various periodicals and nobly transported them to Buxton for me to work on. John Cannon even more heroically did the same with his voluminous archive of parodies and has been generous in responding to the various queries I have put to him. In the United States, I received considerable help and hospitality from Suzanne Segemark and Kelley Crumlish of the Savoy Company of Philadelphia, Ralph MacPhail of Bridgewater College (who has also read most of this book in draft and saved me from several howlers), and Marylu Stevens of the Southeastern Savoyards. Hal Kanthor kindly made available to me material relating to professional productions in North America, and Gayden Wren has been a rich and generous mine of information on the U.S. scene.

Albert Bergeret of the New York G & S Players, Peter Mulloy of Carl Rosa, Ian Martin of D'Oyly Carte, and Jeff Clarke of Opera della Luna have cheerfully subjected themselves to my interrogations. George Hollis, as well as securing for me the supreme accolade of the honorary life presidency of the St. Andrews University Gilbert and Sullivan Society, has encouraged me in many various ways. I have also benefited considerably from conversations and e-mail exchanges with Stephen Turnbull (who has also read and helpfully commented on several draft chapters), Pauline Smith, Peter Featherstone, Richard Suart, Marc Shepherd, Don Smith, Peter Parker, Brian Jones, David Duffey, John Balls, Sarah-Jane Read, Robin Wilson, John Bush Jones, Robert Wardell, Roger Sansom, Matthew Stanhope, Nicholas Hopton, Andrea Atherton, Philip Corbett, Danielle Ryan, Mike Storie, Geoffrey Dixon, David Eden, Alex Shepherd, John Sheppard and Roger and Rosemary Wild. Justin Bender, Mel Moratti, Stuart Maunder, and Milou de Castellane have briefed me about the G & S scene in Australasia, Robert Binder about Jerusalem, and Lorna Hanson about South Africa.

I spent a wonderful day working in the archives of the D'Oyly Carte Opera Company, flanked by the flute part of *The Gondoliers*, an ancient box from L. Gustave: Wig Maker—Private, Historical, Theatrical marked 'Mr Sandford—Shadbolt', and a Mikado hat inscribed 'Mike Ducarel'. Mary Gilhooly, the archivist, and Ian Martin, the general manager, have very kindly let me quote from this wonderful treasure trove of material and reproduce photographs from the D'Oyly Carte Archive. I have also been greatly helped with illustrations by Chris Wain, Janice Stewart, Pret and Donald Houston, Neil Smith, Mark Luff, Peter Mulloy, Jeff Clarke, Alan Wood, Rod Leach and Stephen Wright. The copyright holders of photographs used as illustrations are indicated and acknowledged in brackets at the end of the picture captions.

I must also record my gratitude to the late Anna Russell, Richard Suart, Norry Leonard, Andrew Crowther, Vera Rich, Leon Berger, Arthur Robinson, Simon Rees, Jim Linwood, Malcolm Sircom, Michael Perry, Richard Sturch, Virginia Bottomley, the late Humphrey Carpenter, and John Dryden Burton, managing editor of the *Anglican Digest*, for allowing me to quote copyright material in the parodies chapter.

I have made every effort to trace copyright holders of material that I have quoted. If there are any errors or omissions I can only plead, like Pooh-Bah, for mercy and give an assurance that they will be rectified in any future edition.

CONTENTS

OH JOY!
OH RAPTURE!

◇

ONE

SOMETHING LINGERING: THE ENDURING INFLUENCE OF GILBERT AND SULLIVAN THROUGH THE TWENTIETH CENTURY

When the Mikado regales Ko-Ko and Pooh-Bah with details of the punishment for compassing the death of the heir to the throne, he terrifies them by saying that although he cannot recall the precise details, he knows that it is something lingering. For both their fans and their detractors, Gilbert and Sullivan have a similar quality.

Even if not a single note of their operas had ever sounded again after their first performance, they would still have had a massive influence on British and American culture. They were the principal begetters of what has almost certainly been the dominant theatrical genre of the twentieth century, and arguably its most distinctive cultural icon, the musical. Without the Savoy operas we would never have had *Fiddler on the Roof, Cats,* or *The Lion King.*

Their pioneering role in creating the kind of show that now fills more than half the theatres in the West End and Broadway has always been more readily and enthusiastically recognized in the United States, where musical theatre is treated seriously as an art form, than in Britain, where it is regarded as rather vulgar. In one of his early television shows Danny Kaye saluted their contribution in verse:

> Once, long ago, before Lerner and Loewe,
>   Before Porter, or Gershwin, or Rodgers,
> Most of the tunes with the 'moons' and the 'Junes'
>   Were composed by two old English codgers.

When the International Gilbert and Sullivan Festival visited Philadelphia in 1996, the local Fox news station welcomed 'a tribute to two of Broadway's most prolific songwriters' and described Gilbert and Sullivan as 'the founding fathers of musical theatre who helped create something called Broadway'. Kurt Ganzl's *Book of the Broadway Musical* is subtitled '75 Favorite Shows from *HMS Pinafore* to *Sunset Boulevard*'. John Bush Jones, the most recent historian of American musical theatre, sees Gilbert and Sullivan as 'the primary progenitors of the twentieth century American musical' and credits them not just with providing the model whereby book, music, and lyrics combine to form an integrated whole but also with 'demonstrating that musicals can address contemporary social and political issues without sacrificing entertainment value'. [1] British commentators and critics have generally been less inclined to make these kinds of claim, but Sheridan Morley does acknowledge in his history of the British musical that 'there can be no doubt that it was Gilbert and Sullivan who had made it all possible . . . in writing the first modern hit songs and in writing them exclusively and specifically for the theatre'. [2]

The modern musical bears the lingering imprint of Gilbert and Sullivan's daring and radical innovations in several respects. Perhaps their most revolutionary achievement was to transform the theatre from the haunt of the dissolute working and drinking classes to a wholesome place of entertainment to which middle class families could safely go without a blush or whiff of shame. In the words of the historian David Cannadine, 'They created a new form of entertainment, precisely pitched between the music hall and the concert hall, which was intelligent but not intellectual, tasteful but not pretentious, tuneful but not cloying'. [3] It is thanks to them that we think of musicals as the perfect form of all-age family entertainment.

As well as transforming the conventions of music hall to make musical theatre respectable, Gilbert and Sullivan also changed the conventions of opera to make it accessible. They achieved this first and foremost by establishing parity between words and music. It is no coincidence that their names are inseparable. They introduced the equal partnership between lyricist and composer that was to be one of the hallmarks of the twentieth-century musical. In that respect, as in many others, Rodgers and Hammerstein, Lerner and Loewe, and Rice and Lloyd Webber are their direct heirs. As far as Sullivan was concerned, of course, the music in the Savoy operas was, in reality, subordinate to the words. Most twentieth-century musicals have been similarly word-led, with the lyrics usually being written first and then set to music.

The Savoy operas further broke with the traditions of both music hall and opera in giving prominence to costumes, scenery, and props. They were spectacular as well as tuneful and witty. Audiences may not have left *Iolanthe*, as dismissive critics were later to suggest they left some of the more extravagant Lloyd

4

Webber shows, humming the sets but they did thrill to the sumptuous colours of the peers' robes and the effect created by the fairies' shimmering wings. With his keenness to exploit new technology in the theatre, Gilbert would have thrilled to the crashing chandelier in *Phantom of the Opera* and the helicopter landing in *Miss Saigon*. In a real sense he prepared the way for these spectacular visual effects.

The other great innovation made by Gilbert and Sullivan was the key role that they gave to the chorus. This established the communal dimension which has been such an important feature of much of the most successful and enduring musical theatre, especially notable in the shows of Rodgers and Hammerstein, in many British musicals of the 1960s and 1970s, and in the global megahit *Les Misérables*. It has also, of course, been a major element in the enduring popularity of the Savoy operas with amateur societies. Gilbert and Sullivan created shows that were about communities as well as individuals and in which it is not just the principals who have the fun and the limelight.

It is noticeable, and not surprising, that among the many practitioners of musical theatre in the twentieth century who have openly acknowledged the influence of the Savoy operas on their own work, lyricists hugely predominate over composers. In Johnny Mercer's words 'We all come from Gilbert'. Alan Jay Lerner, lyricist of *My Fair Lady, Gigi,* and *Camelot*, has written that 'Gilbert was the Adam of modern lyric writing. P. G. Wodehouse, Lorenz Hart, Cole Porter, Ira Gershwin, Oscar Hammerstein and their contemporaries and descendants all owe their lyrical, genetic beginning to W. S. Gilbert'. [4] He might have added Noel Coward, who remarked that by the time he was four the lyrics and melodies of 'Take a Pair of Sparkling Eyes', 'Tit Willow' and 'I Have a Song to Sing, O' had been 'fairly inculcated into my bloodstream', but otherwise his list serves as an accurate record of the line of descent through which Gilbert's influence made itself felt on the major lyric writers of the first half of the twentieth century. Wodehouse's indebtedness to Gilbert is well documented, though he preferred writing words to fit an existing tune, believing, unlike his mentor, that 'you get the best results by giving the composer his head and having the lyricist follow him'. [5] For Lorenz Hart, who was compared to Gilbert as early as 1925 by *Variety* magazine, the influence is most apparent in such daring and tongue-twisting rhyming phrases as 'willing ham for Dillingham' and 'Jeritza will shiver when it hits 'er'. Cole Porter, recalling his college days, told an interviewer: 'At Yale, I was rhyme crazy. That was because I was G & S crazy. They had a big influence on my life'.[6]

Ira Gershwin acknowledged a huge indebtedness to the Savoy operas and their style of song. The influence is particularly evident in the patter song like

'Let's Call the Whole Thing Off' and in his ill-fated musical *Strike Up the Band* (1927). When he saw two elderly gentlemen dressed in evening clothes among the pitifully small audience filing into the theatre for one of its final performances, Gershwin quipped to George F. Kaufman, the script writer, 'that's Gilbert and Sullivan coming to fix the show'.[7] Yip Harburg, lyricist of *The Wizard of Oz*, was introduced to the craft of lyric writing through exposure to Gilbert and Sullivan by Ira Gershwin when they were classmates at City College, New York. He was reciting Gilbert's *Bab Ballads*, which were his favourite poems, and was astonished to be told by his friend that they had been set to music. Gershwin invited his classmate home to listen to recordings of the Savoy operas on the family Victrola. 'There were all the lines I knew by heart, put to music!' Harburg recalled. 'I was dumbfounded, staggered'.[8]

Although Oscar Hammerstein was less obviously and consciously influenced by the Savoy style than Lorenz Hart, his collaborations with Richard Rodgers built on and developed the particular innovations and strengths of Gilbert and Sullivan in terms of an integrated approach, word- and plot-led and with a strong sense of community. In many ways, indeed, Rodgers and Hammerstein took musical theatre back to its Savoy roots after a long period when it had drifted more in the direction of operetta, revue, and musical comedy. In their concern to write musical plays where the songs carry forward the plot and develop character and their perfectionism in terms of drilling and rehearsing casts and getting every detail absolutely right, they were, indeed, as they were so often dubbed, modern Savoyards.

Lyricists of the latter part of the twentieth century have also acknowledged their profound debt to Gilbert and Sullivan. Tom Jones told Gayden Wren, the entertainment editor of the New York Times Syndicate, who has made an extensive study of this whole subject, that as a freshman in high school he learned all the patter songs off a recording by Nelson Eddy. Later as a student in the University of Texas, he wrote and performed a parody of *HMS Pinafore* which led directly to subsequent college musicals and his collaboration with Harvey Schmidt in *The Fantasticks* and other professional shows. Sheldon Harnick first discovered the magic of G & S when playing as a teenage violinist for a production of *The Mikado*. He was bowled over by the patter song and Gilbert's mastery of rapid-fire lyrics and way with a comic line:

I think the overall influence exerted on me by Gilbert's work was a heightened awareness of the craft of writing lyrics: the sharpness and inventiveness of the language, the strongly marked rhythmic schemes and the play of wit. I don't mean to suggest that I learned those things through conscious study; I imagine, rather, that I absorbed them through repeatedly hearing (and sometime singing) the lyrics.[9]

Harnick specifically credits Gilbert and Sullivan for the device of having the chorus echo soloists' lines, which he used both in his 1959 show *Fiorello!* and in *Fiddler on the Roof.*

Among contemporary lyricists, Tim Rice has been the most enthusiastic in his acknowledgement of the influence of Gilbert and Sullivan. Introduced to their work at his prep school, he recalls in his autobiography that his only theatrical experiences as a child were school trips to the Savoy operas and that his parents bought a Trixette record player so that the family could listen to D'Oyly Carte performances. He notes that he adored the brilliance of the songs 'primarily but not exclusively because of the words'.[10] The wit and fun of Gilbert's lyrics were very much a model when he was working on *Joseph and the Amazing Technicolor Dreamcoat*, a work which has rightly been compared to *HMS Pinafore* and has many G & S echoes in its zany rhyme schemes and wonderful musical pastiche. Not surprisingly, one of the particular attractions for Rice about the Victorian partnership is the fact that the lyricist was accorded equal stature with the composer—'and of course Gilbert wrote both book and lyrics. . . . Shows that are writer driven are always better'.[11]

Not all modern lyricists are Gilbert and Sullivan fans. Stephen Sondheim finds 'Gilbert's lyrics fussy and self-conscious to an irritating degree, and Sullivan's music rather dull' and Stephen Schwartz 'can't admit to being a huge aficionado' although he acknowledges that there may be some influence on his earlier work.[12] Despite these reservations, both have written deliberate parodies of G & S—Sondheim the British admiral's patter song 'I Come to You with Letters from Her Majesty Victoria' in the 'Please, Hello' song from *Pacific Overtures* and Schwartz 'War Is Science' in *Pippin*. Their lack of enthusiasm almost certainly reflects the fact that both are composers as well as lyricists. The lingering influence of the Savoy operas on twentieth-century musical theatre is much more readily recognized by lyricists than composers and it is Gilbert rather than Sullivan who is almost invariably seen as the key figure. Among composers, the remark made by Jerry Bock, responsible for the score of *Fiddler on the Roof,* is typical: 'It was Gilbert that I admired, that really took me to Sullivan. But Sullivan seems to be more stylistically out of date than Gilbert'. [13] In his extensive trawls around the music theatre world to trace the legacy of the Savoy operas, Gayden Wren has come across only one composer, John Kander, of *Cabaret* and *Chicago* fame, who unashamedly confesses to being influenced by Sullivan—

and significantly the influence acknowledged here is skill in word setting rather than broader melodic or compositional gifts:

> He was extremely meticulous in seeing that every word could be heard by reflecting the natural rhythm of the lyrics in his music. There's a great reciprocity between his music and Gilbert's words. The natural setting of words is very important to me, and I'm sure that comes from Sullivan.[14]

Peter Maxwell Davies is relatively unusual among twentieth-century composers in confessing enthusiasm for the Savoy operas (see page 112). Michael Tippett conducted them with amateur operatic societies and possibly had the hero of *Iolanthe* in mind when constructing the character Strephon in his opera *The Midsummer Marriage*. He included a set of variations on 'I Have a Song to Sing, O' in his 1953 *Divertimento*. Benjamin Britten's early work was compared to that of Sullivan, and critics saw distinct echoes of the Savoy operas in the choral operetta *Paul Bunyan*, on which he collaborated with W. H. Auden, who was himself dismissive of the Victorian duo, describing Sullivan's music as 'so boring'.[15] Neither Britten nor Tippett, however, were conscious imitators or admirers of G & S. Nor is Andrew Lloyd Webber, the contemporary composer who is surely most strikingly similar to Sullivan in style and temperament, with his strong commercial instincts, love of the theatre and high society, gift for parody and pastiche, and combination of accessibility, vulgarity, and deep spiritual yearning. He also follows in Sullivan's footsteps in being loved by audiences but panned by the musical establishment. Lloyd Webber has not acknowledged Sullivan as a significant influence on his work, although as an aficionado of musical theatre from boyhood, dreaming of being the next Richard Rodgers when his contemporaries were dreaming about the Beatles, and dominating the genre over the last thirty years, he is very clearly his heir and successor.

I have begun with this excursus into the world of twentieth-century musicals because it shows how the influence of Gilbert and Sullivan is living and lingering in a way that is not always appreciated, particularly by their fans. I believe it is wrong to say, as Gayden Wren does in his recent book, that 'in terms of theatre history, they represent an evolutionary dead end'.[16] On the contrary, they are the chief begetters and creators of the most buoyant (certainly in commercial terms) branch of modern theatre. It is appropriate that their contribution has been acknowledged in modern musicals from *Memphis Bound* (1945), with its story line of an all-black cast putting on *HMS Pinafore* to raise money to float their showboat off a mud bank, to *Thoroughly Modern Millie* (2003), with its jokes about the fine elbows of a middle-aged woman and on the orphan/often theme and its use of the tune of the 'matter' trio from *Ruddigore* in a number called 'Speed Test' in which Millie takes dictation. The video version of *Nunsense II*, the second of the hugely successful off-Broadway musicals featuring the Little Sisters of Hoboken, is staged on the set of the Inter-Faith Musical Society of Hoboken's production of 'that ever popular Japanese hit, *The Mikado*' sponsored by the Ishizawa Subaru and Sushi Bar.

The musical is not, of course, the only cultural form to show the influence of G & S. Even more direct heirs are those witty and satirical songwriters found on both sides of the Atlantic in the twentieth century like Michael Flanders and Donald Swann in the United Kingdom and Tom Lehrer in the United States. The influence of Gilbert is discernible in a vein of British comedy that runs through John Betjeman's verse via *Monty Python* and *Private Eye* to lunchtime radio quiz shows like *Just a Minute* and television series like *Yes, Minister* and *Have I Got News for You* where the emphasis is on wit, irony, and poking fun at the establishment from within it in a way which manages to be both disrespectful of authority and yet cosily comfortable and urbane.

These and other legacies would indicate the long and lingering influence of Gilbert and Sullivan even if their own works were no longer performed. But of course they are still performed, in great quantity and a huge variety of different forms. They are also still quoted, parodied, recognized, and enjoyed by large numbers of people. For the last hundred years or so the Savoy operas have formed the basis for a distinct bourgeois subculture in much of the English-speaking world, their songs handed down from generation to generation (and particularly from father to son) in a middle-class version of the oral folk tradition. Successive generations have grown up performing them at school, knowing the words of key songs by heart and able to quote and recognize references to them in newspapers, speeches, and sermons. Even though far fewer schools now perform the Savoy operas and general levels of knowledge about history and literature have fallen, G & S remains a significant element in both British and North American middle- and upper-class consciousness. Thanks to television, video, and other new media, it has in recent decades penetrated into popular culture and shed some of its narrow bourgeois base.

To realize the extent to which G & S still permeates British and North American culture, you only have to pick up a newspaper and see how often headline writers and subeditors have recourse to catchphrases like 'the very model of . . .', 'a . . . 's lot is not a happy one' and 'let the punishment fit the crime'. Even sports commentators have been known to indulge in G & S references—a British broadcaster describing the early stages of a long-distance race in the 1972 Olympics noted of the top runners that 'like the Duke of Plaza-Toro, each is trying to lead from behind'. Lines from the Savoy operas crop up regularly in crosswords, radio quiz programmes and on the internet—look up 'destiny' on a website dedicated to definitions of philosophical concepts and you will find 'See how the fates their gifts allot' standing alongside quotations from Nietzsche and Shakespeare. Journalists use the word 'Gilbertian', as, for example, the *Church Times* did to describe the pomp-filled ceremony in St. Paul's Cathedral in December 2002 in which Rowan Williams legally became Archbishop of Canterbury, and expect their readers to know what it means.

Songs from the Savoy operas are regularly quoted and parodied by politicians and pundits (see pages 165–66). The decision by Tony Blair's government first to remove hereditary peers from the House of Lords and then to abolish the office of Lord Chancellor has inspired frequent quotation from *Iolanthe*. In his book, *Farewell My Lords* (1999), the Labour MP, Austin Mitchell, comments that 'the Lords do nothing in particular but they do it very well'. A newspaper article in 2003 by satirist Ian Hislop deploring the abolition of the office of Lord Chancellor for ending 'one of the great running jokes in English political life' quoted extensively from *Iolanthe*, which he noted had immortalized the office, and concluded, 'Audiences find the obvious contemporary parallels in the opera funny and particularly enjoy the absurd figure of the Lord Chancellor, so I am most unhappy at the thought that Blair is going to ruin the fun'.[17]

In the United States, Gilbert's Lord Chancellor has recently proved himself to be a role model in a much more direct way. In 1999, after seeing a production of *Iolanthe*, Chief Justice William Rehnquist had four stripes of gold braid sewn onto each sleeve of his judicial robe to add dignity to his office. In another tribute to the continuing relevance of this particular opera, the organist at the 1998 memorial service for the maverick British Labour politician turned right-wing columnist, Woodrow Wyatt, struck up 'Bow, Bow Ye Lower Middle Classes' as princes and peers filed into St. Margaret's Church, Westminster. The memorial service for the Anglo-American broadcaster and journalist, Alistair Cooke, held in Westminster Abbey in 2004, ended with 'In Friendship's Name' played by the BBC Concert Orchestra. The advisers to John Kerry, Democratic Party candidate in the 2004 United States presidential election, were known as the Pooh-Bahs.

G & S references abound in books. Among those which take their titles from songs are *A Half and Half Affair* (1973), the autobiography of Donald Denman, professor of land economy at Cambridge, Vinetta Colby's *The Singular Anomaly* (1970), a study of women novelists, and two murder mysteries—John Dickson Carr's *The Ghost's High Noon* (1969) and Howard Engel's *A Victim Must Be Found* (1988). There is a small library of 'whodunits' with a G & S theme. Charlotte MacLeod's *The Plain Old Man* (1986) is set in Boston, Massachusetts, during a production of *The Sorcerer*. The detective hero of Nancy Bell's *Biggie and the Mangled Mortician* (1997) is about to take a leading part in a production of *HMS Pinafore* in Job's Crossing, Texas, when he is confronted with the mysterious death of the local undertaker. Kerry Greenwood's *Ruddy Gore: Death by Comic Opera* (1995) tells of dastardly deeds during a performance of *Ruddigore* in Melbourne, Australia, in 1928. Molly Hardwick's *Perish in July* (1989) is set against the background of an amateur production of *The Yeomen of the Guard*. In Roberta Morrell's *Vengeance Dire* (2001) the leading lady of the Castlethorpe Gilbert and Sullivan Players is murdered during a production of *The Pirates of Penzance*. Joan Spencer, heroine of Sara Hoskinson Frommer's *Murder and Sullivan* (1997), is recruited to play viola in a production of *Ruddigore* in Oliver, Indiana, and finds herself investigating the mysterious death on stage on the opening night of the actor playing Sir Roderic Murgatroyd. *Death at the Opera*, one of Gladys Mitchell's Mrs. Bradley mysteries, turned into a highly successful BBC television series in 2000 starring Diana Rigg, involves Mrs. Bradley returning to her old finishing school to see an all-female production of *The Mikado* which is enlivened by the murder of one of the teachers waiting to go on as Ko-Ko. Despite sharing my surname, the feisty lady detective is not an enthusiastic Savoyard. When the headmaster expresses the hope that she likes Gilbert and Sullivan, she tartly replies 'Frankly, Doctor, I wish they'd never met'.

G & S has even provided the background for a fictional sex scene. In Jo Ann Ross's *Tempting Fate* (1987), one of a series of 'compelling stories of passionate romance for today's woman', the two leading characters debate the merits of the partnership as they listen to *The Mikado* before indulging in torrid lovemaking. Donovan (the man) champions Sullivan while his partner, Brooke, prefers Gilbert. Following their frolicking, Brooke suggests they listen to *HMS Pinafore*. In less racy mode, Tony Rounsefell's novel *The Donnington Diaries* (1996) tells how a stately home is saved through the performance of a Savoy opera.

Several films have included G & S references and performances of their songs. In *The Producers* (1967) one of the singers auditioning for the musical *Springtime for Hitler* gets as far as 'A vantering minstel hi' before he is unceremoniously stopped. John Wayne and Lauren Bacall sing 'Tit Willow' in *The Shootist* (1976). The plot of *Foul Play* (1978) centres on an assassination attempt on the pope while he is attending a performance of *The Mikado*. *Chariots of Fire* (1980) shows the Olympic athlete Harold Abrahams joining the Gilbert and Sullivan society to the strains of 'The Soldiers of Our Queen' when he goes up to Cambridge and later watching his wife-to-be, Sybil Gordon, a principal soprano with the D'Oyly Carte, singing 'Three Little Maids'. In Steven Spielberg's *Raiders of the Lost Ark* (1981) Sallah sings 'A British Tar Is a Soaring Soul' as he and Indiana Jones embark for Egypt. In *Porterhouse Blue* (1987) the reactionary atmosphere of the Cambridge college is confirmed by a scene of the dean sitting in his room listening to 'A Wandering Minstrel' on a windup gramophone. Themes from the Savoy operas crop up continually in *The Hand That Rocks the*

Cradle (1992), even providing tunes for the alarm clocks in the home where father (Matt McCoy) and daughter (Madeline Zima) also sing 'I Am the Captain of the Pinafore' together. *Wyatt Earp* (1994) recalls the true story of how the famed lawman met his future wife when she was playing in an early touring production of *Pinafore* and features two numbers from the opera. One of the most poignant scenes in *Wilde* (2001) has Lord Alfred Douglas singing 'Ah, Leave Me Not to Pine Alone and Desolate' to Oscar Wilde. This melody is then used as a refrain throughout the rest of the film, notably in the scene where the two men first make love. In *Peter Pan* (2003) Mr. Darling sings 'When I Was a Lad' with his children.

Many of these cinematic quotations are there to add period flavour and give an atmosphere of nostalgia and quaintness. This is true of the recent use of 'I Am the Very Model of a Modern Major General' in a scene involving a ventriloquist's dummy in *Beautiful* (2000) and as a party piece delivered by a man transported in a time warp from the 1870s to the present day in *Kate and Leopold* (2001). But G & S songs are not just used in historic contexts. The major general's song is sung in space in *Star Trek: The Next Generation* (1987). It also helps a character in the television sci-fi series *Babylon 5* relieve the tedium of a long space journey. In *Star Trek Insurrection* (1998) a stirring rendition of 'A British Tar Is a Soaring Soul' brings Lieutenant Commander Data out of a zombie-like malfunction which threatens to wreck the universe. Recalling that Data had been rehearsing a production of *HMS Pinafore* before embarking on a mission to the race of Ba'ku, Captain Picard begins the song after all other means of rousing the comatose commander have failed. Mr. Worf enthusiastically joins in, despite having responded to Picard's question as to whether he knows Gilbert and Sullivan: 'No sir, I have not had the chance to meet all the new crew members yet', and the familiar strains are enough to snap Data out of his malfunction as he lustily adds his voice to the trio. These, and other recent references, underline the strong contemporary feel and appeal of G & S, especially in the United States, and the extent to which it is still seen as a morale-booster and source of divine emollient.

One recent film in particular has had a huge impact in promoting and popularizing Gilbert and Sullivan. *Topsy-Turvy*, released in the United States in 1999, grossed over $5,000,000 in box office receipts, was voted fourth best film of the year, and won two Oscars. It came out in Britain in 2000 and gained plaudits from critics and filmgoers alike. Beautifully crafted and meticulously researched, it focuses on the characters of and relationship between composer and librettist and the backstage life of the D'Oyly Carte Opera Company during the making of *The Mikado*. Its slow pace and period detail seem a world away from the bleak gritty contemporary reality and *ciné-verité* usually associated with its director,

Mike Leigh, but he is a self-confessed G & S addict who first fell in love with the Savoy magic when he was taken to see a D'Oyly Carte *Mikado* at the age of six.

In Britain, radio has been the most consistently G & S-conscious medium, perhaps reinforcing the image of both as slightly worthy and old-fashioned. Radio soap operas have periodically acknowledged the continuing appeal of the Savoy operas over the last five decades, from the episode of *Mrs. Dale's Diary* in May 1961 featuring a tea party to commemorate the fiftieth anniversary of Gilbert's death to the performance of *The Mikado* in place of the usual Ambridge Christmas pantomime which provided *The Archers* with one of its main story lines in the winter of 2000–2001. A memorable 1999 episode of *The Archers* featured Julia Pargetter celebrating her eightieth birthday by singing 'The Sun Whose Rays Are All Ablaze'. Scarcely a week goes by without some allusion to or snatch of G & S being heard on BBC Radio 4, be it in a question on 'Brain of Britain', a request on 'Desert Island Discs', a song used in a play to give a period atmosphere, or a discussion in a current affairs programme—the edition of the flagship *Today* programme which went out on the morning that I began revising this chapter included a discussion about evolution in which an eminent geneticist quoted from 'A Lady Fair of Lineage High' from *Princess Ida* to explain Darwin's theory of the descent of man. Like headline writers, radio producers still turn to songs from the Savoy operas for programme titles and to establish a mood or set a tone. 'When Our Gallant Norman Foes' with its chilling reference to 'The screw may twist and the rack may turn' was used in this way to introduce a debate on corporal punishment in schools in 1996, although 'Sing Hey the Cat o'Nine Tails and the Tar' might have been more appropriate.

The BBC's other main domestic stations also continue to reflect and acknowledge Gilbert and Sullivan's hold on the British psyche. Radio 2 broadcast superb specially recorded productions of the complete Savoy cycle in 1989, and despite its more recent virtual abandonment of all pre-1960s music, it still finds a place for songs from the operas on 'Friday Night Is Music Night' and 'Your Hundred Best Tunes'. It has also been responsible for one of the more imaginative recent pieces of G & S 'product placement' on the airwaves when it broadcast in its 'Pause for Thought' slot during 2003 a series of religious reflections by Dr. John Florance on such phrases as 'Things are seldom what they seem', 'To let the punishment fit the crime', and 'When every one is somebody, then no one's anybody'. Radio 3 is also generous if somewhat sporadic in the airtime that it devotes to G & S. In the space of three days in the summer of 2000, for example, it provided an hour-long feature programme, a further hour of archive material devoted to the Savoy operas, and a live relay of *The Gondoliers* from the Proms. Britain's national independent classical music station, Classic FM, has also tuned into the G & S zeitgeist, not least with somewhat bizarre Christmas productions of favourite Savoy operas with celebrity casts drawn from the world of politics.

In the United States, children's television programmes and cartoon series reflect the continuing hold of G & S in popular awareness and culture. An episode of *Clarissa*, the mid-1990s series about a young teenager, featured a high school performance of *The Pirates of Penzance* with Clarissa, inevitably, in the role of Mabel (or May Bell as she insisted on pronouncing it) and her good friend Sam as a pirate. I cannot imagine a similar plot line in a contemporary British teenage soap like *Grange Hill*, and it confirms my sense that among young people G & S is probably better known nowadays in the United States than in the United Kingdom. Further confirmation of this state of affairs, and perhaps a contributory factor to it, is the prominent role accorded to songs from the Savoy operas in *The Simpsons*. In 'Deep Space Homer', Barney Gumble, the local Springfield drunk, displays his newfound lack of dependence on the bottle by back flipping while singing 'I Am the Very Model of a Modern Major General'. 'Cape Feare' offers two acts of Savoyard homage—the first when Homer leads his family while on a car journey in singing 'Three Little Maids' from the FBI Light opera songbook and the second when Bart manages to stave off annihilation at the hands of Sideshow Bob by getting him to sing through the entire score of *HMS Pinafore* while their boat glides slowly towards safety and the waiting police.

What really establishes beyond any doubt the continuing 'street cred' of Gilbert and Sullivan is their regular quotation in television soap operas. Their songs have been heard on *Neighbours*, *The Flying Doctors*, *Emmerdale Farm*, and *Coronation Street*, where a particularly poignant scene in a 1997 episode featured the sudden death through a heart attack of Derek Wilton as he was listening to a tape of John Reed singing 'Tit Willow'. Frasier has sung 'Three Little Maids' falsetto over the phone and played Colonel Fairfax. An episode of *West Wing* shown in 2000 and entitled 'And It's Surely to Their Credit' introduced the character of Ainsley, a Republican attorney hired by President Bartlett, who is president of her local Gilbert and Sullivan society. Her colleagues decorate her office with posters of the Savoy operas and welcome her into the White House with a chorus of 'For He Himself Has Said It'. She shows herself to be actuated by an overwhelming sense of duty and is asked at one point if she has stepped out of *The Pirates of Penzance*.

All of this confirms that Gilbert and Sullivan is still very much part of mainstream popular culture on both sides of the Atlantic. The stars who have performed or recorded G & S numbers over the last half-century include Danny Kaye, Stubby Kaye, Groucho Marx, Nelson Eddy, Frankie Howerd, Tommy Steele, Stanley Holloway, Vincent Price, Sonny and Cher, and the Muppets. Alistair Cooke has recorded all four parts of the *Mikado* madrigal. Michael Barry-more has sung the major general's song on television with a parrot perched on his shoulder. G & S has been camped up by Hinge and Bracket, treated as folk music by Peter, Paul, and Mary, syncopated by the Black and White Minstrels, and turned into virtuoso pieces by brass bands and male voice choirs. There have been all-black and cross-dressed productions, cartoon and puppet ver-sions. Britain's first permanent puppet theatre, 'The Harlequin' at Rhos-on-Sea in North Wales, has had *The Mikado* in its repertoire since 1961 and *Ruddigore* since 1971.

It has also, thank goodness, continued to be performed more or less straight by amateur and professional companies, schools, and university societies across the English-speaking world and beyond, and this more than anything else ac-counts for its endurance throughout the twentieth century. The performance history of G & S over the last five decades, covered in some detail in the next four chapters of this book, gives a mixed picture. The D'Oyly Carte Opera Company, in both its old and new incarnations, has struggled, many amateur operatic societies have forsaken the Savoy operas for musicals, and schools have increasingly opted for *Guys and Dolls* or *Grease* in preference to *The Gondoliers*. Yet, measured in terms of professional performances, recordings, and general levels of scholarly activity and interest, G & S is in a healthier state in the first decade of the twenty-first century than at any other time in its history.

In the United Kingdom, even after the D'Oyly Carte's cessation of produc-tions, three professional companies remain largely devoted to performing the Savoy operas—Carl Rosa, Opera della Luna, and the Gilbert and Sullivan Opera Company created for the Buxton G & S Festival. Jonathan Miller's *Mikado* has been one of English National Opera's greatest successes, revived in London on an almost annual basis and seen in New York, Venice, and the Netherlands. In the United States, the 'Piramikafore' trinity are in the repertoire of around 25 re-gional opera companies. The variety of productions has never been greater. The updated version of *Pirates* which opened in New York's Central Park in 1980 and transferred to Broadway in 1981 has spawned a whole series of up-tempo treat-ments, not least in Australia where Simon Gallaher's innovative Essgee versions are among the biggest box office draws. Yiddish translations of 'Piramikafore' have won huge acclaim and a gay version of *Pinafore* played for nine months in Los Angeles before transferring to Chicago and New York. More traditional productions are regularly mounted by major opera houses around the English-speaking world. Perhaps the most striking and encouraging feature of recent years has been the penetration of G & S into the repertory of opera companies in Continental Europe. *Die Piraten von Penzance* has played for two seasons at the Vienna Volksoper. *HMS Pinafore* has been staged several times in Denmark and *The Yeomen of the Guard* in Sweden, *El Mikado* has been performed and recorded in Catalonia and *Trial by Jury* put on in Estonia. There have been three German translations of *The Mikado* since 1960. Further afield, the strains of 'Miya Sama' have been heard in Penang, China, and in the Japanese town of Chichibu.

The works of Gilbert and Sullivan, indeed, remain more vibrant and enduring than the musicals which they have inspired. What Stuart Maunder has written about Australia is equally valid elsewhere: '*Cats* is a whisker in comparison, *The Phantom of the Opera* a mere shadow, *Les Miserables* particularly glum—there is no theatrical phenomenon with the staying power of G & S'.[18] It helps considerably, of course, that unlike most musicals, the Savoy operas are out of copyright and can be performed by both amateur and professional companies free of charge. This is undoubtedly one of the reasons why they remain so popular with amateur societies, schools, and colleges, and it also partly explains the huge number of recordings. Certainly no musicals, nor operas, have been more recorded. It is an extraordinary tribute to their enduring popular appeal that three leading High Street retailers in the United Kingdom, Boots, Marks & Spencer, and W. H. Smith, have all marketed their own brand recordings of complete operas or highlights, as has the *Reader's Digest*, that bastion of middle-brow taste. The G & S Archive on the web lists 55 recordings of *The Mikado* alone, the oldest made in 1906 and the most recent in 2001. They include four BBC versions and twenty-one film, television, or video productions—including one made by Hungarian Television and a German version set in a brothel. Currently available on CD are nineteen complete recordings of *The Mikado*, seventeen of *HMS Pinafore* and sixteen of *The Pirates of Penzance*, not counting Joseph Papp's version. There are also several recordings of most of the operas on video and DVD.

This level of ubiquity and availability is remarkable for a 'product' that is now more than a hundred years old. Gilbert and Sullivan belongs to a cultural era and milieu which has proved remarkably enduring. Among their late Victorian contemporaries still very much around today are the Wimbledon tennis championships (first played in 1877), Test Match cricket (1877), and the Promenade Concerts (1895). The Savoy operas are virtually contemporary with the stories of Sherlock Holmes and the novels of Thomas Hardy, both of which also receive regular airings on radio and television. Much else from this era has almost disappeared, however, either submerged by the tide of political correctness and post-imperial guilt like the Royal Tournament (1880) and the manly adventure stories of Rider Haggard and G. A. Henty, or simply past their sell-by date like the songs of the music hall and the plays of Arthur Wing Pinero.

Yet for all this evidence of their remarkable powers of endurance, there remains a distinct problem about Gilbert and Sullivan. In the country of their birth they are not quite kosher. Indeed, they are regarded by many within the arts world and the cultural establishment as distinctly infra-dig. This attitude has manifested itself in several ways over recent decades—the refusal of the Arts Council to fund either the new or the old D'Oyly Carte companies; the complete absence of G & S from the repertoire of a subsidised National Theatre which can happily stage *Guys and Dolls*, *South Pacific*, and *Me and My Girl*; the fact that the Royal Opera House, Covent Garden, will put on Sondheim's *Sweeney Todd* but not *The Yeomen of the Guard*. It is expressed in withering reviews in the quality press, like that by Meredith Oaks in the *Independent* of a concert performance of *Pinafore* at the Royal Festival Hall which took issue with the idea that 'Gilbert and Sullivan's bone-china classics of English insouciance' are just innocent fun: ' I can think of lots of things more innocent, and more fun, than Sullivan's leering, inane rip-offs of real music, or Gilbert's pert, complacent rhymes'.[19] This dismissive attitude even surfaces on Radio 4. The *Today* programme used the release of *Topsy-Turvy* to mount a full-scale assault, with presenter Edward Stourton beginning his interview with Mike Leigh 'Gilbert and Sullivan—most people think they're pretty ghastly, don't they?' and music critic Michael White dismissing the Savoy operas as 'high Victorian nothingness' and suggesting that 'Gilbert and Sullivan are only for consenting adults behind closed doors'.[20]

The trouble is that G & S falls between two stools with neither the kudos to count as high culture nor the proletarian credentials to make it trendy and fashionable. It suffers from being at once too accessible and too subtle and from being perceived as irredeemably middlebrow and middle-class. Meredith Oaks concluded his review with a comment that cuts to the heart of the objection that so many critics have to G & S: 'There's a thin line between English middle-class self-mockery and English middle-class self-congratulation, and the famous closing anthem 'For he is an Englishman' places *HMS Pinafore* flagrantly on the wrong side of it'. It is perhaps some small consolation to G & S fans that other late Victorian survivals attract similar comments. The Wimbledon tennis championships have recently been slated for being 'smothered in that cloying middle-class/middle-England/middle-of-the-afternoon-on-a-sunny-day smugness'.[21]

This is a peculiarly British perception. In the United States Gilbert and Sullivan is regarded as high culture. This was brought home to me when I attended a performance by the New York Gilbert and Sullivan Players in Scranton, Pennsylvania, which was promoted as part of a cultural season of grand opera and ballet. It is altogether more of an intellectual and upper-class taste in North

America, with fans predominantly to be found among college graduates (and particularly those from East Coast and Ivy League schools) in contrast to the United Kingdom, where it has a wider social appeal stretching well down into the station occupied by Captain Corcoran in the lower middle class. In Britain, indeed, G & S and the middle classes have suffered something of the same stigma, so accurately described by Hilaire Belloc in his characterization of 'the people in between' who are 'underdone and harassed, and out of place and mean and horribly embarrassed'. I have never met an American who is embarrassed about liking G & S. In Britain, by contrast, as the journalist Susannah Herbert has observed:

> For as long as I can remember, it's been unacceptable in cultivated circles to confess to a passion for *HMS Pinafore* or *Patience* or *The Pirates of Penzance*. Unless you actually want to badge yourself in public as a provincial bourgeois, middle-brow, imperial nostalgist, you were best keeping mum.[22]

Even Mike Leigh admitted when *Topsy-Turvy* came out that as a drama student in London in the 1960s he had keep quiet about his enthusiasm for G & S—'it became a closet thing which I didn't publicly talk about'.[23]

What is the explanation for this state of affairs? It clearly goes back to the snobbish prejudice which led to Sullivan being cold-shouldered by the Victorian musical establishment. Its persistence today, I suspect, may have something to do with the number of G & S fans in that somewhat forgotten and despised class, once in the mainstream of British life, but increasingly edged out in the Cool Britannia of café latte, bottled water, and designer clothes. They are the quiet, unassuming people who are being overtaken in the race of life by the raucous, the brash, and the young. They live in untrendy places like Streatham and Derby, have dandruff, wear anoraks, go to church, drink bitter, and still stand for the national anthem. It is all too easy to caricature G & S fans and it is all too easy to patronize them—and maybe, like Captain Corcoran, I am the last person who has. The trouble is that this becomes a self-fulfilling process. Because they feel patronized and put down, devotees of G & S often react by becoming more obsessional and cultlike, seeing everyone in conspiracy against them and being fiercely protective of their idols and highly sensitive to any criticism. This syndrome and the reaction it has provoked are well described by the distinguished music and theatre critic Philip Hope Wallace:

> The Gilbert and Sullivan operas have been for so long a feature of the English landscape that we find some difficulty in considering them from a dispassionately critical point of view. Their immense popularity hardened

too quickly into a cult. The faithful never missed a visit of the D'Oyly Carte Opera Company, demanded countless encores to every patter song, never cared how meagre or mediocre were the sounds that came from the pit, and burned to copy the whole proceedings, down to the smallest bit of 'business', in their next production of their own amateur operatic society. Every musical boy has some jovial uncle who rammed Gilbert and Sullivan down his throat since childhood; no wonder that he should grow up to associate an enthusiasm for this form of art with indifference to all others. As a result, there has been among the more intelligent a violent reaction, and the Savoy operas have long been regarded in some quarters as unmentionable.[24]

There is no doubt that the enduring appeal of Gilbert and Sullivan both to their devoted fans and to the wider public is partly a matter of nostalgia. They seem to breathe the innocence, naivety, and fun of a long vanished age. Again, there is a subtle transatlantic difference here. For North Americans the datedness of the Savoy operas is part of their quaintness. For many of the British fans, there is a more wistful sense of yearning and even mourning for the values of a lost age of innocent enjoyment.

For their critics, the lingering appeal of Gilbert and Sullivan is a key symptom of the British disease of living in the past and failing to confront the realities of the present, let alone the future. In a letter to *The Times* in December 1990 Sir Graham Hills, principal of the University of Strathclyde, proposed, apparently in all seriousness, a moratorium for at least five years on performances of the Savoy operas on the following grounds:

> They engender in the British (and especially in the English) nostalgic fondness for Britain's imperial past which is a serious obstacle to change and reform. Everything associated with that past, from lord chancellors and the like in fancy dress to light-hearted, bone-headed military men in scarlet, gives credence to the idea that great wealth flows effortlessly and unceasingly from such cultivated minds. The facts are that our wealth-creating apparatus, in the form of business and industry, continues to decline almost monotonically, and has done so since those operas were first performed. [25]

Hills has since admitted to me that he is himself a G & S fan and has been since he sang in school performances. He enjoyed *Topsy-Turvy*, finding it 'a delightful depiction of both the pedantic Gilbert and the romantic Sullivan', but still stands by the main point in his letter. If we want to inhabit 'the museum of Britain where we all dress as beefeaters and parade to the music of G & S' then

FIGURE 1.1 G & S meets modern technology. Seattle Yeomen of the Guard greet the arrival of Concorde, 2003 *(R. Wesley Aman/Seattle G & S Society)*

so be it – 'I just hope we have thought it through'.[26] I can see his point. There is an extent to which the enduring hold of G & S, its recent renaissance, and its future prospects are an aspect of the whole burgeoning heritage industry that is gradually turning Britain into one big theme park (see page 200).

In the United States there are no such worries about a fondness for Gilbert and Sullivan standing in the way of technological innovation and economic progress. Indeed, rather the reverse is true and they are quite happily integrated and combined. A good example of this occurred recently in Seattle when the Museum of Flight took delivery of a British Airways Concorde supersonic aeroplane on its retirement from service. The museum wanted a display of British colour and pageantry to greet Concorde's arrival. The local British-American Chamber of Commerce suggested a call to the Seattle Gilbert and Sullivan Society, who provided four Yeomen of the Guard in full costume. Somehow in the North American context there is nothing incongruous about using G & S-inspired 'Olde English' nostalgia to celebrate the wonders of modern aerospace technology. In Britain, such juxtaposition would somehow jar.

The historian David Cannadine, one of very few British academics to have analysed the whole Gilbert and Sullivan phenomenon, places a heavy emphasis on the nostalgia factor. He describes their operas as a 'paean of praise to national pride and the established order' and finds them 'obsessed with the personnel and rituals of monarchy' and excessively admiring of the army and navy and the forces of law and order. He believes that the Savoy operas encouraged a British faith in institutions and especially in the police. Indeed, he credits them with creating the image of the British bobby as 'decent, dutiful, well-meaning and incorruptible—even if not over-bright', taken up and perpetuated in detective stories and early television programmes like *Dixon of Dock Green*. Even in their own day, he argues, they were nostalgic, representing 'a deliberate and very successful cultivation of anachronism'—'the commercial and entrepreneurial bourgeoisie hardly appears at all ... the working class are invariably picturesque and dutiful: rustic maidens, country bumpkins and jolly jack tars. The settings are almost always pastoral and sylvan ... the press and pace of urban life hardly intrude'. [27]

Cannadine is certainly right about the patriotic strain in Gilbert and Sullivan, although like so much else it is not without its topsy-turvy ambiguity. It is not quite clear how seriously 'He Is an Englishman' is meant to be taken nor whether 'When Britain Really Ruled the Waves' is a piece of patriotic sentiment or a send-up of a national institution. There is no doubt, however, of the extent to which the continuing appeal of G & S goes with displays of patriotic feeling. Performances of the Savoy operas are among the very few public occasions left now where the British national anthem is sung. Interestingly, this happens, if anything, more often in the United States than in the United Kingdom. The programme for the annual Ohio Light Opera summer festival at Wooster College reminds patrons that 'in keeping with the tradition established at the Savoy Theatre in London, we will sing "God Save the Queen" before each Gilbert and Sullivan performance'. The Savoy Company of Philadelphia goes one better, requiring its audiences to sing two verses before every performance and also installing a look-alike Queen Victoria in the Royal Box. "God Save the Queen" is the recommended audition piece for students wishing to join the Harvard University G & S Society. For Americans, singing this song is part of the quaint, Anglophile, rather cultured and elevated Gilbert and Sullivan experience. For the British it is more embarrassing. At the last night of the Proms introduced at the Buxton G & S Festival in 2003, the audience in the Opera House waved their Union Jacks and sung their way through 'Jerusalem' and 'Land of Hope and Glory' rather self-consciously, keen to show their affection for their country but also aware of the nationalistic, xenophobic associations that such songs now have in the United Kingdom.

This raises another interesting difference about the lingering appeal of G & S on either side of the Atlantic. North Americans love G & S because they see it as quintessentially English. It is often accompanied by a strong Anglophilia (and it is *Anglo*-philia—Gilbert and Sullivan does not appeal half as much to those Americans who love Scotland and hardly at all to those who are Hibernophiles). Much the same is true, I suspect, of British ex-pats among whom there has traditionally been a strong G & S following, and of immigrants who have fallen in love with all things English. It is notable that the case for the 'Englishness' of Gilbert and Sullivan has been most forcefully made by an adopted Englishman, the Hungarian-born writer George Mikes. At the root of their continuing popularity for him is the fact that Gilbert, 'the most English of Englishmen', has perhaps come closer than anyone else to producing an English weltanschauung or philosophical way of looking at the world:

> It is an attractive *Weltanschauung* which respects decency and good taste but, apart from these, takes nothing seriously. . . . Gilbert, in true English vein, accepted reality and society as it was, just managed to laugh at it heartily. . . . He was the satirist who meant to *preserve* society; the court jester who was a pillar of the establishment. The epitome of Englishness: self-admiration tempered with self-mockery'.[28]

Among those born and living in the United Kingdom, however, I am not sure that the Britishness, or Englishness, of Gilbert and Sullivan, is a major factor in its popularity. Enthusiasm for G & S has not just been confined to the English — it has been popular in Scotland for much of the twentieth century and to a lesser extent also in Wales and Ireland. It will be interesting to see whether in the current climate of much greater individual national cultural identity, it will be perceived more and more as an English cultural phenomenon and lose its wider British appeal. Certainly a graph of cultural, political, and religious trends in Scotland would show G & S performances among schools and amateur operatic societies, support for the Conservative and Unionist Party, and membership of the Church of Scotland all peaking in the mid-1950s and steadily declining since. But G & S has arguably held up better north of the border than either Unionism or organised Christianity. There are still a number of Scottish amateur societies dedicated to performing only the Savoy operas, with Edinburgh leading the field as one of the best in the United Kingdom. Despite the interpolation of a burst of 'Oh Flower of Scotland' into 'He Is an Englishman' in the Edinburgh society's 2000 production of *Pinafore*, a Scottish journalist still found herself wondering 'why Edinburgh has one of the liveliest Gilbert and Sullivan scenes in Britain' and 'what makes Scots turn out to play at Union Jack waving?' when 'there is something so amazingly English about this whole G & S business'.[29] The answer, I hope, may have something to do with a sense that in its understated, self-deprecating way G & S stands for something that is quintessentially British, rather than just narrowly English, and still worth celebrating.

If part of the reason for Gilbert and Sullivan's lingering appeal lies in nostalgia and patriotism, even more significant is what might be called the comfort factor.

What I have already called its quality of 'divine emollient' could from a less en-thusiastic perspective be dismissed as the musical equivalent of comfort food. It is relatively undemanding and serves as an instant pick-me-up, particularly in our disordered and angst-ridden age. Its characters exist in a self-contained, make-believe world where, on the whole, order prevails and virtue is, indeed, triumphant—the same is true of the world of Sherlock Holmes—and I won-der if the popularity of the Harry Potter stories is not partly attributable to the fact that they have a similar quality. This aspect is very clearly brought out in this description by self-confessed (North American) 'Gilbert and Sullivan Ad-dict' Paul Kresh of his first experience of a D'Oyly Carte performance:

> During the intermission the aunt who took me to this iniquitous spectacle encountered an old lady who informed her that she had been to every single performance of *Iolanthe* since the troupe had hit our shores, and in-tended to be in her seat day-in and day-out until the D'Oyly Carte people departed the city. When pressed for reasons, poor woman, she explained that in the on-stage world of G & S everything was safe, scintillating, com-fortable and predictable, while outside, the ugly grey weather of events, where dictators threatened and the nations raged against each other, made her constantly nervous.[30]

This comfort factor may well explain why G & S has actually increased its ap-peal over recent years at a time of increasing uncertainty and dislocation. Robert Stopford, Bishop of London, referred during his sermon at the D'Oyly Carte centenary service at St. Paul's Church, Covent Garden in 1975 to 'the joy which the operas have given, and can give, in times of stress'. David Cannadine has argued that the operas became less 'comfortingly and relevantly traditional' in the radical and confrontational Britain of the 1980s and early 1990s than they had in 'the more emollient and consensual inter-war years':

> The House of Lords was very largely a political irrelevance, the aristocracy had become the proprietors of safari parks or photographers' studios, and life peerages were given out to members of all social classes. With Britain no longer an imperial power, the army and the navy seemed increasingly tangential to national life. The legal profession was on the brink of the most systematic reform since the time of Gilbert and Sullivan themselves; and with the rapidly rising crime rates, and countless allegations of police corruption and brutality, the constabulary were no longer as appreciatively or as affectionately regarded as once they were.[31]

In the late 1990s and early 2000s, by contrast, heightened levels of anxiety and tension have surely made the comforting and traditional nature of G & S even more appealing, at the same time as debates in Britain about reforming the House of Lords and abolishing the office of Lord Chancellor have given them a new topicality.

The comfort factor (or divine emollient quality) in Gilbert and Sullivan was very clearly evident in the aftermath of the terrorist attacks of 11 September 2001. The New York City Opera production of *The Mikado* opened, as scheduled, four days later. Richard Suart, starring as Ko-Ko, describes the atmosphere of the opening night:

> With an audience who were not quite sure that they should be going out to enjoy themselves, and a cast distinctly in two minds as to whether they were ready yet to entertain people, we all met on stage before curtain-up— singers, dancers, dressers, stage-hands, management, the lot. The curtain went up, the American flag was lowered from the flies and the general manager spoke to the audience. We then all joined in to sing the Star Spangled Banner, everyone in the theatre. It broke the ice. The performance began and soon the audience began to relax and enjoy themselves.
>
> Immediately after the attacks, I wondered how on earth I could help. What could I possibly do? Nothing in me was trained to offer any assistance. But although I felt useless at first, I began to realize that New Yorkers needed desperately to get away from the television screen; they needed to be transported into another world for a few short hours, and why not Titipu?[32]

A week later the Philadelphia Savoy Company went ahead with a long-planned concert to celebrate their centenary. Among those invited to take part were the chorus of the Blue Hill Troupe from New York City, who had lost one of their members in the World Trade Center attack. Cynthia Morey, who directed the concert, wondered if they would want to come in the circumstances. 'It appeared that they not only wanted to—they needed to'.[33]

In addition to offering the reassurance and escapism of innocent enjoyment in frightening and bewildering times, G & S also provides more than a little magic. Perhaps this is another link with Harry Potter. It is a very wholesome, almost childlike kind of magic. Maybe that is why Gilbert and Sullivan is so often put on at Christmas. There have long been Christmas G & S seasons at the Savoy Theatre, and in 2003 a new production of *Pirates* was put on there over the holiday period in tandem with that other traditional Christmas offering, J. M. Barrie's *Peter Pan*. Television and radio schedulers link G & S with the festive season. On Christmas Day 1996 Classic FM broadcast *Iolanthe* with the dialogue delivered by leading politicians of the day: Lord Healey as the Lord Chancellor, Clare Short as Queen of the Fairies, Edwina Currie as Iolanthe, and Lord Archer as Tolloller. Channel 4 screened Barry Purves's brilliant animated film *Gilbert and Sullivan—The Very Models* on Christmas Day 1998, and the BBC chose Christmas Day 2002 for the first British television showing of *Topsy-Turvy*. It is, of course, possible to interpret this scheduling in several different ways. Is G & S regarded as a suitably solid and traditional companion for the Queen and the carol services on this most traditional and family-oriented of days, is it simply seen as bland and undemanding fare for an audience sated on Christmas pudding and sweet sherry, or is there a recognition of its magical fairy-tale qualities and aptness for the season when grim reality is suspended and we are allowed to dream dreams and weave spells?

There is yet another way of interpreting the television schedulers' fondness for putting Gilbert and Sullivan on at Christmas. Does it belong to a ghetto, albeit of a special and sacred kind, cut off from the normal world—rather like the Queen, in fact? This view, or something very like it, is found among the more ardent and obsessional G & S fans for whom the Savoy operas are a kind of sacred icon, to be treated with the utmost reverence. An advert for a course on operetta at the University of Liverpool's Centre for Continuing Education promises that 'After the rise of the Viennese operetta, we shall admire, compare and judge the music of those who followed ... with that sacred institution of Gilbert and Sullivan'. The use of the term 'sacred' here is telling—there is more than a whiff of the holy grail about the operas in the eyes of many of their fans who are fiercely protective of these relics and the way they are handed down to future generations. At the heart of this attitude of reverence is that holy of holies, the G & S tradition.

What does tradition mean in the context of Gilbert and Sullivan? Few are better qualified to answer this question than Geoffrey Dixon, longtime performer, producer, and student of G & S and self-confessed 'traditionalist', responsible for such examples of devotion to the cult as *The Gilbert and Sullivan Photofinder*, a 234-page index to published illustrations of the Savoy operas, and *The Gilbert and Sullivan Sorting System*, a guide on how to arrange a G & S collection. For him, 'it depends heavily on abstract matters such as charm, wholesomeness, precision and simplicity'. These are qualities which he, like a good many G & S fans, feels are in short supply nowadays:

> We live in a self-indulgent, 'in-yer-face' period where reticence, honesty, discipline and good manners are no longer put forward as virtues. Much popular entertainment, particularly on film and television, is unwhole-

some, loud, garish and immoderate and is presented in language which, if it can be heard at all, is indistinct, lazy, ugly and scatalogical. Any attempt to make the Savoy operas 'relevant' to all this is doomed to failure. [34]

Dixon and his fellow traditionalists regard the Savoy operas in much the same way that members of the Prayer Book Society regard the Book of Common Prayer. They are sacred icons which must be treated not just with respect but with reverence:

> The text should be delivered in an acceptable standard English accent— a Scouse *Iolanthe* or a Scots *Gondoliers* can be nothing more than gimmicky. . . . Gilbert's dialogue is spare, elegant and densely packed and needs to be delivered with deliberation, relish, clarity, attack and point— not thrown away in the hoarse, throaty whisper which is all too prevalent in the mass media today.[35]

Above all, perhaps, the essence of G & S tradition is attention to detail, wholesomeness, and respect for the integrity of the original. Quoting Gilbert's own dictum about treating a farcical subject in a thoroughly serious manner, Dixon defines the tradition in these terms:

> It does not really matter whether Yum-Yum is on Nanki-Poo's right at the end of 'Were you not to Ko-Ko Plighted' but it does matter that Captain Corcoran's uniform should be correct in every detail as that of a Captain of the Royal Navy of the period. It does not really matter whether Don Alhambra is standing or seated for his second act song but it does matter that Phoebe be not portrayed as a sleazy tart. . . . There is no need to thrash around restlessly trying to make the operas 'relevant' or 'different'. They are what they are and hold sufficient of value to ensure their continuance.[36]

For over a hundred years this intriguing mixture of obsessional attention to detail, extreme moral propriety, pure diction, and studied determination to avoid relevance and innovation was maintained and enforced by the D'Oyly Carte Company. Its survival into the penultimate decade of the twentieth century as guardian of an almost unchanging tradition of innocent enjoyment is one of the strangest elements of the whole Gilbert and Sullivan phenomenon and its remarkable powers of endurance.

༄

TWO

A THING OF SHREDS AND PATCHES:
THE D'OYLY CARTE OPERA COMPANY, 1961–1982

From its foundation in 1875 until the expiry of copyright on Gilbert's works at the end of 1961, the D'Oyly Carte Opera Company had a monopoly on the professional performance of Gilbert and Sullivan in the United Kingdom. No other professional productions were allowed and even the insertion of a song from one of the Savoy operas into a pantomime or revue was strictly forbidden. Any amateur company wishing to perform G & S had to obtain the company's permission, pay a royalty of 10 percent of its takings and hire D'Oyly Carte band parts and prompt books, which were expected to be followed in every detail.

Few theatrical companies have so jealously guarded their repertoire or kept it so exclusive and confined. There have been others dedicated primarily to performing the works of one author, like the Royal Shakespeare Company, but they have generally embraced other authors and different styles of production. The D'Oyly Carte stuck to G & S alone and performed it in a style which followed many of Gilbert's own directions and bits of 'business' added by early performers. In doing so, it delighted its fans who were sticklers for tradition and derived much of their pleasure from seeing familiar faces doing things in a familiar way. For them the thrill lay in the utterly predictable rather than the unexpected. It was this aspect of the (in this case North American) D'Oyly Carte audience that fascinated the young Paul Kresh on his first visit to a performance by the company:

> I remember little of what occurred on stage; for me, the real show was the audience. Every man-jack of them was prepared to rush on stage and fill in for Martyn Green as the Lord Chancellor, or for anyone else in the cast who might happen to fluff so much as a single line or be struck dumb by sudden indisposition or failure of memory. Next to me sat a woman who mumbled along with the cast every song in the score and every word of the

spoken dialogue of the entire book. Others sat equipped with oversized musical scores in which they buried their noses, seldom glancing up at the stage at all or smiling, no matter how hilarious the capers of the various pompous peers and the chorus of electrically lighted fairies. When a particular ballad, madrigal, or tongue-twisting tour de force such as the Lord Chancellor's nightmare song struck their fancy, these addicts got completely out of hand, rising with no decorum from their seats to clap their hands and cheer and cry for encores, some of which held up the action almost interminably.[1]

It is hard to think of any other performing group with such a loyal and conservative following. The prospect of anyone other than the D'Oyly Carte performing G & S filled many with horror. In 1959 Dorothy Alderley, a 72-year-old spinster from Oxford who had gone to her first Savoy opera in 1922 and seen *The Mikado* and *The Gondoliers* each 98 times, gathered half a million signatures for a petition to Parliament to extend the copyright and turn the D'Oyly Carte into a nationalised monopoly with the exclusive right to perform G & S in perpetuity. Alarmed that Danny Kaye had already recorded a version of the nightmare song from *Iolanthe* in which the second-class steamer from Harwich had become 'the Bronx subway', she greatly feared the 'Americanisation' of the operas, with Frank Sinatra being cast as the defendant in *Trial by Jury* and *The Gondoliers* reworked as 'The Road to Venice' starring Bob Hope and Bing Crosby. Her petition was presented in the House of Commons by her local MP and won some sympathy but not enough to bring about what would have been an unprecedented move to give legal protection to a national cultural institution.

As the day of the copyright's expiry loomed, there was a deep air of foreboding among Savoyards as to what might ensue, epitomised by the editorial in the January 1961 issue of the *Gilbert and Sullivan Journal*:

> We may, perhaps, have ephemeral perpetrations that would debase the operas. Perhaps public opinion can be left to look after these; after all, they will not be Gilbert and Sullivan Operas as we understand the term. Perhaps we have greater reason to consider more responsible and artistic productions which may do more than full justice to Sullivan at the expense of his collaborator. . . . Too great an emphasis on the music (not composed for operatic singers in the narrowest sense of that term) may well upset the interdependent balance of words and music, while to employ a lavish style of production would deprive the operas of much of the simple charm of style inherent in that designed by their creators.[2]

These sentiments say much about the mentality of the D'Oyly Carte fans and their view and expectation of the company. They were emphatic that G & S was not opera and that the words should have priority over the music. Indeed, in a classic expression of the British love of amateurism and the second-rate, they did not want the singing to be too good or the productions too lavish. They believed rather that G & S should be done in the D'Oyly Carte way, with what they called 'simple charm'.

The company itself commissioned a report by consultants who took a very different view of how it should respond to the post-copyright challenge:

> In our view the D'Oyly Carte Opera Company can only hope to maintain its place in the musical life of the country by radical re-organisation and re-thinking. Its statement that "we are essentially a travelling repertory company, and fully recognise the artistic, technical and economic limits of such an organisation" has little validity in 1961 and cannot be expected to inspire public confidence.[3]

Calling for 'a fresh approach and a new appraisal', the consultants specifically suggested among other initiatives a G & S festival season during the 1962 Edinburgh Festival, competitions for young singers and for the design of a new production, and the commissioning of a new operetta from a young British composer and librettist.

In the event, the company chose not to go down this route but rather to follow the promptings of its fans and continue in its role as keeper and transmitter of the holy grail of G & S tradition. The only significant change made to adjust to the new situation created by the ending of the copyright was the creation of a charitable trust to which Bridget D'Oyly Carte gave over her own rights to the operas, the company's scenery, costumes, band parts, prompt books, royalties from recordings, and other assets. The Trust, a body of establishment figures led by Antony Tuke, chairman of Barclays Bank, promptly assigned to Miss D'Oyly Carte the theatrical presentation of the Savoy operas by a limited company of which she was chairman and managing director. Thus the hold of the D'Oyly Carte family was maintained. The new Trust's conservatism is evident in an article written by its first president, Sir Malcolm Sargent, in the official D'Oyly Carte journal, the *Savoyard*:

> If there were producers living who were better at producing Gilbert and Sullivan than Gilbert himself was, then I am sure that the D'Oyly Carte tradition would cease. . . . But I see no producer living whose productions

have lasted more than a few years as against Gilbert's survival for over fifty. Indeed of the new productions that I have seen my impression is that the music is lost in over-production—the stage is kept too 'busy' for the wit of the libretto and the charm of the lyrics to make their full appeal –in short, the producer has taken the pessimistic attitude of modern 'musicals' that the music and poetry is too weak to stand alone and must be bolstered up by clever choreography, décor, lighting, etc.[4]

Tellingly, Sargent comes to the same conclusion as the editor of the *Gilbert and Sullivan Journal*, although in his view it is the music as much as the words that suffer from overlavish and modern productions. He also makes much of the fact that the D'Oyly Carte tradition preserves Gilbert's own production values and style. This combined commitment to simplicity and tradition underlay the company's approach to performing Gilbert and Sullivan throughout its last twenty-one years. Quite apart from ideological considerations, it was a manifesto suited to an organisation that was increasingly strapped for cash and unable to afford the clever choreography, décor, and lighting against which Sargent railed.

In opting to continue simple, traditional productions, the new Trust was, of course, doing exactly what its devoted fans wanted. Their support was regarded as crucial to the D'Oyly Carte's success in the postmonopoly era and it was harnessed in all sorts of ways. A new scheme of associate membership was established in 1961 with the benefits of priority booking, reduction on the cost of hiring band parts, and subscription to the *Savoyard* which became a key link between fans and the company. The fans also provided moderately priced 'digs' for company members on tour. In the words of principal soprano Cynthia Morey, 'providing you did not mind talking shop for the whole of your stay, they nearly always offered a good deal'.[5] The relationship with amateur performers was also carefully cultivated. After the copyright expired, most amateur societies continued to hire their band parts from the D'Oyly Carte and still looked to it as a model and mentor for their productions. Throughout the 1960s and 1970s the *Savoyard* carried several pages of closely printed lists of forthcoming amateur shows. Many retired company members found congenial employment coaching and directing amateurs. George Cook, who retired as principal bass in 1969, set up a business hiring complete sets of fans for *The Mikado*. He was not the only singer to cash in on the (other kind of) fans' devotion—principal soprano Joyce Wright made hand-painted lampshades depicting figures from the operas which were advertised through the *Savoyard*.

As far as their devotees were concerned, one of the most distinctive and attractive features of the D'Oyly Carte was its strong family atmosphere, reinforced by the number of marriages in the company and the fact that so many people stayed with it for so long. There were some particularly impressive examples of long service. Harry Haste served as the company's master carpenter from 1919 to 1962. Cis Blain, the touring wardrobe mistress, presided over 2,000 costumes stored on the top floor of a terraced house in Camberwell for forty-nine years until her retirement in 1971. Isidore Godfrey joined the company in 1925 and retired in 1968, having conducted, on his calculation, 12,000 performances, including 3,000 of *The Mikado*. Several singers were given administrative jobs once they retired from the stage, prompting the adage 'old tenors never die—they simply join the management'. Bert Newby started as a chorister in 1946, became a principal tenor and went on to be stage manager, director of productions, and finally company manager until his death in 1979. Gordon Mackenzie joined as a chorister in 1954 and went on to be assistant manager, company manager, and business manager until the company's closure in 1982. James Marsland went from being a tenor chorister to assistant producer, and Leonard Osborn from tenor soloist to production director.

The family feeling was also fostered by the thirty-five weeks each year that company members spent on tour. For Valerie Masterson, principal soprano from 1964 to 1971, this was one of the most striking features of being with the D'Oyly Carte—'people didn't have flats or houses to go back to—touring was your life. We moved around together on the train, or increasingly in caravans'. [6] She was one of many who married a fellow-member of the touring company— in her case the principal flautist Andrew March. The experience of touring could produce tension as well as romance between singers and orchestra members. A management memo from 1976 records that a chorister 'when discussing the between show meal arrangements for back-to-back shows, asked that meals could be prepared separately for orchestra and artists, as naturally the orchestra were always able to get to the food first, and sometimes would not leave sufficient for the artists'. [7] On the whole, however, the experience of being together so much engendered a huge sense of camaraderie. Peter Riley, who began as props and baggage master in 1965 and ended up as deputy general manager, once told me that he felt the best description of what it was like to be in the D'Oyly Carte was Dodie Smith's definition of the family as 'that dear octopus from whose tentacles we never quite escape nor, in our inmost hearts, ever quite wish to'. [8]

For those within it, the D'Oyly Carte was a very Victorian family run on strictly hierarchical lines and firm moral principles. Not for nothing was it known as the 'The Savoy Boarding School' or the 'D'Oyly Carte Sunday School'. Much of this tone was set by Bridget D'Oyly Carte, who presided over the company as a rather remote *mater familias*. Shy and reclusive by nature, she had never expected to succeed her father in running the family firm. Her own instincts were perhaps to innovate and experiment but she went along with the extreme caution and conservatism of the fans and the company's senior management. Although she personally supervised soloists' auditions, regularly helped to stuff envelopes with flyers for the coming season, and enjoyed perching on one of the wickerwork costume baskets chatting to the wardrobe staff, she was generally regarded as aloof and distant. During six years with the company in the 1950s Cynthia Morey never once met Miss Carte, as she was always known (Dame Bridget after 1975): 'She always seemed to be guarded by an impenetrable band of protectors who made access virtually impossible. If anything, after the Trust formed in 1961, it was worse'.[9] According to Paul Seeley, the company's repetiteur until its closure, 'after the formation of the Trust she became a virtual stranger to most members of the Company'. [10]

The Victorian boarding school atmosphere was reinforced by the senior management. The company was run from offices in the Savoy Hotel presided over by the Pickwickian figure of Albert Truelove, company secretary, and Frederic Lloyd, the monocled general manager whose paternalistic style is evident in the numerous memos which he wrote to Bridget D'Oyly Carte. These ranged in subject matter from the desirability 'if only from a psychological point of view' of having the entire company inoculated against influenza to the personal foibles of company members, such as the principal contralto who did not wish to join a tour to America 'as she disliked the flight to Rome where so many members of the company were inebriated' and who 'hates the idea of going to Scotland as she does not like the country and is too far away from home'.[11] Every member of the company was assessed at an annual 'field day' and given an annual report by the production director, musical director, and company manager. The comments in these reports, which were not seen by their subjects, were often very personal with remarks like 'curious personality but nevertheless is the only true contralto of the belting quality in the company'.

The company was run with a strict regard for respectability and moral propriety. Wherever possible, ladies and gentlemen had dressing rooms on different sides of the stage. Both on and off stage artistes observed a strict dress code. John Reed recalls that 'you never saw girls coming to rehearsals in trousers' and for recording sessions in the 1960s the male chorus were expected to wear suits and many of the ladies wore hats. Cynthia Morey remembers small semicircles of pleated organdie being stitched on the front of the contadines' dresses for *The Gondoliers* 'in case the slightest hint of cleavage might be detected'. Male company members were invariably referred to by their surnames and females were very much seen and treated as 'the ladies of the D'Oyly Carte as opposed to the girls in the chorus'. While there were nicknames for some of the more

FIGURE 2.1 The ladies of the D'Oyly Carte. The female *Pinafore* chorus perched on the ancient wicker props skips before one of the last performances before closure, 1981 (*Author's collection*)

prominent and long-serving figures, John Reed recalls that 'it took me years to dare call Anne Drummond-Grant Drummy or Isidore Godfrey Goddy'.[12]

Until the mid-1960s the company did most of its touring by train. Provided the company bought sixty seats, the scenery, costumes, and props could travel free in three goods waggons at the rear. Sunday morning train calls saw the ladies of the D'Oyly Carte kitted out in best suits, hats, gloves, and long umbrellas. Separate reserved compartments were allocated to principals, ladies of the chorus, gentlemen of the chorus, wardrobe staff, stage management, and orchestra, so preserving the delicate social distinctions which Gilbert had made so much of in the operas.

Discipline was rigorously enforced. The company's standard contract included a clause to the effect that 'the artist shall not introduce into his performance any material not previously approved by Bridget D'Oyly Carte and shall not without such consent alter the music, words, or business of the part which he is playing'. Company managers frequently issued admonishments addressed to 'the Ladies and Gentlemen of the Chorus'. A typical one, dating from 1971, begins: 'I am deeply concerned about the recent bad and unprofessional behaviour of some of the Chorus, not only in the wings but on-stage as well. After numerous warnings and repeated requests for silence in the wings, there are still those of you who persistently chatter and create a general nuisance'. In 1978 three members of the male chorus were called in to Frederic Lloyd's office and carpeted for 'continuous misbehaviour during performances on stage. This consists of not singing Gilbert's written script and substituting (according to other chorus members) other words (sometimes rude)'.[13]

For chorus members in particular the regime was punishing. They were expected to be on stage for 270 nights a year (usually made up of 35 weeks on tour followed by a London season of up to 13 weeks). A request by choristers in 1976 to be allowed some nights off was turned down. The accompanying managerial memo notes, 'if we did agree, out of 270 nights suggest three off which should never be at the beginning or end of the week'. In 1977, in response to union demands, each chorus member was allowed one night off per week but another notice 'to the ladies and gentlemen of the chorus' required that 'on the day of your night off, you will telephone Stage Management between 12 noon and 12.30 pm to check that it is in order for you take your night off'. Requests by chorus members for time off were generally turned down, as in the case of a Scottish tenor who asked to be allowed off the second act of *Pirates of Penzance* on Christmas Eve so he could drive back home in time for the festive season. Although he pointed out that the tenors are only on stage for the last ten minutes of the act, the management insisted that, Frederic-like, he must do his duty. Backstage staff were subject to even more draconian rules, with girls in the wardrobe department being allowed to talk to each other for only six minutes in the morning and six in the afternoon.

Coming from performing musicals, Kenneth Sandford, the company's principal baritone from 1957 until 1982, was struck by the very different atmosphere prevailing in the D'Oyly Carte. He found 'a kind of upper class gentility pervading the principals' dressing rooms—a sort of public school ambience—and the cloister-like quiet backstage, as if the company was taking part in some time-honoured ritual far too serious to warrant any light-hearted banter'. He was also struck by the management's distance from and general indifference to the artists. Negotiating as Equity representative to secure a share of recording royalties for the artistes, he was somewhat nonplussed when the company manager responded 'Damn it all, Sandford. Miss Carte provides the orchestra, the chorus, the scenery and the props. All you've got to do is go on stage and sing'.[14]

Money was a perpetual bone of contention between management and staff. It was always in short supply and the company had a reputation for being parsimonious, if not actually mean. D'Oyly Carte artistes were for the most part tremendously loyal and prepared to work for salaries considerably lower than in other branches of the profession. A precise and somewhat miserly scale of payments was drawn up for those playing small parts. In 1975, for example, the parts of the foreman in *Trial by Jury*, Fleta in *Iolanthe*, Go-To in *The Mikado*, and the first citizen in *Yeomen* attracted the paltry sum of 75 pence apiece, while those playing the four speaking ghosts in *Ruddigore* each received twenty pence for their moment of stardom and the carpenter in *Pinafore* the princely sum of £1.25. By 1982 these payments had risen to £1.43, 44 pence and £2.20, respectively.

The problem of money, or more precisely the lack of it, dominated the last twenty-one years of the company's existence. Touring became increasingly expensive as people switched from travelling by train to car or caravan. As a result, sets and costumes had to be transported by lorry, with drivers insisting on being paid throughout the tour. Every effort was made to keep costs down. A 'unit set' designed by Peter Goffin provided a basic frame into which different backcloths could be slotted and enabled the company to tour with nine lorries instead of twenty. In the costume and property departments a philosophy of make do and mend prevailed. Many of the prop baskets were more than thirty years old. Costumes were lovingly preserved and patched up so that they could be used season after season. The robes made for Tolloller and Mountararat in *Iolanthe* in the 1920s were only finally retired in 1968. *Ruddigore* costumes dating from 1947 were still in use when the company closed in 1982. When costumes eventually became worn out, embroidery, buttons, and anything else that might be reuseable were painstakingly removed and kept. The D'Oyly Carte Company was literally becoming a thing of shreds and patches.

Much rested on the commitment and ésprit de corps of the artistes who were expected to give eight performances a week (six evenings and two matinees), sometimes involving six different operas, for forty-eight weeks of the year. It is not surprising that several found the sheer grind too much. During its final twenty-five years the company was made up of two distinct groups—those who used it as a launching-pad for their careers and moved on to other opera companies and those who stayed for a long time. In the first category were Valerie Masterson, Tom Round, Cynthia Morey, and John Fryatt. The second was dominated by John Reed, who joined in 1951 and remained until 1979, and Kenneth Sandford, with the company from 1957 until its demise in 1982, and included long-serving choristers like Beti Lloyd-Jones (1956–1982). For this latter group, the D'Oyly Carte was their life. Even those who passed through it more briefly found that it gave them a unique experience and wonderful training. Sunday School it may have been but it was one where players were taught how to wear a costume, move on stage, and articulate good and clear diction. Drilling in this last skill never stopped. Principals, even well on in their careers, would have the producer coming round to their dressing room to tell them that the second word in the third line of their solo had not been as clearly articulated as it should have been.

In a way that perhaps only a company committed to Gilbert and Sullivan could, the D'Oyly Carte straddled the worlds of light entertainment and opera and of amateur and professional performance. It took singers from the Black and White Minstrels, like Alan Spencer, and sent others into careers in grand opera, like Thomas Lawlor and Valerie Masterson. Its position somewhere in between these two worlds was symbolised by the location of its London performing base in the later 1960s and throughout the 1970s in Sadler's Wells Theatre, a solid if slightly uncomfortable and shabby island of middle-class restraint and respectability stranded between the brash commercialism of the West End and the trendy fringe theatres of Islington and Hampstead. Many of the singers were recruited from amateur societies and were familiar with G & S, which was probably just as well, given how quickly they had to master their roles. Several had joined the company as a direct result of attending a D'Oyly Carte performance. After seeing them in Leicester, Cynthia Morey resolved 'This is what I must do with my life' and wrote straight off for an audition. Thomas Round went to a performance in Hammersmith while on thirty-six-hour wartime leave from the RAF: 'That day changed my life for ever. As soon as the overture finished, I knew that was what I wanted to do. I had replaced the tenor in my mind's eye'. He asked for an audition at the end of the show and was given one immediately. [15]

Those who successfully passed the D'Oyly Carte auditions—for which Isidore Godfrey's standard opening question was 'Have you got a bright English song?'—found themselves on a steep learning curve. Whether joining as principals or chorus members, new recruits had two weeks of music rehearsals with the company repetiteur and two weeks with the assistant producer being drilled in dialogue, movement, and dancing. In this time, up to seven operas had to be learned before the newcomers joined the rest of the company for a week of full rehearsal before the start of the new touring season. Throughout this brief but intensive period of training the emphasis was on precise conformity to the moves and business laid down in the prompt books and, in the words of one weary chorister, on 'diction, diction, diction'. New soloists had the sense of stepping into someone else's shoes—almost literally, as wherever possible their predecessor's costumes would be adjusted to fit them to avoid the cost of replacements. John Reed recalls that 'when a new person was chosen, we always felt it was basically because the costume fitted them. You stepped into a whole set of roles because they had been done by your predecessor, regardless of whether they were suitable or not'. In this and in other respects there was relatively little scope for new soloists to display their creativity. In Reed's words, 'You had to speak up for yourself a bit. Otherwise, D'Oyly Carte would have walked right over you'.[16] Nonetheless, he found ways of gradually introducing his own bits of 'business' as in the encore of 'Never Mind the Why and Wherefore' for which he bought a lifebelt, asked Kenneth Sandford to hold it in the wings, and reappeared with it over his shoulders after apparently jumping into the sea. Sandford himself recalled that 'Every so often Peggy Ann Jones and I would say 'Wouldn't it be nice if we changed things a tiny bit. So one month we would move an extra foot across the stage. No one would notice until the understudies did it and then when the director queried it the understudy would say 'Oh, but Mr Sandford does it'.[17]

With this underlying commitment to keeping things largely unchanged, it is not surprising that when asked what effect the lifting of copyright would have on the company, Bridget D'Oyly Carte responded 'very little, I should imagine'. Her sanguine view seemed to be confirmed by the success of the 1961–62 London winter season, which lasted for fifteen weeks and took the company back to the Savoy Theatre. Malcolm Sargent returned as guest conductor for several performances and *Pinafore* was spruced up with new costumes for the female

FIGURE 2.2 Classic D'Oyly Carte. John Reed leads the company in *HMS Pinafore* on the eve of the expiry of copyright, 1961 *(John Blomfield/D'Oyly Carte Archive)*

chorus designed by Peter Goffin. The impact of the first non-D'Oyly Carte professional productions—Sadler's Wells' *Iolanthe* and *Mikado* and Tyrone Guthrie's
Pinafore and *Pirates*—was much less than had been feared and did no damage
to the company's box office takings.

The winter of 1962–63 saw a successful North American tour, which began
with a fourteen-hour nonstop flight from London to New York in a chartered
DC 7. Some critics identified weaknesses that were to be mentioned more and
more in the coming years. The *Chicago Daily News* found *The Gondoliers* 'a curious combination of quaint, old-fashioned charm and outmoded mustiness'
and 'amazingly dull in long stretches', and the *Toronto Daily Star* complained of
'poor singing, weak acting, static and unimaginative staging, timid and capri-
cious conducting, lack lustre orchestral playing, a mumbling frozen chorus,
amateurish dancing, colourless costumes, old-fashioned sets and irrational lighting'. It put much of the blame for these failings on the frenetic schedule in which
the artists were performing five shows in forty-eight hours and concluded 'it's a
wonder they could stumble on stage, let alone act or sing'.[18] These criticisms
aside, however, the company was generally well received across the Atlantic and
made further North American tours in 1964–65, 1966–67, 1968, 1976, and 1978.

Some critics nearer home were also worried that the company was over-
stretching itself. Stan Meares, writing in the *Gilbert and Sullivan Journal* in 1966,
complained that the orchestra 'lacks quality, and its strings and brass are grim,
the size of the chorus has been reduced and the principals are over-strained by
having to sing every night'. He also criticised the 'dull, unimaginative and tired
sets'.[19] For many of its fans, however, the mid-1960s constituted a golden age for
the D'Oyly Carte. The 1963–64 London season, which lasted sixteen weeks, was
the company's longest for thirty-seven years. There was a burst of recordings—
Gondoliers and *Patience* in 1961, *Ruddigore* in 1962, *Yeomen* and *Trial by Jury* in
1964, *Princess Ida* in 1965, *Sorcerer* in 1966, and *Pirates* in 1968—featuring a
strong team of soloists led by John Reed, Kenneth Sandford, Donald Adams,
Thomas Round, Valerie Masterson, Jean Hindmarsh, and Gillian Knight. The
company's *Patience*, televised on BBC 2 on 27 December 1965, was the first full-
length Gilbert and Sullivan opera shown on British television, and D'Oyly
Carte singers also provided the soundtrack for an animated film of *Ruddigore*
released in 1967.

The 1960s also brought two innovative new productions by Anthony Besch,
an internationally renowned opera director who had fallen in love with G & S
when he first saw *The Mikado* at the age of eight. His 1964 *Mikado* departed significantly from the blockings in Gilbert's prompt books and the traditional
'business' that had accrued over the years while keeping enough familiar gags to
keep the fans happy. Designer Disley Jones retained Charles Ricketts's 1926 cos-

tumes but devised a new set with fibre-glass translucent panels and a garden bridge with moulded rocks. Restaged by Stuart Burge, this production was filmed at Golders Green Hippodrome in 1966, providing a relatively rare permanent record of D'Oyly Carte in what many considered to be its prime.

In 1968 Besch was responsible for a new production of the *Gondoliers*. The action was updated by a century, with the scenery, designed by John Stoddard, resembling a nineteenth-century engraving with crosshatch shading. More radically, as Roberta Morrell has noted, 'Besch broke down the rigid, synchronised blocking for the chorus and introduced natural movement and gesture, immediately creating a realism previously unknown to the company'.[20] His major rethink of the characterisation of the principal roles had an especially liberating effect on Kenneth Sandford, playing the Grand Inquisitor, who had been schooled in the D'Oyly Carte tradition of 'talking out front and not to people on stage. You had to purse your lips and speak to the audience with no reference to anyone else on the stage'.[21] Besch encouraged him to humanise Don Alhambra, making him a flirtatious old gentleman with a distinct eye for the ladies, and relate to other performers on stage. The changes did not go down well with 'Snookie' Fancourt, the widow of the company's longtime principal bass, who had coached numerous soloists in the traditional ways. She complained to Sandford after the first performance, 'He's no longer a "grand" Inquisitor'. As far as he was concerned, however, he had at last been freed from the stuffiness and preciousness of the old D'Oyly Carte approach and allowed to develop a real character. The Grand Inquisitor was not the only role that was humanised in the mid-sixties—the youthful Gillian Knight, who took over the principal contralto roles, brought a very different approach from the 'battle-axes' who had played them before.

Besch's *Gondoliers* showed that the company was capable of innovation and a fresh approach to the operas. Inevitably it attracted criticism from die-hard traditionalists who complained in the pages of the *Savoyard* that it 'dragged Gilbert and Sullivan down to the level of a musical comedy'.[22] Particular exception was taken to the Duke and his party eating spaghetti during Don Alhambra's song 'I Stole the Prince', which was seen as a vulgar distraction. This piece of business allowed huge scope for practical jokes. Jon Ellison, who played the obsequious waiter who brings on the plate of spaghetti, concealed in it on various occasions a glass eye, a set of false teeth, a bloodied finger, a beetle, and a spider. It also presented Peter Riley, as stage manager, with the problem of sourcing a supply of spaghetti in each tour venue:

> There was usually an Italian restaurant near the theatre but in the wilds of Wimbledon there was a dearth of such establishments and the nearest

supply was a five mile taxi journey away. We had to put it in a thermos flask and I don't think it tasted very good by the time it reached the stage. One night it didn't arrive at all so I sent a ham sandwich on instead. Miss D'Oyly Carte suggested that it would be much easier to use false spaghetti made out of white knitting wool but it wouldn't have been as realistic. Eventually we took to heating up tins on a hot-plate back-stage.[23]

The 1970s started well for the company when it made its first sally into Continental Europe for ninety years with a visit to Denmark in 1970. *The Sorcerer* was revived in 1971 for the first time since 1940 when the scenery and costumes had been destroyed during the Blitz. Michael Heyland's new production, with sets by the cartoonist Osbert Lancaster, was notable for giving the chorus individual characters to develop. In 1973 *HMS Pinafore* was televised. The *Savoyard* announced an agreement with Associated Television to record all the operas for television and release them on videocassettes but in the event no others were filmed. The following year the company took *The Mikado* to Rome, and in 1975 it celebrated its centenary with a return to the Savoy Theatre for a season of all the surviving operas. At the end of the performance of *The Sorcerer* on 25 March Harold Wilson, the Prime Minister and a D'Oyly Carte trustee, came on to the stage and said: 'This is part of our national birthright'. A fully staged production of *Utopia Limited*, revived for the first time since 1893, proved so popular that four further performances were given at the Royal Festival Hall and a concert performance of *The Grand Duke* was given with television newsreader Richard Baker as the narrator. These two operas were subsequently recorded under the baton of Royston Nash, principal conductor from 1971 to 1979. *Princess Ida* was restaged for the 1976–77 season at Sadler's Wells by Leonard Osborn.

The Queen's silver jubilee in 1977 was marked by a new production of *Iolanthe* by Michael Heyland. Designer Bruno Santini created a shimmering magic effect with a silver cobweb strung across the stage for the fairies' entrance. At Harold Wilson's suggestion, there was also a command performance of *HMS Pinafore* in Windsor Castle. It cemented close links between the royal family and the D'Oyly Carte Opera Company. Prince Charles saw *The Mikado* in 1960 and remarked to John Reed at the end on the ugliness of Katisha. The Queen has seen *Ruddigore, Mikado, Gondoliers,* and *Pinafore* performed by the D'Oyly Carte, as well as watching her eldest son, Prince Charles, playing the role of the Pirate King in *Pirates* at Gordonstoun School and attending the Tower of London production of *Yeomen* and Scottish Opera's *Gondoliers*. The patriotic and monarchical connection was further reinforced by the release of a special LP in jubilee year entitled 'If Patriotic Sentiment Is Wanted' featuring such songs as

FIGURE 2.3 Silver Jubilee *Iolanthe*. Patricia Leonard as the Fairy Queen and John Reed as the Lord Chancellor, 1977 *(Reg Wilson/D'Oyly Carte Archive)*

'The Soldiers of Our Queen', 'He Is an Englishman', 'When Britain Really Ruled the Waves', and 'A Regular Royal Queen'.

Despite all these successes, there were growing rumblings of discontent from company members through the 1970s that things were not as they had once been. Two senior artistes, Beti Lloyd-Jones and Jon Ellison, complained to the management in 1973 that 'the standard of productions was dropping and that tradition was going at the expense of doing anything for a cheap laugh'.[24] An action plan arising from comments made in the company suggestion box in the late 1970s points to another growing problem:

> Devise some way of preventing Principals becoming bored and apathetic in their approach to roles—this also applies to some members of the chorus. It *does* show from the front, and gives the overall appearance that we don't care—not true.[25]

The company was facing an increasing number of new challenges. Provincial theatres were closing down, especially the older type which had a reasonable orchestra pit. Touring digs were more difficult to find. A different kind of singer was coming into the D'Oyly Carte, recruited from music or drama college rather than from an amateur society, with less feel for and familiarity with Gilbert and Sullivan and a view of the company simply as a stepping stone to a contract with a 'proper' opera house. In general, both principals and choristers were staying for shorter and shorter periods. Trade union attitudes were replacing the old loyalty and family feeling. The Musicians' Union demanded opera rates for the orchestra and insisted that a full band was toured, putting an end to the old practice of touring a small orchestra and picking up extra players locally without the need to pay them travel and subsistence costs. Choristers were no longer prepared to work for 20 percent below Equity minimum wages. John Reed was shocked by the new militant attitude displayed at the beginning of the company's seventeen-week tour of Australia and New Zealand in 1979. Everyone had enjoyed a relaxing week by the beach after being flown out, except for Reed himself, who had been sent on a gruelling promotional tour of the cities where they would be performing. At the end of their first rehearsal, conductor Fraser Goulding asked the chorus to stay on for a few minutes just to polish the act 2 finale. The Equity representative promptly stood up and said 'You know that means we'll be going into overtime'. Reed says: 'I never thought we would get to that stage. When I think of how we used to go on far into the evening working on things to get them right and never thought of overtime. I realized that was the time to go'.[26] He left the company quietly but suddenly at the end of the tour, which turned out to be the company's last trip abroad.

Above all, the financial problems that had long dogged the company were becoming insuperable. By the late 1970s D'Oyly Carte was losing £2,000 a week. To survive, it needed some element of public subsidy. This meant going to the Arts Council, the public body which already dispensed funding on a large scale to other opera companies—indeed 21 percent of its total budget went to supporting the five national opera companies in the United Kingdom. The D'Oyly Carte felt it had a strong case as the only real touring opera company left. It could claim a substantial national audience—350,000 people attended its performances in 1979. Prompted by the D'Oyly Carte's first tentative approach that year about the possibility of public funding, the Arts Council set up a working party to 'examine the demand for light opera in the United Kingdom and to propose suitable methods for meeting any demand so identified, with particular reference to touring possibilities'.

The working party's report, published in January 1981, identified the peculiarly British prejudice which regards 'light' opera as fundamentally 'inferior' to serious opera, noting that 'this distinction between serious and light is smaller and more "factual" on the continent and in Eastern Europe: in Britain it is almost moral'.[27] Describing this as an example of the British class system that 'brings out the worst in people—snobbishness, conceit and defensiveness', it went on to point out that the creation of the Arts Council had made the distinction worse by encouraging the view that while serious opera required state subsidy, light opera should pay for itself commercially.

The bulk of the report was devoted to the plight of the D'Oyly Carte. It had a distinctly equivocal tone, insisting that 'not one member of the committee was anxious to see the destruction of a great tradition', yet at the same time betraying the anti-G & S and anti-D'Oyly Carte bias found in the British arts establishment throughout the twentieth century:

> Several members of the Committee began the Enquiry unashamedly of the belief (or prejudice) that D'Oyly Carte was an anachronism: like a splendid old actress well past her prime, waddling away into the distance to a well deserved and peaceful death. They were instinctively inclined to help her on her way and by no means to bring her back to the limelight. Gilbert and Sullivan, they reckoned, would survive very nicely, thank you, without the stifling ministrations of a theatrical management and tradition rooted and remaining in the nineteenth century.[28]

This candid admission of a preconceived prejudice prepared the way for a sustained assault on the standards of the company. 'Frankly, we heard many criticisms', the report noted, 'and there is no doubt comparisons with subsidised national opera companies in terms of production and musical standards have been unfavourable'. Nine specific shortcomings were listed:

Technically, the productions are unsophisticated.

Twentieth century marketing techniques have passed D'Oyly Carte by.

A newly revived production looks under-rehearsed.

Musically the performances are variable and have fallen off with small orchestras making, frankly, a rather thin sound.

The rigidity of the repertoire occasionally means wooden or tired performances.

The slavishness of some of the 'business' is now meaningless and frequently automatic, with excessive devotion to the printed word.

Some theatre managers believe that the audiences are not only getting smaller but also older and there is not enough evidence of a new, young audience coming along.

Some of the older members of the Company are due for a rest.

The dancing, by and large, is non-existent.[29]

It could have been worse. An unpublished memo written by Richard Pulford, the Arts Council's deputy secretary-general, after seeing a D'Oyly Carte production of *Pirates* was considerably more damning: 'The spoken words were simply awful—fourth rate panto stuff. The general level of characterisation was distressingly low. The production suffered the worst excesses of obsessional stage symmetry I have ever seen on the professional stage; every choral gesture in clockwork motion'. The working party's report was not wholly negative. It paid tribute to the company's remarkable achievement in mounting eight performances a week for up to forty-eight weeks of the year, thirty-five of them on tour: 'Week in, week out, the Company sets down in Bristol or Sunderland or Eastbourne or Liverpool, does acceptable business at worst and splendidly at best, and generally is welcomed as an essential part of each theatre's annual programme'.[30]

In many ways, the report argued, D'Oyly Carte was a victim of its own success, or rather its stringent financial control, which the report admitted was 'the most striking feature of the company's administration'. It pointed out that the company had first tentatively approached the Arts Council about funding in 1967, arguing that without it they would collapse. 'Ironically, it seems to weaken the company's case that they have managed to survive the last twelve years and avoid bankruptcy'.[31] The loyal fan base was noted, as was the fact that other opera companies performing G & S since the expiry of copyright had often had rather disappointing audiences. 'There is real evidence that if it is Gilbert and Sullivan you want to see, it is D'Oyly Carte you like to see doing it'.[32] The working party were also impressed 'that the D'Oyly Carte productions over the years and still today are a much-used bridge by audiences making the nervous journey from "pop" into serious music and grand opera' and they conceded, despite their many criticisms, that 'the productions are trim and exceptionally well-maintained, some of the soloists are first-rate and the chorus work is sound. That all this should still be available without subsidy is little short of miraculous'.[33]

The report calculated that a subsidised national opera company touring Gilbert and Sullivan for thirty-five weeks a year would probably cost the Arts Council £1,000,000 (an eighth of the annual subsidy given to the Royal Opera House). It argued, however, that the D'Oyly Carte Company was a very much more commercial animal than the subsidised national opera companies. Its box office takings provided 80 percent of total income, whereas for Covent Garden and the English National Opera the comparable figure was only around 25 percent. Helping D'Oyly Carte must be about encouraging its commercialism and not swamping it with public subsidy—to give it an annual £1,000,000 grant would be 'killing it with kindness'. The company was uniquely well placed to

seek commercial sponsorship—as a known quantity with an established repertoire, it could be 'hawked about like a tennis tournament or cricket competition
to the highest bidder'.[34]

In keeping with its overall tone, the report's conclusion was distinctly equivocal. It pointed out that 'there are frankly some who believe that death has already set in for D'Oyly Carte. They are simply clinging on by the grace of an elderly public and an elderly tradition, supported by royalties and hires from
amateur performances'. There was, too, the genuine worry that 'an injection of
public money into an organisation recognised by its own directors to be in decline will act merely as a temporary life-support machine, keeping the heart
pumping (at great expense) when nature demands that the patient has, in every
other sense, died'.[35] Significant public subsidy would also weaken the company's
resolve in the market place and strengthen the negotiating hand of the unions.
But this argument was counterbalanced by what the working party felt was ultimately a more powerful case for the defence:

> The greatest fear, however, and in our view overriding all others is that the
> D'Oyly Carte could disappear, and the loss would be felt in almost every
> major provincial city in the country as well as in London. . . . We have de-
> tected in the Company's evidence the mild but clear hint that if they do not
> get some indication of help soon they might prefer to call it a day in the
> next year or two while the company is still a dignified and beloved institu-
> tion, rather than dwindle unhappily to a shabby end.[36]

The working party concluded that 'the D'Oyly Carte should be supported,
sparingly'. It suggested an Arts Council grant of between £50,000 and £100,000
a year tied to specific expenditure, for additional musicians, guest directors, or
a new production, and not simply to be set against the general annual deficit. At
the end of a given period, perhaps three years, the council should make a hard-
nosed reassessment of the company's state of health and if significant improve-
ment had not taken place, it might be best to accept that 'the Company's brave
and glorious history is at an end'.

The Arts Council rejected the report's recommendation of limited financial
support for D'Oyly Carte on the grounds that 'it has been the Council's consis-
tent policy to subsidise companies only after they have reached acceptable standards, and it does not feel able to make an exception in this case'.[37] The company found itself in a catch-22 situation. It fully conceded that its standards
needed improving—especially in regard to size of orchestra and chorus—but
the only way to do this was by being granted a fraction of the huge subsidy given
to other national and touring opera companies. Yet the Arts Council was refus-

ing it the wherewithal to raise its standards. An appeal from leading luminaries of the classical music world including Sir Adrian Boult, Sir Geraint Evans, and Dame Heather Harper failed to move the council and drew the response from Sir Roy Shaw, the secretary general, that it was not prepared to offer support to an organisation whose work had been assessed as unsatisfactory.

News of the Arts Council's refusal of funding in February 1981 provoked a huge outcry. *The Times* thundered:

> If Burbage's Mermaid Theatre company were still in existence, still performing Shakespeare with pious attention to the dictates of the great man's prompt-book, we would undoubtedly cherish and sustain it even if its performances were somewhat short on that verve which goes with innovation, and its casting organized according to the principle of Buggins' turn. The Russians still cherish Chekhov's original stage company, and the Japanese make their hereditary grand masters of the Noh drama into National Artistic Monuments, a status roughly equivalent to a Grade One listing. The nearest thing we have to such a continuity of house tradition is the D'Oyly Carte Opera Company, which has been playing Gilbert and Sullivan for the past 105 years, and is now threatened with extinction. . . . It is an extremely difficult not to say dangerous thing to put a pistol at the head of the Duke of Plaza Toro and threaten to shoot unless industry pays up.[38]

A correspondent to the newspaper complained that

> Russian ballet, Italian opera, German lieder and French farce are subsidised to the hilt together with a 'rag-bag' of latter day cacophonous pantonics not dissimilar in sound to the noises made by orchestras permanently trying to get into tune, whereas the only Company devoted exclusively to bringing British opera to as wide an audience as possible is being killed off by a tiny minority of intransigent dispensers of tax payers' money who have expressed the opinion that performances are wooden—an opinion not shared by the vast majority of those audiences who (unlike critics and VIPs) actually hand over hard cash for their seats.

He went on to warn the government: 'A survey of most Tories of my acquaintance has revealed that some 60 percent are Gilbert and Sullivan devotees who are to a man (and woman) very angry indeed; in fact, angered to the extent that almost all are prepared to ditch this Government at the next election if the situation is not retrieved'.[39]

However disgruntled many Tory voters may have been about this issue, Margaret Thatcher's government was riding high in the opinion polls and there was no imminent prospect of a general election at which the pro-D'Oyly Carte vote could be mobilised. The Tory victory in 1979 had certainly not helped the company's cause—Mrs Thatcher was no great fan of G & S and she was strongly opposed to public subsidies of all kinds—but the Arts Council was wholly independent of the government and not under direct political control. As prime minister in 1975, Harold Wilson had written to his minister for the arts, Hugh Jenkins, 'I believe you will agree with me that Gilbert and Sullivan is part of the national heritage. . . . and that the D'Oyly Carte Opera Company is an indispensable part of all that Gilbert and Sullivan represents. . . . It is to my mind unthinkable that it should be allowed to go out of existence for lack of modest financial support'.[40] Even this plea from on high, however, had failed to elicit any funding.

The Arts Council's refusal to accept its own working party's recommendation and support the D'Oyly Carte was a huge blow to company morale. Alastair Donkin, who had forsaken a safe job with Shropshire County Council to become one of the youngest principals, saw it as 'a piece of pure artistic snobbery'. Kenneth Sandford told me: 'One gets the impression that in the establishment it is a bit infra-dig to appreciate the genius of these two men, when really they can stand up and be counted among the greats'. Principal bass John Ayldon disputed the accusation that the company was elderly—'I'm one of the oldest members of the company and I'm 37'. Various money-saving and money-raising ideas were made in the company suggestion box: 'Only put on understudies when the principal is really ill—saves £10 a time— and we might enlist the help and support of the many influential and well-known people who have been associated with the company. MPs such as Clement Freud, Harold Wilson, Betty Boothroyd, and Enoch Powell see our shows regularly and have expressed an interest in saving the company'.[41] Harold Wilson did, in fact, become involved in efforts to save the company, joining artistes, suitably attired in their *Iolanthe* costumes, outside the House of Lords to publicise its plight. The former Bishop of London, Robert Stopford, a dedicated Savoyard who had been chairman of D'Oyly Carte Trust, attempted to mobilise the establishment with 'a letter to *The Times* signed by Lord Chancellors, Bishops, major generals and so on'. Lord Elwyn Jones, a former Lord Chancellor and keen Savoyard, assured him, 'You won't have any difficulty with the Lord Chancellors because there are only three of us'.[42]

The company itself was inundated with letters and offers of support. A Save D'Oyly Carte campaign was launched and a new group, 'The Friends of D'Oyly

FIGURE 2.4 'I'm one of the oldest members of the Company and I'm 37'. John Ayldon applying his Dick Deadeye makeup for one of the last performances, 1981 *(Author's collection)*

Carte', was set up in March 1981 to replace the associate members. Over the next twenty-two years the Friends would raise over £300,000 for the D'Oyly Carte Opera Trust. In the short term, however, their efforts were not enough to stem the tide of bankruptcy which was rapidly engulfing the company. Onstage appeals for money and collecting boxes rattled in theatre foyers after every performance showed just how desperate the situation was. By May 1981, when the company had set itself the target of raising £200,000 if it was to survive, it had received donations of only £16,000, a grant of £35,000 from the Greater London Council, and £50,000 as part of regular sponsorship from Barclays Bank. It was now losing £4000 a week and its trading deficit for the six months from 1 April to 30 September 1981 was £223,000. The costs of maintaining a full-scale company were unsustainable. In what turned out to be its final season D'Oyly Carte was employing 101 people full-time: eleven soloists, thirty-two chorus members, a twenty-three-piece orchestra, eighteen touring staff, thirteen London office staff, and four in the London wardrobe and stores. It was also transporting six juggernaut-loads of scenery and props around the country. The scrimping and saving which it had always practised was now being stretched to the limits. The chorus in 1981 were paid £66 a week, nearly 20 percent less than equity minimum of £77. *The Gondoliers* had to be dropped from the repertoire because

FIGURE 2.5 Harold Wilson and Lord Elwyn Jones join James Conroy-Ward and the peers' chorus outside the House of Lords, 1981 *(Author's collection)*

the scenery was literally falling to bits and the company could not afford the £55,000 replacement costs. Heather Perkins, the wig mistress, told a journalist: 'You would not believe how the wigs are held together. It is a full-time job keeping them in one piece. I dread the time when one will disintegrate on stage beyond repair'.[43] In a grim mood, the trustees decided to extend the contracts of artistes and staff to February 1982 in the hope that some major injection of money might still materialise to stave off what looked increasingly like closure.

In fact, a potential saviour did emerge in the summer of 1981 in the unlikely figure of George Walker, former East End boxer turned nightclub owner and film impresario. Discovering that only the Beatles had been more recorded than Gilbert and Sullivan, Walker hit on the idea of filming the D'Oyly Carte productions for the booming home entertainment and video market and signed a £100,000 contract to record their performances at the Adelphi Theatre. This was seen as a lifeline by the management of the ailing company. Frederic Lloyd told Dame Bridget: 'It is essential that we undertake these video recordings if possible because if we do not do so I think the company will have to close down'.[44] When he saw the D'Oyly Carte artistes on stage, however, Walker decided that they were too elderly and hired the Ambrosian Opera Chorus for the chorus roles. He was persuaded by Judith de Paul, the American producer brought in to supervise the project, that it needed big-name transatlantic stars in the solo parts. Even the D'Oyly Carte orchestra was rejected in favour of the London Symphony Orchestra, conducted by Alexander Faris. When the cast list for the recordings appeared, there was not a single current D'Oyly Carte name on it. The company got the £100,000 promised, which allowed it to keep going for the six weeks which would have been spent filming but the whole experience was a massive blow to its morale.

Various last-ditch options to save the company were floated following this debacle. Hotel and catering magnate Charles (later Lord) Forte offered at least £50,000 but the trustees were uneasy that his offer, made just as he was bidding for the Savoy Hotel, came with strings attached. Talks were held with potential North American backers, leading to fears that the company might leave Britain for a permanent base in the United States, but no one materialised and U.S. union rules would in any case have prevented British artists from working there for more than thirteen weeks a year. Hugh Wontner, a trustee and chairman of the Savoy Hotel, suggested that D'Oyly Carte should seek to obtain the United Kingdom rights to perform Joseph Papp's updated version of *The Pirates of Penzance*, which was doing very successful business on Broadway, but this was not pursued.

The final London season opened on 18 November 1981 at the Adelphi Theatre in the Strand, following two weeks in Manchester and two in Nottingham, where the company played to 88 percent capacity houses. Alexander Faris was brought in as musical director, with Charles Mackerras as guest conductor for two performances of *Pirates*. Former artistes including John Reed and Valerie Masterson returned to make guest appearances. In a start-of-season message to the company Dame Bridget reflected on the ups and downs of her thirty-three-year reign over the family business and noted that 'possibly at the end of the copyright in 1961, or again at our centenary year 1975, I could have decided to close our activities down but at that time all was going well and inflation had not taken over'. While conceding that 'the moment has now come when a new approach is obviously necessary' she went on: 'I believe this need not be the end of a tradition, but can be the beginning of a continuously developing one, for tradition is never static and, in our case, never in fact has been. . . . I see re-organisation is now needed, and the future does require, as you will realise, an imaginative, constructive attitude. It is for the Trustees to decide how best this can be arrived at'.[45]

In fact, the trustees had little option but to bite the bullet and on 10 December 1981 they pronounced the long-expected death sentence and announced that the D'Oyly Carte would close at the end of the London season. The last night on 27 February 1982 was a typically understated occasion. The programme made no reference to this being the final performance and simply billed it as 'an evening of excerpts from the D'Oyly Carte repertoire'. Supporters came from far and wide—eighteen at least flew in specially from the United States, two of whom told me, 'We will leave tomorrow morning, crying all the way home. It is their perfectionism; they do it the way we feel it should always be done'. At the end of the performance the frail and diminutive figure of Dame Bridget rose in her box to acknowledge the cheers and thank everyone for the support given to her family over three generations. Yet hardly had she resumed her seat than Frederic Lloyd was on stage telling the audience of a plan to launch a new-look D'Oyly Carte later in the year with money from Lord Forte and raised through the efforts of a new committee headed by Dame Vera Lynn, the popular British singer known during the Second World War as 'the forces' sweetheart', and Tory MP Norman St. John Stevas.

Despite this ray of hope, there was a general sense on both sides of the curtain that an era had ended and that the D'Oyly Carte had finally breathed its last. In a way it was a wonder that it survived so long in a world in which its Victorian values and style seemed increasingly anachronistic—it was only in its final year that the company got around to employing a publicity and marketing officer. The fans on that last night were distraught, as many have been ever since. Even now, more than twenty years on, some have still not really come to terms with its demise and regard it as the greatest tragedy ever to have befallen Gilbert and Sullivan. For them the reappearance of the old company's former stars on stage at the Buxton G & S Festival brings back a golden age and the recordings made in the 1960s and 1970s remain definitive interpretations. Others are not so sure. Reviewing the 2003 reissue of these recordings, David Nice repeats criticisms made at the time, finding them full of 'wretched bit-part players, fluttery leading ladies, gravelly baritones and a contralto who apes the matron'. Even more heretically in the eyes of those of us who worshipped them, he also finds that 'the two linchpins come to seem less attractive now that we enjoy more subtle characterisations: John Reed, king of patter, is about Good Diction and little else, while Kenneth Sandford throws away some of the words and tends to flatness'.[46]

For members of the company the last night also brought ambivalent feelings. Not one of the trustees or the management came backstage to bid farewell to the artists or wish them good luck for the future. Yet despite the criticisms and gripes that many of them had about the D'Oyly Carte, almost everyone connected with it views their time there with affection. Even those who were in the company for a relatively short time and left it long ago, like Cynthia Morey, still feel the pull of 'the old D'Oyly Carte magic':

What is this strange bond that still exists between old D'Oyly Carte members? When we worked for the company we all felt the same annoyance at the autocratic management, the suppression of individuality, the same rigid discipline—but somehow this all fades into insignificance and only the pleasant memories remain. My own later and much longer association with far more efficiently run companies has left me with no comparable nostalgia.

What is this peculiar magic that exists between us? I can only think that the unique family atmosphere engendered by the company's direct descent from its creators, Gilbert, Sullivan and the remarkable Richard D'Oyly Carte, followed by his widow, Helen, his son Rupert, and finally his granddaughter Bridget, may be the answer. Once you have been part of that family it seems impossible to sever the connection. We recognise this, and often joke about it, but I'm fairly sure that most of us in our heart of hearts are proud to have been part of the great D'Oyly Carte tradition.[47]

~

THREE

UNFRIENDED, UNPROTECTED, AND ALONE: THE NEW D'OYLY CARTE, 1988–2003

The old D'Oyly Carte company survived for 107 years, its successor for just fifteen before announcing in May 2003 that it was ceasing performing for the foreseeable future. For most of that time, it was in the state that Major General Stanley feared for himself if the pirates of Penzance robbed him of his daughters—unfriended, unprotected, and alone. Castigated by traditionalists and fans of the old company, it never really established a house style and was if anything even more shamefully treated by the Arts Council than its predecessor had been.

The closure of the old company in 1982 did not mean the name or the familiar faces of D'Oyly Carte disappearing from view. A group of singers led by Kenneth Sandford, Geoffrey Shovelton, and John Ayldon toured the country, initially using the name 'G & S à la Carte' and, after lengthy negotiations with the trustees, 'Magic of D'Oyly Carte'. A new group, 'The London Savoyards', also gave fully staged performances in the capital. In 1985 there were full productions of *Yeomen* at the Barbican and of *Pirates*, *Pinafore*, and *Mikado* at the Alhambra Theatre, Bradford, and the Theatre Royal, Nottingham, using the old company's scenery. Although nothing came of the much-trumpeted initiative led by Dame Vera Lynn and Norman St. John Stevas or the promises of Lord Forte, the D'Oyly Carte Trust remained in being as did the Friends of D'Oyly Carte, run by the redoubtable Margaret Bowden. A skeleton staff were kept on in a South London office from where the business of hiring out band parts continued, but gradually the company disposed of its most prized assets. In January 1984 1,500 costumes were auctioned off, giving G & S fans the opportunity to acquire treasured heirlooms.

Dame Bridget D'Oyly Carte died in 1985, leaving a legacy of £1 million to fund a new performing company. To this sum was added the £50,000 raised by

Friends of D'Oyly Carte and a substantial grant from Sir Michael Bishop, chairman of British Midland Airways, who went on to become the new company's main sponsor and chairman of the D'Oyly Carte Trust from 1989. This provided enough capital to get the show on the road again and in 1987 Richard Condon, the effervescent Irish manager of the Theatre Royal, Norwich, was appointed general manager and Bramwell Tovey, former conductor of Sadler's Wells Royal Ballet, music director, with a brief to set up a new performing company.

Over 700 singers and 250 instrumentalists were auditioned. Among those from the old D'Oyly Carte taken on for the first season of the new company were Gillian Knight, Jill Pert, and Gareth Jones, who came in completely by accident. He happened to be walking past the theatre where the men were being auditioned, saw that there was no queue and walked straight in. As a result of his audition, he was given the parts of the Lieutenant in *Yeomen* and Private Willis in *Iolanthe*. He 'later heard that the queue for the women went right down to the Embankment Gardens'.[1] Jones went on to play twelve different roles with the new D'Oyly Carte. There was some bad feeling among other members of the old company who were not chosen and who were told that they could no longer use the D'Oyly Carte name for their presentations. They reverted briefly to 'G & S à la Carte' and then took up the name 'The Magic of Gilbert and Sullivan'.

The new company's initial public utterances suggested that it would be both traditional and innovative. Richard Baker, who had been recruited as a trustee during the interregnum, announced at the press launch, held at the Savoy Hotel on 1 March 1988, that 'while all that is good in Gilbert and Sullivan tradition should be respected, fresh vision is called for if the Company is to build a new audience'. Richard Condon announced that he was already studying the feasibility of taking the company not only to the United States, Canada, and Australia, as in 'the old days' but to countries like Japan: 'A much wider and very receptive world is waiting out there for the real thing'.[2]

The new D'Oyly Carte Opera Company opened at the Grand Theatre, Sunderland, on 28 April 1988 and went on to tour nine other provincial theatres with productions of *Iolanthe* and *The Yeomen of the Guard*, before moving to the Cambridge Theatre, London, in the summer. *Iolanthe* was played straight despite the fact that the director, Peter Walker, had spent two years as production director of *The Rocky Horror Show*. It was set in the 1920s, an idea which appealed to Lord Wilson although he suggested that 'the entry of the peers should be in peers' robes and coronets. The entry always has a really electrifying effect—blazers and straw hats would not be at all the same—anyone could have worn them, even Three Men in a Boat! Also, peers' robes would have been worn in the '20s, so would not be incongruous'.[3] This advice was followed and

FIGURE 3.1 Richard Suart
as the Lord Chancellor
(*Carl Rosa Opera*)

the familiar peers' costumes of the old company, which had not been auctioned off, were brought back into service.

Vocally as well as visually, the production was a delight and included several familiar figures from the old D'Oyly Carte, notably Gillian Knight as the Fairy Queen and Vivian Tierney as a bubbly and boisterous Phyllis. The Lord Chancellor was played by Richard Suart, who has gone on to establish himself as the leading contemporary exponent of the patter roles. Unlike the old D'Oyly Carte patter men, he is a trained singer, having been a Cambridge choral scholar and a student at the Royal Academy of Music. His first G & S role was understudying Derek Hammond Stroud's Bunthorne in the 1984 English National Opera (ENO) tour of *Patience* in the United States, but he was never required to go on stage. He then understudied Ko-Ko in the 1986–87 and 1988–89 performances of Jonathan Miller's *Mikado*. During the 1990s he continued to sing Ko-Ko with

ENO, sang and recorded the Lord Chancellor and the Duke of Plaza Toro for the new D'Oyly Carte, appeared as King Gama in Ken Russell's infamous ENO production of *Princess Ida,* and performed and recorded Jack Point for Welsh National Opera. More recently he has sung with both Carl Rosa Opera and Opera della Luna. He has also developed his one-man show, 'A Matter of Patter' and taken part in numerous concert performances and overseas productions of G & S in places as far apart as Vancouver, Venice, Penang, and the Netherlands.

The other opening production, Christopher Renshaw's *Yeomen,* was also broadly traditional and recognisably 'D'Oyly Carte', not least because it used the old company's yeomen's costumes, which had been excluded from the sale. The curtain rose to reveal a dark, cavernous chamber instead of the old cardboard cutout of the Tower of London and towards the end of the first act this set was flown to reveal a stark courtyard with the executioner's block dominating the stage. The female principals were particularly strong, with Gillian Knight as Dame Carruthers, Thora Ker as Phoebe, and Deborah Rees as Elsie Maynard. The production also introduced two male soloists who were to be key figures in the early years of the new company—patter man Eric Roberts as a very Welsh Jack Point and tenor Philip Creasy as a dashing and nonchalantly cavalier Colonel Fairfax.

The musical standard of the new company was particularly high, with a rich and full sound from the orchestra and a very strong chorus. The choreography was also notably livelier than that of the old régime. Nonetheless, a number of traditionalists and those associated with the old D'Oyly Carte found fault with the new one, perhaps goaded by an ill-chosen remark by Richard Condon in the programme for the opening productions which accused the old company of having 'lost direction' and 'failed to keep pace with the changes and developments in operatic and musical tastes that would have been second nature to Gilbert, Sullivan and D'Oyly Carte'.

Reviewing *Yeomen,* Paul Seeley, repetiteur with the old company, found it 'devoid of acting and diction, the hallmark of D'Oyly Carte tradition'. He objected to 'the abandon within which this leg-flashing Phoebe rams Shad-bolt's nose to her cleavage: an excellent idea for a *Carry On* film farce—but for W. S. Gilbert, no thank you'.[4]

This kind of criticism went on dogging the new D'Oyly Carte company. It was relatively muted in respect of the two 1989 offerings, John Wells's *Mikado* and Keith Warner's *Pirates,* which went to the Savoy Theatre for a thirteen-week autumn season. Both were broadly traditional, with Marie-Jeanne Lecca's colourful and beautifully lit set for *Pirates* resembling a Victorian toy theatre. But the 1990 double bill of *Pinafore* and *Trial by Jury* brought the offended traditionalists out in force. The director, Andrew Wickes, had an excellent G & S pedigree, having directed *Thespis* at school, four Savoy operas at Cambridge, and *Pinafore* for Kent Opera, as well as having sung Dick Deadeye and the Mikado. He restored Cousin Hebe's dialogue and reinstated the original *Pinafore* finale, establishing a fidelity to the original text and a commitment to restore lost material that was to mark several of the new company's productions. But other aspects of the double bill seemed gimmicky and gratuitous. Although the sailors in *Pinafore*, which was unusually played before *Trial*, belonged firmly to Nelson's time, the female chorus were dressed in clothes of the 1940s and Buttercup made her entrance accompanied by two charladies. *Trial by Jury* was played unashamedly for laughs—a heavily pregnant Angelina had a balloon stuffed in her dress which was burst at the end of the show. The old D'Oyly Carte brigade were not amused. Frederic Lloyd deplored 'the vulgar portrayal of the Plaintiff' and noted that 'the antics and costumes of the jury were in very poor taste'.[5] A letter somewhat masochistically published in the company's newsletter complained about the 'offensive vulgarity' of *Pinafore* and *Trial* and concluded that 'to use Dame Bridget's generous legacy to produce Gilbert and Sullivan operas as you have done is a monstrous betrayal of her trust and abuse of the name of D'Oyly Carte'.[6]

In 1991 the company, now feeling sufficiently well established to drop the word 'new' from its title, moved its base to Birmingham, lured by the city council, who provided office space, rehearsal rooms, scenery storage, and an annual grant of £125,000 for five years. The decision was made to turn it into a national light opera company with a repertoire extending beyond G & S. Serious consideration was given to changing the name to the Birmingham Light Opera Company but it was decided the cachet of D'Oyly Carte was still worth keeping. This seemed to be confirmed when British Rail named an intercity locomotive 'The D'Oyly Carte Opera Company' on the grounds that the company, like the train, was forever on the move across the length and breadth of the country.

The first Birmingham season opened with a bizarre production of *The Gondoliers* by Tim Hopkins where attention was constantly diverted from the words and music by silly gimmicks and a distracting set. In the first act the cast had to perform on a steeply raked block of undulating orange waves and contend with a fascist-like red and white banner, an exclamation mark in its centre, which was pulled across the stage at every opportunity and for no apparent reason. At one point a joke rat scampered across the stage and during the singing of 'A Regular Royal Queen' a corgi dressed as the Queen drove on in a kiddie car. The production was greeted by boos from a small section of the first-night audience and castigated by most critics. Benedict Nightingale wrote in *The Times* that the director 'has found a way of escaping from traditionalism more destructive than traditionalism itself and of packaging the opera so gaudily that nobody can see the contents for the wrapping paper'.[7] Perhaps the most perceptive criticism came from David Eden:

> Any remaining links with the traditions of the old D'Oyly Carte Company have been broken. Musical values are to the fore, and all traces of respect for the Gilbertian stagecraft have been abandoned. So much for the Revolution—long overdue and desperately necessary; the Terror takes the form of a deconstructionist production which substitutes a series of mostly philistine gimmicks for the intellectual effort that might have resulted in a coherent reinterpretation.[8]

Eden's remarks pinpoint two significant features of the new company—its high concern for musical values and its tendency to indulge in rather vulgar gimmickry. Unfortunately, and perhaps inevitably, it was the latter feature which was picked up by G & S devotees. The other 1991 production, Andrew Wickes's *Iolanthe*, which was an object lesson in how the Savoy operas should be performed with stage business enhancing rather than distracting from the music and dialogue handled with impeccable timing and the right degree of understatement, was very little noticed as everyone rushed to heap calumny on *The Gondoliers.*

Somewhat bruised by all the criticism but determined to press on with modern, innovative productions, the company celebrated the 150th anniversary of Sullivan's birth in 1992 with a thirty-five-week tour of 21 theatres featuring another *Mikado* and another *Yeomen*, both directed by Andrew Wickes. John Rath played the Mikado perched on mechanical stilts and Fenton Gray portrayed Ko-Ko as a bespectacled mixture of Arthur Askey and Woody Allen. *Yeomen* had a minimum of extraneous business and distraction, with Fenton Gray as Jack Point cast as a tragic hunchback in the mould of Rigoletto. An educational project was launched in the same year under Michael Jefferson's direction. More than three hundred children from Birmingham took part in a one-day festival, a celebration day was held at Lichfield Cathedral, a six-week course in voice production was mounted for a school in Bristol, and projects were run in more than a dozen schools where children composed, produced and performed their own mini-operettas. The older generation were not neglected, with workshops for the over-fifties leading to performances of *Pirates.* As a direct result of these and other initiatives, membership of the Friends of D'Oyly Carte increased by 10 percent. Yet the company was continually dogged by sniping criticisms from devotees of the old D'Oyly Carte for whom they could do nothing right. Robin

FIGURE 3.2 Jill Pert as
Katisha in the 1992
D'Oyly Carte production
of *Mikado (Alan Wood)*

Wilson, a rare friend and supporter of both the old and new companies, tried
to draw a line under this in the Christmas 1992 issue of the Friends' newsletter:

> It would be helpful if the distinctions between the old and the new
> companies could be increasingly blurred. Ever since it started in the 1870s,
> the D'Oyly Carte Company has continually been changing its perform-
> ance styles to cope with changing audiences and the current productions
> are simply part of this continuous change. If the productions can continue
> to attract the audiences of the 1990s, and as long as people watch them
> with an open mind, rather than always hankering after the past, the Com-
> pany should have a bright future.[9]

In 1993 the company made its first foray into the non–G & S repertoire with a
raunchy co-production with Opera North of Offenbach's *Orpheus in the Under-
world.* This departure from tradition brought the company its first-ever grant

from the Arts Council, a modest £30,000 for the *Orpheus* tour, which covered just half a week's running costs. There was a sense of optimism and new beginnings in the air. The programme for the *Orpheus* tour, which covered 24 venues and also featured another production of *Pirates*, this time directed by Stuart Maunder, contained a questionnaire asking audience members to list in order of preference which composers they would like to see added to the repertoire. Strauss, Lehar, Offenbach, Romberg, Novello, and Coward were specifically mentioned. 'For a brief moment', *The Times* critic Rodney Milnes noted, 'the inviting prospect of a national operetta company with a rep stretching from Offenbach to Sondheim floats into view'.[10]

Needless to say, *Orpheus* did not go down well with die-hard G & S traditionalists, who seem to have forgotten that it was not unprecedented—the D'Oyly Carte had performed Offenbach's *Grand Duchess of Gerolstein* in its 1897–98 season. It did not help when Bill Clancy, the company's marketing manager, called the new show 'a sexy romp' and described it 'an operatic Rocky Horror Show'. One of several outraged correspondents pointed out that 'the Savoy operas were produced to clean up the stage and protect us from the sexual immoralities imported from France'.[11] Devotees of the old company were not made any happier when the new general manager, Ray Brown, spoke of his 'desire to sweep away the memory of too many years of sub-standard, albeit well-meaning amateurism fettered to an alarmingly limited repertoire'.[12]

Realising that it was dangerous to alienate the traditional G & S fan base, the company made very clear that it was committed to doing more of the Savoy operas as well as other things. The autumn 1993 *Friends'* magazine promised recordings in 1994 of *Trial by Jury, Sorcerer, Pinafore, Ida, Ruddigore, Utopia, Grand Duke,* and *Cox and Box,* and the summer 1994 issue announced that 'a director and designer are presently carrying out a feasibility study with a view to producing the entire canon by the turn of the century'. Yet despite this buoyant rhetoric, the mid-1990s were a period of retreat for the company. A promised production of *The Sorcerer* for 1993 never materialised. Instead, the old favourites were brought out yet again—*Pirates* in 1993; a new *Pinafore*, directed by Martin Duncan, in 1994; *Mikado*, directed by Fenton Gray and based on Wickes's production, in 1995–96; and a revival of Wickes's 1991 *Iolanthe*, also directed by Fenton Gray, in 1997–98. The 1994 spring and summer seasons were abandoned, leaving just a short autumn tour, and subsequent seasons were shorter than in the early years. The only non–G & S shows mounted were *Die Fledermaus* in 1994, *La Vie Parisienne* in 1995–96, and *The Count of Luxembourg* in 1997–98.

The company played similarly safe in terms of its recordings. Despite its promises, the more obscure G & S works were not committed to disc. In all, the new D'Oyly Carte recorded seven operas: *Pirates* and *Mikado* in 1990; *Iolanthe* and *Gondoliers* in 1991; *Yeomen* in 1993, with the 'lost' songs 'A Laughing Boy' and 'When Jealous Torments' and the verses for the third and fourth yeomen in the act 1 finale included; *Patience* in 1994, complete with the Duke's song and an earlier version of the act 2 finale reconstructed by David Russell Hulme; and *Pinafore* in 2000, with dialogue and the recently reconstructed 'Reflect, My Child'. Even this valuable service to the cause of G & S in bringing hitherto neglected material into the public domain won few plaudits from the increasingly vociferous critics in whose eyes the new D'Oyly Carte seemed irretrievably damned.

Part of the reason that the new company failed to win over a substantial and vocal minority of the old D'Oyly Carte's fans was undoubtedly its very different management style. In contrast to the understated, diffident, almost apologetic approach of the old company, the new one was full of marketing hype, describing itself as 'a renowned company offering a quality product', promoting the Savoy operas as 'the world's best-loved musicals', and constantly promising far more than it could deliver. This did not go down well with those of a more conservative and traditional bent who tend to dominate the world of G & S appreciation societies and publications. They had other gripes as well. Concluding his history of the original company, published in 1994, Tony Joseph noted, 'The new D'Oyly Carte Company is not a rebirth of the old but something quite different. Apart from performing G & S, the only feature the two companies share is the name'. He found two things particularly lacking:

> One is any real feeling within the new company for its origins, its traditions, for the D'Oyly Carte past . . . and the second thing lacking, the thing that ultimately, throughout its existence, made the old D'Oyly Carte company so special, was the feeling it engendered of continuity, of family: of the rapport that developed, generation after generation, between performers and audiences who in so many instances got to know—and became friends with—each other in a very special way'.[13]

Marc Shepherd has pointed to two further weaknesses:

> The first is that because the new company does not perform year-round, the old concept of 'being a member of D'Oyly Carte' no longer exists: after each season, the performers disperse. . . . The second is that the new D'Oyly Carte has no concept of a repertory. None of their productions has had a life of more than two seasons, and many have lasted only one. Even within a given season, the two operas that they typically put on have different directors and largely different casts.[14]

Is the G & S audience so wedded to familiarity that it simply wants to see the same production with the same singers back year after year? Certainly that was a large part of the appeal of the old D'Oyly Carte for its fans and undoubtedly both the lack of any identifiable house style and of continuity among its artistes were contributory factors in the new company's failure to build a brand loyalty and a strong fan base. In the early days it did look as though it was going to have a nucleus of regular performers in the likes of Philip Creasy, Terence Sharpe, and John Rath but as its seasons became shorter, it became increasingly difficult to hold on to singers. Turnover of staff at the management and creative levels was, if anything, even more rapid and certainly did not make for continuity or stability. Richard Condon resigned in 1989 and was replaced as general manager in 1990 by Ray Brown, a former principal trombonist with the City of Birmingham Symphony Orchestra who came to D'Oyly Carte from running Capital Radio's Wren Orchestra. The company went through three musical directors in its first five years—Bramwell Tovey stayed for only two seasons and was replaced in 1990 by John Pryce Jones, previously head of music with Scottish Opera. He left with some acrimony in 1992 when the size of the touring band was reduced from twenty-seven to twenty-four players, with two extra for *Yeomen* (the orchestra was later increased to thirty) and John Owen Edwards took over. The turnover of directors was even more rapid. Had the company held on to Andrew Wickes, it might well have developed a house style. As it was, virtually every season brought a brand new production with a different director. Overall, between 1988 and 2003, there were four different productions of the *Mikado* and *Iolanthe*, three of *Yeomen*, *Pirates*, and *Pinafore*, and one of *Gondoliers* but not a single *Sorcerer*, *Ruddigore*, *Patience*, or *Ida*. As Bill Clancy admitted in one of his less upbeat statements to the press, 'of the 13 operas, only six now have box-office potential'.[15]

At root, the key problem for the new D'Oyly Carte, as for the old, was financial. In 1990 and 1991 the company toured ninety-six people for a total of thirty weeks and lost £25,000 a week. Reductions in the size of orchestra and chorus in 1992 brought the touring company down to seventy-two, but it was still an impossible operation without significant subsidy. Birmingham's support and significant help from Sir Michael Bishop just about kept the company afloat but the Arts Council remained adamantly set against G & S in general and the D'Oyly Carte in particular. The 1993 touring grant for *Orpheus* was a one-off, and all the company received for its 1994–95 season was a derisory £18,000. Although its ticket prices were 35 percent less than the average for touring opera companies it was also much more self-sufficient. In 1994–95, for example, it was relying on a subsidy of just £2.50 for every seat sold—the comparable figure for Scottish Opera was £33.

The financial problems came to a head in the summer of 1996 when Birmingham City Council decided not to renew its subsidy. An annual loss of over £500,000 now loomed and the company announced that it would have to suspend performances. Anthony Steen, Tory MP for South Hams, raised its plight in Parliament in July 1996 and attempted through a procedural motion to prevent the House of Commons adjourning for the summer recess until the government promised £500,000 to secure the immediate future of 'one of the most peculiar and important of British institutions'. Having pointed out that D'Oyly Carte covered 80 percent of its costs through box office receipts, private sponsorship, and local authority support, in contrast to the Royal Opera House, which depended for 80 percent of its income on the Arts Council, he waxed lyrical about the merits of G & S:

> Tens of thousands of people want an evening's entertainment in a language they understand. It is no good going to grand opera and listening to Italian, French or German—most of the tens of thousands of people in the provinces want to hear a light operetta in English. From Birmingham to Glasgow and from Coventry to Plymouth, people flood to theatres in their droves and leave feeling better and happier. Whenever I go to see a Gilbert and Sullivan production, I come out to a merry mood, whistling some of the infectious tunes.[16]

At this point, the veteran left-wing Labour MP, Denis Skinner, cried out 'Go on—whistle them'. Steen declined to take up this challenge 'although it is tempting' but instead launched into his peroration that 'Gilbert and Sullivan is as much part of the British culture as cream teas, cricket at Lord's or the unpredictability of the weather'. This mixture of nostalgia, political incorrectness, and old-fashioned patriotism was hardly calculated to win round the Arts Council. Rather more effective was a grilling given to Lord Gowrie, its chairman, at the end of 1996 by what the *Times* described as 'Parliament's equivalent of the parish fete committee: its Gilbert and Sullivan fans'. The paper reported that 'in between flicking pellets at Gowrie's la-di-dah tastes' the ad-hoc group of MPs, led by Anthony Steen and including Conservative Party chairman Norman Fowler and former Home Secretary Kenneth Baker, 'aimed to secure the cultural credibility of G & S'.[17] This 'gang of G & S–humming Tory grandees' clearly got their message over. In January 1997 the Arts Council announced a £250,000 rescue package to save D'Oyly Carte from extinction.

This enabled the company to resume performances with a tour in the autumn of 1997 but as a strictly one-off payment, it offered no long-term security. Hopes were raised when a Newcastle entrepreneur, Karl Watkin, offered to install D'Oyly Carte in the city's 128-year-old Tyne Theatre and Opera House, which he was hoping to restore, but this project fell through and the company instead relocated to Wolverhampton. Its financial problems were not helped by a sharp drop in the annual amount raised from the Friends, down from £25,000 in the early years to just over £8000 in 1997.

Early in 1998 the company announced that the projected autumn tour had been cancelled and the end seemed nigh, with the new D'Oyly Carte facing closure just ten years after it had reopened. Its plight was debated in both houses of Parliament on 1 April, a date whose appropriateness was not lost on those who took part. There was rare cross-party unanimity with Conservative, Labour, and Liberal Democrat members united in deploring the prospect of the company folding and imploring the Arts Council to assist it. There was ample opportunity for quotation from the works of the masters, with the sentry's song from *Iolanthe* being invoked in several speeches in both houses and extracts used from the nightmare song, 'I Have a Song to Sing, O', 'Conceive Me if You Can' and 'When I Was a Lad'.

Introducing the Commons debate, Martin Bell, the independent MP for Tatton and former BBC journalist, began:

> This is not the weightiest issue ever to come before the House, nor is it negligible. It speaks to our theatre, our music, our tradition, our identity, our sense of history and our sense of humour. We British—I almost said we English; as we have had so many Scottish and Welsh debates lately, let us have an English one—we English have no Mozart, no Puccini, no Wagner, but, my goodness, we have Gilbert and Sullivan, who have entertained and illuminated our country and the world for more than 120 years and whose legacy is now in danger. The D'Oyly Carte Company is in danger of extinction unless we act to save it. The time is short, the threat is real; this is the place and this is the time to sound the alarm bells.[18]

He went on to point out that the company needed just £500,000 to stave off bankruptcy and closure, a small enough sum when set against the £12 million of public funding which went every year to English National Opera and the £8 million which Covent Garden received. Bell then touched on the central issue of the low esteem in which G & S was held by the cultural establishment:

> Perhaps the D'Oyly Carte Opera is too popular; perhaps it is too accessible; perhaps people like it too much. Perhaps if it wrapped up bricks in muslin or islands in plastic, it would be deemed worthy of Arts Council funding. Perhaps if it cross-dressed the cast of *The Gondoliers* or had the

crew of *HMS Pinafore* clad in black leathers and chains, it would be deemed worthy of Arts Council funding. However, it does not do that: it brings light opera to the people and performs the magic of the stage in loved productions that people understand.

I sense cultural élitism and snobbery being deployed by the mandarins and Pooh-Bahs of the arts establishment. Their coded accusation is apparently that the company's repertoire is 'unchallenging'—what a weasel word that is.

MPs across the political spectrum lined up to proclaim their fondness for G & S and reminisce as to how and where they had first encountered it. Austin Mitchell, Labour MP for Grimsby, confessed that 'I came to know Gilbert and Sullivan's work at Manchester University. As a humble working-class lad, I considered it to be positively upper class. However, the Arts Council considers it to be middle-brow and down-market. It is as simple as that'.[19] Simon Hughes, Liberal Democrat MP for Bermondsey, proudly declared:

I am the product of a Gilbert and Sullivan upbringing. For a very high price I shall reveal a photograph of me at the age of thirteen dressed in a costume as Katisha. When I was at school, I went to London to see D'Oyly Carte and found it inspirational. It was the first non-children's performance that I saw in the theatre. At home, we sung the scores round the piano with family and friends. It was an easy, accessible and enjoyable activity, but it was also educative—dare I say, it was my first introduction to politics.[20]

Patricia Hewitt, Labour MP for Leicester West and the only woman to speak in the Commons debate, noted that she had been brought up on *The Mikado* and *The Messiah* 'and had the great good fortune as a schoolgirl to sing in productions of both'. Sir Patrick Cormack, Conservative MP for South Staffordshire, recalled that he had gained his love for G & S 'at the Theatre Royal, Cleethorpes, when at the age of eight I was taken by my parents to see *The Mikado*'. He then turned on 'the Arts Council snobs who think poetry shouldn't rhyme and music shouldn't have tunes' and suggested that 'if tinned turds at the Serpentine are worthy of public subsidy, surely Gilbert and Sullivan, that wonderful marriage of marvellous music and superb verse, deserves Arts Council help'.[21]

Other contributors to the debate produced statistical evidence to support the D'Oyly Carte's case. Barry Gardiner, MP for Brent North, pointed out that since 1988 the company had performed for one million people in forty major provincial theatres around the United Kingdom and taken £8.5 million at the box office. Ronnie Fearn, Liberal Democrat MP for Southport, commended its role in inspiring amateurs and noted that it played to 80 percent capacity houses com-pared to the Royal Opera's 45 percent. Summing up the debate, Anthony Steen returned with gusto to the themes he had raised in the House two years previ-ously. He praised the company for the enterprising deal it had struck with Harry Ramsden's fish and chip shop in Nottingham to perform once a month to cus-tomers enjoying their fish suppers. He observed that 'if the D'Oyly Carte were a Stockhausen quartet playing in a wine bar in Ludlow or Cheltenham, the Arts Council would be throwing money at it'. Speaking as a classically trained pi-anist, he testified to the fact that Gilbert and Sullivan was regarded by the cul-tural and musical establishment as 'low-brow, down-market, popular and not musically correct'. The Arts Council had strung the company along with prom-ises of lottery funding yet had given it next to nothing. By contrast, English Na-tional Opera's debts of £6.8 million had been written off. The truth was, he con-cluded, that 'the Arts Council wants to kill off the D'Oyly Carte, and it has nearly succeeded'.[22]

The degree of unanimity expressed in this debate is striking. Not a single MP ventured to suggest that Gilbert and Sullivan was past its sell-by date, or the D'Oyly Carte unworthy of public funding. It shows the huge affection still felt for Gilbert and Sullivan by middle-class, middle-aged men who gained their love of it from their parents or at school or university. It also indicates the ex-tent to which, thirty-seven years after the expiry of the copyright and sixteen years after the demise of the old company, the future of Gilbert and Sullivan was still being equated with the fortunes of the D'Oyly Carte Opera Company. The debate also underlines the continuing patriotic associations of both institu-tions. Simon Hughes observed: 'This company is the best of British and it tells us about Britain'. Tom Clarke, a Scot who as minister for tourism replied to the debate on behalf of the government, upbraided Patrick Cormack for describing Gilbert and Sullivan as 'quintessentially English'. He pointed to its strong appeal north of the border and in Wales and cautioned, 'we should not limit the influ-ence of Gilbert and Sullivan to England'.[23]

Despite his own enthusiasm, Clarke was able to offer nothing in the way of hard cash. He merely reiterated the standard government line that the Arts Council was an independent body which had the right to decide how it allo-cated its funds. With long-term public funding apparently unobtainable, D'Oyly Carte started looking to the private sector and found a saviour in the impresario Raymond Gubbay, himself a Gilbert and Sullivan devotee, who of-fered to promote and underwrite short G & S seasons in London. In 1998 the company made the decision to sign up with him and stop trying to chase a per-manent public subsidy. This meant a major change of direction, abandoning its touring role and its hopes of becoming a national light opera company and relocating in London to operate on a strictly commercial basis in a slimmed-down form. A one-week revival of Fenton Gray's *Mikado* at the Royal Festival Hall in September 1998 was followed by a Christmas season of *Pirates* at the Queen's Theatre, and the following year *Pinafore* was presented at the Royal Festival Hall. These productions drew the inevitable complaints from purists who found them altogether too racy. The reviewer of the *Mikado* in the *Gilbert and Sullivan News* found it 'brash and vulgarised' and complained, 'I was not prepared, particularly as there were so many children in the audience, for Pitti-Sing to call Peep-Bo a "smart ass" nor for Ko-Ko to say "bugger the flowers that bloom in the spring" and what was utterly reprehensible was the interpolation into the Mikado's song of filthy innuendoes about President Clinton's alleged activities in the White House'.[24]

The new arrangement initially worked well even if it meant abandoning all non–G & S productions and concentrating on an even smaller repertoire of the most popular Savoy operas. Gubbay made clear that he wanted star names from television in the cast, and in 2000 the company returned to the Savoy Theatre for the first time in eleven years for a nine-week run of Martin Duncan's *Pinafore*, with Sam Kelly of BBC Television's *Porridge* and *'Allo 'Allo* as Sir Joseph Porter. Later in the year and also at the Savoy a new *Mikado* directed by Ian Judge played for eighteen weeks, the longest single run for any traditionally performed G & S opera in London since 1902. An eleven-week nationwide autumn tour of *Pinafore* brought two D'Oyly Carte companies playing simultaneously for the first time since 1927. In 2001, a revival of Stuart Maunder's *Pirates* at the Savoy received considerable publicity when an actress turned down for a part in the chorus because she would have been heavily pregnant by the end of the show's run accused the company of sexual discrimination. Ian Martin, who had taken over in 1998 as the third general manager in ten years, defended the decision on the grounds that 'we were casting for the ladies chorus who play the teenage virginal daughters of General Stanley and scream every time they see a man. It would not make sense to have one who was obviously pregnant'. [25]

The next year proved a bumper year, with a new *Iolanthe* directed by Martin Connor running at the Savoy from February 2002, followed by a new *Yeomen* directed by Ian Talbot until June, a hastily mounted revival of the 2000 production of *Mikado*, starring Jasper Carrott as Ko-Ko and then Martin Duncan's *Pinafore* again. The reviews for all four shows were highly favourable—Rodney Milnes began his of *Iolanthe* by reflecting that 'there are few greater pleasures in life than a really good performance of Gilbert and Sullivan, and this was one such'.[26] With the shows running virtually back-to-back, D'Oyly Carte was performing almost continually at the Savoy from February 2002 to March 2003. 'How delightful to see so many D'Oyly Carte productions in one year', a correspondent to the company newsletter wrote; ' I am reminded of times past'.[27] Ironically, this achievement, which did, indeed, recall the old glory days and guaranteed stalwarts like Gareth Jones forty-five weeks of continuous employment, was the company's undoing. In Ian Martin's words, 'We got greedy and over-ambitious. It was a mistake to be on in London for so long. It led people to think that D'Oyly Carte was always going to be there so the imperative to book went and ticket sales fell off'.[28] Faced with half-empty houses, Raymond Gubbay got cold feet and pulled out.

Following the announcement in 2003 of a cessation in productions, the company sold off its sets and props while keeping its costumes for hiring out to amateurs. Also retained was the hire library for vocal scores, prompt books, and band parts, many dating from the 1950s and 1960s, providing a last tangible link with the old company whose retired members had laboriously copied them out by hand. In 2003 there were 224 loans of the band parts. They went as far afield as Bulawayo (for a performance of *Trial by Jury* by the national symphony orchestra) in Zimbabwe, as well as to France, Belgium, Germany, and Ireland. The majority of hires were to amateur societies in the United Kingdom paying £125 for a standard set of orchestral parts dispatched one month before performance and to be returned within a week afterwards. As well as supporting the amateur G & S scene in this way, the company has also recently embarked on a series of master classes in London at which aspiring singers can learn from professional soloists and musical director John Owen Edwards.

In fact, G & S enthusiasts have much to thank the resurrected D'Oyly Carte company for. It has provided employment for several well-loved exponents of G & S, notably Gareth Jones, Jill Pert, and Gillian Knight, and fostered and developed the talents of the patter song trio of Richard Suart, Eric Roberts, and Simon Butteriss. It has helped to train many young performers straight out of music or drama college in the combination of skills required to perform G & S well. It has made significant efforts to attract a younger audience for Gilbert and Sullivan with its educational initiatives and updated productions and brought a new approach to the Savoy operas, exemplified in the words of Martin Duncan, whose *Pinafore* is generally adjudged one of the company's most successful shows: 'When I approached this operetta, which is, in fact, simply a wonderful musical, I had to trust the piece. I didn't think of it as something dusty or Victorian. I treated it like any other musical'.[29]

While it has undoubtedly sought to present the operas in a way that it thinks would have contemporary appeal, the new D'Oyly Carte company has also treated them with considerable respect, especially from a musical point of view. It generally had a larger orchestra in the pit than the old company and resolutely refused to go with the modern trend for miking singers and artificial amplification. Its performances have often been more faithful to Sullivan's original scoring and it has restored several 'lost' songs. Ironically, it has also proved more assiduous than the old company ever was in preserving and caring for its archives. The D'Oyly Carte archives have had a rather chequered and peripatetic history, being moved from the Savoy Hotel to various company offices and then back again to the hotel for a brief period. In 2000 Ian Martin managed to gather them together in the new company's south London offices and to employ a professional archivist, Mary Gilhooly, to catalogue and look after them. He also located and saved papers relating to the last twenty years of the old company which had been left to languish in filing cabinets in the Savoy Hotel laundry on Clapham Road. Receiving a call that they were about to be tipped into a builder's skip, he went round in his car and rescued them in the nick of time.

None of this activity has earned any plaudits or gratitude from the die-hard fans of the old D'Oyly Carte who have continued to snipe away at the new company. The *Gilbert and Sullivan News* review of the 2002 *Yeomen* complained of the 'inappropriate' high-kick dance routine which turned the Yeomen warders, 'who used to convey dignity' into Tiller girls and protested that 'Dame Carruthers starts to undo her bodice and make suggestive signs to Sergeant Meryll in "Rapture, Rapture". WSG must be turning in his grave—funny, yes maybe, but Gilbert and Sullivan from the D'Oyly Carte, no'.[30] A highly positive review in the *Sunday Telegraph* of the 2002–3 *Pinafore* which compared the new company favourably to the old elicited the response, 'the new D'Oyly Carte lack the humour, pathos and vividness of the old. The directors try to be clever and modern, but you can't improve a Victorian piece of furniture by grafting on some Ikea features'.[31]

Only one thing has been more destructive of the company's morale than the constant attacks by die-hard traditionalists and fans of the old company: the persistent hostility and prejudice against it displayed by the cultural establishment and the Arts Council in particular. In the words of Ian Martin, who has worked for the company right through its troubled existence:

The Arts Council just kept moving the goal posts. Every time we applied for funding there was a different reason for turning us down—either there was too much G & S in the amateur sector, or there were other companies doing G & S, or the work we were doing wasn't good enough or we weren't doing enough non–G & S. The company felt it had done everything they asked us to do. We diversified into non–G & S and got ourselves on the way to being a British light opera company, we improved musical standards and freshened productions to appeal to a younger audience. It really wore me down over the fifteen years—so much bigotry and prejudice against us both from the Arts Council on one side and the die-hard traditionalists and fans of the old company on the other.[32]

The new D'Oyly Carte company has, like its predecessor, been a victim of the persistent cultural snobbery and prejudice against Gilbert and Sullivan in Britain. It has lived through many false dawns and unfulfilled promises. There was real hope in the mid-1990s that it would become the British, or at least English, equivalent of the Vienna *Volksoper*, the French *Opéra Comique*, or perhaps even more the Danish National Opera, with a specific remit to tour light opera through the country. I remember so many exciting conversations with successive music directors and company managers about the works it might perform: John Pryce Jones telling me in 1991 that he wanted to do Offenbach's *The Brigands* with its English libretto by Gilbert, Ray Brown enthusing in 1992 about *Kismet,* John Owen Edwards proposing a double bill in 1993 of Edward German's *Merrie England* and *Tom Jones.* Then there were the grand plans for overseas tours. Just three months after it opened the company announced a £7.5 million ten-year touring deal in the United States, starting with an eight-week visit to the United States in 1990. This never came off. Nor did the proposal to take *Mikado* to Moscow in 1990, *Gondoliers* to Rome and Florence in 1991, and to go further afield to Russia, Australia, and Hong Kong. The company's only overseas engagements have been very brief visits to Los Angeles in 1990 and New Haven, Connecticut, in 2000.

At this time it is not clear what the future holds and when and if the D'Oyly Carte will perform again. If its story has been a rather sad one, however, there have been plenty of other professional companies who have had much happier experiences performing G & S in recent decades and whose success suggests that there is still considerable life, and box office potential, in the old duo yet.

FOUR

VIRTUE IS TRIUMPHANT ONLY IN THEATRICAL PERFORMANCES: PROFESSIONAL PRODUCTIONS OF GILBERT AND SULLIVAN, 1961–2004

This chapter is not intended to provide an exhaustive catalogue of professional performances of Gilbert and Sullivan since 1961. It offers rather a decade-by-decade survey of the most significant productions and trends, not just in the United Kingdom and the United States but also in Australasia and Continental Europe. On the whole, it is confined to reasonably 'straight' productions—the more offbeat and heavily altered versions will be covered in chapter 8.

Competitors lost no time in challenging the D'Oyly Carte monopoly in the United Kingdom once the copyright restrictions ended. On 1 January 1962 Sadler's Wells Opera staged *Iolanthe* at the Theatre Royal, Stratford-on-Avon. Directed by Frank Hauser, who admitted he had never seen any Gilbert and Sullivan, it starred Elizabeth Harwood as Phyllis, Patricia Kern as Iolanthe, and Eric Shilling as the Lord Chancellor. The style was fairly traditional, although Bridget D'Oyly Carte fretted that the act 1 set 'looked exactly like one of Messrs. Lyons Easter window displays of boiled sweets! Incredibly fussy and rather vulgar' and there were complaints from traditionalists that the peers, rather than being 'dignified and stately, were used as a vehicle for humour' and that 'the sophisticated fairies introduced a sexuality reminiscent of what Gilbert and Sullivan tried to sweep off the stage'.[1] The production transferred to London, toured to Brussels, Hamburg, and Stuttgart in 1962, and Berlin and Prague in 1966 and was revived at the London Coliseum when the company moved there in 1968. Sadler's Wells also staged a fairly traditional *Mikado* in 1962, with John Wakefield as Nanki-Poo, Marion Studholme as Yum-Yum, and Clive Revill as Ko-Ko. Both productions were recorded under the musical direction of Alexander Faris, adding to a G & S LP list that had recently been boosted by the recordings made between 1956 and 1962 by Sir Malcolm Sargent with soloists like Owen Brannigan, Geraint Evans, Richard Lewis, and John Cameron.

The other initial competition to D'Oyly Carte came in the shape of productions of *Pinafore* and *Pirates* which opened at Her Majesty's Theatre in London in February 1962. Directed by Tyrone Guthrie, they had first been performed at the Stratford Shakespeare Festival, Ontario, Canada, which has remained an important venue for innovative G & S performances. They, too, were fairly conservative, although traditionalists were outraged when a short-sighted Sir Joseph Porter attempted to pinch Josephine and ended up pinching one of the guns, a 'lewd gesture' which they insisted would never have appeared in a D'Oyly Carte production.

The 1962 City of London Festival included an outdoor production of *The Yeomen of the Guard* at the Tower of London with a cast including Kenneth Sandford and Thomas Round from the D'Oyly Carte and John Cameron as Jack Point. 'A Laughing Boy but Yesterday' and 'Rapture, Rapture', dropped from D'Oyly Carte productions, were restored. Director Anthony Besch had initially hoped to stage the opera on Tower Green but this was thwarted by the ancient regulation that after the nightly Ceremony of the Keys no visitors were allowed on the premises. So he switched to the moat on the west side with the Tower forming a natural backdrop. Designer Peter Rice constructed a huge timber staircase from the top of the battlements leading down to the execution scaffold on which the main performance took place. The production, revived in 1964 and 1966, created a welcome precedent for staging the Savoy operas in their proper locations. *Pinafore* has been performed on various nineteenth-century battleships, although never, as far as I am aware, on HMS Victory and *Pirates* has had numerous stagings at the outdoor Minack Theatre on the Cornish coast. *Princess Ida* has been put on at least once in an all-female educational establishment when the students of Mary Baldwin College, Staunton, Virginia, performed it as a co-production with Washington and Lee, a neighbouring all-male college, in 1986. We still await *Iolanthe* performed on Palace Green, Westminster, with the Houses of Parliament as the backdrop.

There was a steady trickle of televised performances of G & S through the 1960s. A truncated version of the Sadler's Wells *Mikado* running to just over an hour and broadcast on Christmas Eve 1962 was the first screening of any Savoy opera on British television. The Stratford, Ontario, production of *The Gondoliers* was televised in 1962, shortened versions of the Sadler's Wells *Iolanthe* and Besch's *Yeomen* in 1964, and the D'Oyly Carte *Patience* in 1965. In October 1963 Czechoslovakian television transmitted a production of *Gondoliers* that had run in repertoire over the previous twelve months at the Prague Operetta Theatre. This was not the only G & S production in Eastern Europe — *Yeomen* was performed at Olomouc in Moldavia the same year as part of a workers' theatrical festival. A *Radioduffusion–Télévision-Française* production of *Mikado* in a translation by Tony Mayer in January 1965 constituted the first professional performance of G & S in France since a D'Oyly Carte touring company had performed in Calais and Boulogne in 1887. On Boxing Day 1969 *Pinafore* was shown on Danish television in a production by the Royal Theatre, Copenhagen, which had been running successfully for more than a decade. The same company also staged *Trial* and *Pirates* in Danish translations.

In 1966 BBC radio broadcast complete versions of all thirteen extant Savoy operas conducted by Stanford Robinson. The inspiration and much of the direction came from Peter Pratt, formerly of the D'Oyly Carte, who sang and spoke many of the patter roles. Most of the other roles were split between singers and actors. Among the famous names involved were the husband-and-wife team of Timothy West and Prunella Scales, who spoke the parts of King Gama and Princess Ida, respectively. Broadcast on alternate Sundays, reinforcing the sacred aura of G & S, the series was repeated in 1967. There were regular live relays of the operas on radio throughout the 1960s. Television began to take a more irreverent approach towards the end of the decade with an updated *Mikado* by Alan Melville entitled *Titipu* on BBC 2 over Christmas 1967 and a similar reworking of *Iolanthe* the following year with the comedy actor Patrick Cargill playing the Lord Chancellor.

Scottish Opera ventured into G & S in 1968 with a production of *Gondoliers* starring Ian Wallace and Bill McCue, and Kent Opera toured *Pinafore* in 1969. The growing influence of hippydom and 'flower power' inevitably worked its way into performances of *Patience*. A Toronto production had the maidens addressing Bunthorne as 'Maharishi'. John Cox contemplated a similar updating for Sadler's Wells in 1969 but decided in the end to play it straight. His production, with Emile Belcourt as Grosvenor and Derek Hammond-Stroud as Bunthorne, remained in the repertoire of English National Opera (as Sadler's Wells was renamed in 1974) until 1984. It was performed at the Proms in 1976 and toured to Vienna and the United States in 1984. It was also taken into the repertoire of Australian Opera where it remained for a considerable time, being revived in 1995 and shown on Australian television in 1996. It has most recently been revived by West Australian Opera in 1999.

Australia enjoyed something of a G & S boom in the 1960s. Throughout the period of the copyright professional productions were a monopoly of J. C. Williamson Theatres, who were licensed by D'Oyly Carte and stuck closely to their style. Williamson did very well out of this arrangement and coined the adage 'If you need money, then put on G & S', which became something of a mantra in Australian theatrical circles. The ending of the copyright brought a number of other professional performing groups into the field, the most successful being the Elizabethan Trust Opera Company, which presented *Iolanthe*, *Pinafore*, *Pirates*, and *Yeomen* in Sydney, Adelaide, and Brisbane in 1969. It kept costs low by recycling costumes and sets from previous productions—most of the *Yeomen* costumes had first been used in *Faust*—and took the operas to Melbourne and Canberra in 1970. The singers and orchestra brought together for these productions formed the nucleus of Australian Opera. Stephen Hall, the director, was also responsible for new productions of *Gondoliers* and *Mikado* in 1971, and his *Pinafore* and *Iolanthe* were revived in 1976 for the new Sydney Opera House, with *Iolanthe* being televised from there.

The 1970s saw considerably fewer new professional productions in Britain, perhaps because the initial excitement generated by the expiry of the copyright was wearing off. Kent Opera followed a successful *Pinafore* with a short-lived production of *Ruddigore* in 1970. Television continued to feature regular G & S performances, with both the D'Oyly Carte *Pinafore* (on ITV) and *Mikado* (on BBC) being shown over Christmas 1973 and *Trial* and *Yeomen* the following Christmas. On the Continent, *Der Gaukler von London*, a German translation of *Yeomen*, was performed at Kassel in Germany in 1973 and *Pinafore* was staged at the same venue the following year. *Mikado* returned to Russia, where it had regularly played in the 1880s and 1890s, in a new translation by Anatoly Orelovich for the Odessa Operetta Theatre in 1978. Also in 1978 Besch's *Yeomen* was revived for the 900th anniversary of the Tower of London, with rock-and-roll pioneer turned musical comedy star Tommy Steele as Jack Point. It was filmed at Shepperton Studios for broadcast on independent television the following Christmas and subsequently released on video.

The most significant event in terms of professional performance of G & S in the 1970s occurred in the United States. This was the foundation in 1974 by Albert Bergeret of the New York Gilbert and Sullivan Players (NYGASP). Bergeret began his lifelong love affair with G & S while a student in the late 1960s at Columbia University, where he majored in music, learned the entire Savoy repertory, and fulfilled just about every role he could with the Gilbert and Sullivan Society, including soloist, chorister, designer, director, conductor, and vice-president. After graduation, he got together a group of Columbia alumni to perform on a semiprofessional basis. Eventually, running the company became his full-time job, although his singers are still semipros and fit in their G & S performances around other work commitments, on occasions literally—one of his regular soloists who is also a supernumerary at the Metropolitan Opera sang the Counsel in *Trial by Jury* between going on in the first and last acts of *Tannhäuser*.

When NYGASP started, its budget was just $35 for photocopying flyers. Now it is over $2 million a year although Bergeret is the only full-timer with the company, which has a three-week season in New York every January and around twenty-five performances on tour during the rest of the year, mostly in the northeast and Canada but also as far afield as Georgia and Florida. In 2004 the company brought *Pirates* and *Iolanthe* to Britain for the Buxton G & S festival. Scenery and costumes are kept in a warehouse in Newark—Bergeret is particularly proud of the unique folding sets that he has invented using interfacing panels and coffin locks—and loaded on to a twenty-four-foot Ryder truck. Singers and orchestra are transported by bus. There are hairy stories of twenty-hour journeys to distant venues with the truck arriving late, leaving just two hours to erect the complex set in a strange theatre. The company regularly does one-night stands and because of their other commitments, it is rare to have the same people on stage and in the pit for consecutive performances. Out of 300 hopefuls who audition every year, Bergeret picks a team that will provide him with at least three people to cover every soloist's role and chorus slot. He describes the whole operation as 'constantly juggling the jigsaw puzzle' and often has to make last-minute switches of cast. During a recent performance of *Pirates* in Georgia the second trombone was required to leave the pit and go on stage for the second act to cover for a pirate who had just suffered a bereavement.

Widely recognised as the leading professional G & S repertory company in the United States, NYGASP has performed the entire canon of extant Savoy operas. The usual pattern is for each season to feature two of the 'Piramikafore' trio together with one of the slightly less popular works. It also has a significant educational outreach and runs performing workshops in several schools. Bergeret maintains that he is not a G & S fanatic—'I'm interested in communicating thoughts and theatrical values to an audience and I happen to use G & S to do that'— but admits that his ambition is to have a permanent G & S repertory company on the lines of the old D'Oyly Carte. Given his enthusiasm and seemingly boundless energy, it does not seem an impossible dream. When I met him during preparations for a one-night performance of *Pirates* in Scranton, Pennsylvania, he was up a ladder on stage fixing the set. After personally checking the lighting cues, props, and backcloth, he dived down to his dressing room to pick up a wad of cheques, which he personally distributed to the artistes and orchestra members, who are all paid per performance. After a sound check with the orchestra, he changed into his tuxedo to meet the evening's sponsors and then stepped into the pit to conduct the show, which he had also directed and rehearsed. Musically strong ('Poor Wandering One' had the longest and most complex cadenza I have ever heard) and with the accent on slick choreography and Broadway-style routines—the reprise of 'With Cat-like Tread' had the pirates donning sparkling silver bowlers—the diction was faultless and the whole effect highly polished and full of high-level energy.[2]

The most important event in terms of G & S performance in the 1980s also took place in the United States. On 15 July 1980 a new production of *Pirates* opened the New York Shakespeare Festival in the Delacorte Theatre in New York's Central Park. Directed by Wilford Leach and produced by Joseph Papp, who had been responsible for the supremely successful Broadway musical *A Chorus Line*, it was the first major professional production to treat G & S as though it were a Broadway musical. Gilbert's words were largely unaltered but Sullivan's orchestrations were ditched in favour of arrangements by William Elliott, there was no overture, the singers were miked, and synthesisers replaced strings in the pit. The soloists were actors and pop stars rather than trained opera singers—George Rose as the major general, Patricia Routledge (later to make her name as Hyacinth Bucket in the television series 'Keeping Up Appearances') as Ruth, Linda Ronstadt as Mabel, and Kevin Kline as the pirate king. Several liberties were taken with the score—'My Eyes Are Fully Open' from *Ruddigore* and 'Sorry Her Lot' from *Pinafore* were added to the second act—but there was also a touch of authenticity, with part of the original 1879 New York finale being restored by operetta scholar Richard Traubner.

Papp's *Pirates*, as it has come to be known, was hugely successful. It moved to Broadway in 1981, where it had 787 performances, the longest run ever achieved by any production of a Gilbert and Sullivan opera, toured the United States, and was filmed with Angela Lansbury as Ruth. The stage version came to London in May 1982 with a production at the Theatre Royal, Drury Lane, in which veteran comedian George Cole was joined by rock stars Bonnie Langford and Pamela Stephenson. The Manchester production launched the career of Michael Ball, who played Frederic. Critics enthused about its energy, youthfulness, and exuberance. Despite the synthesisers and the amplified pop voices, it managed to keep faith with the spirit of the original and offended traditionalists less than many other updated productions. It has been regularly revived on both sides of the Atlantic—a British revival in 2000 transferred from the West Yorkshire Playhouse, Leeds, to the Open Air Theatre in Regent's Park, London—and has also become well established in the repertoire of amateur and student societies.

No other production has had as much lasting impact or influence. Papp's *Pirates* affected the style of countless professional G & S productions in many countries throughout the 1980s and 1990s. It also helped to promote G & S in places where it had been little performed and bring it to the attention of a much wider and younger audience. It was hugely successful in Germany, playing initially at Dortmund in 1994 and enjoying a four-month run in 1996 at the

Theater des Westens, Berlin, where it received standing ovations and endless cheers. In the finale of the German version Ruth reappeared as Queen Elizabeth II, apologizing for Queen Victoria's absence 'due to death'. One German critic observed, 'what was being cheered was without doubt not so much the piece (after all, who is interested in pirates, the bourgeoisie in Victorian England, or forgotten works by Gilbert and Sullivan?) as the triumph of the director and choreographer' and another concluded: 'Opera, operetta or musical? In the end, it's irrelevant. The various elements are all satirically combined to produce a top-quality non-stop spectacle, entertaining but harmless, filled with exuberant delight, punning rhymes and delicious parodies'.[3]

A co-production with Victoria State Opera starring Jon English as the pirate king, June Bronhill as Ruth, and Simon Gallaher as Frederic toured Australia and New Zealand for almost three years from 1984 and clocked up over 700 performances. Gallaher went on to form his own company, which staged *Mikado* and *Pinafore* with himself in the tenor leads. Building on Papp's model and musical style, he formed Essgee Entertainment in 1994 to produce a new version of *Pirates* which grossed over $13,000,000 and played to over 350,000 people. The video of this show is the top-selling music video in Australian history. Gallaher's Papp-style *Mikado* (1995) and *Pinafore* (1997) have both been highly successful and continue to tour Australasia. The Essgee shows make heavy use of synthesiser-based accompaniment (the orchestration is for three keyboards, percussion, guitar, and drums) and material imported from other operas—in the case of *Pirates*, 'You Understand' from *Ruddigore* becomes a trio for Ruth, Frederic, and the Pirate King. The women's chorus is replaced by a trio called 'the fabulous Singlettes', who sing in 1950s close harmony style and there is always a megamix medley of reprised numbers at the end. Gallaher's response to those who object to such innovations is 'Time to move on. Let your hair down and don't take life so seriously'.

It is strange that apart from the Essgee productions, there have been few attempts to do a 'Papp' on the other Savoy operas. Although there have been many updated versions, they lack the panache, energy, star casting, and staying power of his *Pirates*. Advance publicity for a version of *Utopia Ltd* planned for the Adelphi Theatre in 1982 and starring the veteran music hall and radio comedian Charlie Chester promised that 'the rhythms and sound of Latin music will invade the score transforming, but retaining, the genius of Sullivan into the pulsating and dynamic sound of today', but the show never came off. Perhaps *Pirates* lends itself uniquely to this kind of treatment, being more like a Broadway musical than any other Savoy opera. Indeed, Papp's own experience tends to confirm this. He and Leach had originally thought of doing *Mikado* but found that it was not suitable for the kind of treatment they wanted. Nor was *Pinafore*, which they turned to next: 'So then there was *Pirates* and that was perfect. It's such an optimistic piece and is as well crafted as a top American musical. Why it even has an eleven o'clock number as we call it in the trade'.[4]

Aside from Papp's *Pirates*, the 1980s saw a number of much more conventional G & S productions in the United States by newly established opera companies. Glimmerglass Opera, which had been founded in 1975 by a group of academics who had summer homes around Cooperstown in New York State, performed *Pinafore* in 1981 and 1989 and *Pirates* in 1987. Ohio Light Opera, founded in 1979 to provide a showcase and training ground for young singers and instrumentalists embarking on professional careers, concentrated entirely on G & S for its first four years. Although it extended its repertoire in 1983 to cover operetta, it has continued to present at least one Savoy opera (and usually two) in its annual summer season and prides itself on having performed the entire canon. By 2004 it had achieved twelve productions of *Pinafore*; eleven of *Mikado* and *Pirates*; seven of *Gondoliers*, *Yeomen*, and *Trial*; six of *Iolanthe*, *Patience*, and *Ruddigore*; five of *Sorcerer* and *Utopia*; four of *Ida*; and one of *Grand Duke*. The Southeastern Savoyards were formed in Atlanta in 1980 initially as a largely amateur performing group but rapidly became professional. Between 1980 and 1998, when they diversified into non–G & S works, their tally was ten performances of *Mikado*; seven of *Pirates*; five of *Pinafore* and *Iolanthe*; four of *Gondoliers*; and three of *Ruddigore*, *Patience*, and *Trial*.

In Britain, the most important and long-lasting production from this period was the video series made by George Walker in 1982. This lavish operation had a total budget of $15 million and a team of 700 people involved in filming all the operas except *Utopia* and *Grand Duke*. Walker's approach was unashamedly populist. He said of the libretti 'they're so good, it would cost a quarter of a million dollars to get someone to write that kind of script now' and told me that he saw G & S as 'like a Hollywood musical—that's how it should be treated— *Iolanthe* reminds me of *Oklahoma*'.[5] He brought in high-quality directors like John Cox, responsible for Southern Television's recordings of Glyndebourne operas, and put the music in the capable hands of Alexander Faris and the London Symphony Orchestra. Judith de Paul, the American producer hired to supervise the project, insisted on having big names who would appeal on both sides of the Atlantic for the character parts and cast Vincent Price, star of countless Hammer horror films, as Sir Despard Murgatroyd; Joel Grey, master of ceremonies in the film *Cabaret*, as Jack Point; William Conrad, the television detective Cannon, as the Mikado; Frankie Howerd as Sir Joseph Porter; and Keith Michell as Robin Oakapple, Major General Stanley, and Don Alhambra.

The finished result—'22 hours of exquisite programming' in Miss de Paul's words—was more traditional than the celebrity casting and show-business ap-

FIGURE 4.1 'Like a *Hollywood* musical'. George Walker surrounded by sailors during the filming of the Brent Walker *Pinafore*, 1981 *(Author's collection)*

FIGURE 4.2 Peter Marshall as Captain Corcoran and Frankie Howerd as Sir Joseph Porter in the Brent Walker *Pinafore*, 1981 *(Brent Walker Film Productions Ltd.)*

proach might suggest. Most of the key singing roles were given to established opera singers like Ann Hood, Derek Hammond-Stroud, and Eric Shilling, though none, pointedly, went to anyone from the existing D'Oyly Carte company. Dialogue and music were both treated with considerable respect, although there were some cuts, and the staging was generally both picturesque and appropriate. For the American market, the videos were packaged with introductions by Douglas Fairbanks Jr. They are still selling today and have had regular showings on British television since *Pirates* was first screened on BBC 1 on 22 December 1982. The Brent Walker videos spawned a number of professional stage productions featuring well-known faces from television. A summer season of *HMS Pinafore* in 1982 at the Queen Elizabeth Hall, London, for example, featured Frank Thornton from the BBC television programme *Are You Being Served?* as Sir Joseph Porter.

The year 1983 saw the emergence of a new British light opera company partly to fill the gap left by the demise of the D'Oyly Carte in the previous year. New Sadler's Wells Opera put G & S at the centre of its repertoire, and its opening season included a *Mikado* directed by Christopher Renshaw with Donald Adams in the title role. Ko-Ko was played by Nickolas Grace, who had made his name as the mincing Anthony Blanche in the highly successful television adaptation of Evelyn Waugh's *Brideshead Revisited*. Despite some novel touches—the 'train of little ladies' entered on a toy train made up of vases and teapots, and the Mikado and Katisha were stuck on an enormous mantel-shelf as they meted out justice—it was a fairly traditional production and suggested that the new company was not going to rock any boats.

The following year New Sadler's Wells mounted two more Renshaw productions, *Pinafore*, with Nickolas Grace as Sir Joseph, and *Gondoliers*, with John Fryatt as the Duke of Plaza-Toro and Donald Adams as Don Alhambra. In 1987 a centenary production of *Ruddigore*, directed by Ian Judge and starring Marilyn Hill-Smith as Rose Maybud, David Hillman as Dick Dauntless, Gordon Sandison as Robin, and Linda Ormiston as Mad Margaret, played to full houses over a seven-week tour. Thanks to scholarly research on the autograph score by David Russell Hulme, several 'lost' songs were restored and the excellent recording of this production produced by John Yap included the march of the ancestors and song for Sir Roderic and chorus 'By the Curse Upon Our Race' in the act 2 ghost scene, Sir Ruthven's song 'For Thirty Five Years' and the original act 2 finale. *Pinafore* was also revived and recorded in 1987 with the inclusion of the quotation from 'Rule Britannia' that Sullivan introduced in the finale of the 1887 revival to celebrate Queen Victoria's Golden Jubilee. Also recorded for the first time was Sir Joseph Porter's 'Here, Take Her Sir' recitative from act 2. For a while it looked as though the new company would take over the old D'Oyly

Carte mantle, as well as offering operetta classics like *Countess Maritza* and *The Count of Luxembourg* but it, too, fell victim to cultural snobbery and prejudice against light opera and folded in 1988.

Meanwhile, two of Britain's major established opera companies were tackling G & S in exciting ways. Scottish Opera put on *Iolanthe* in 1986, with Ricki Fulton as the Lord Chancellor and Gillian Knight as the Queen of the Fairies, in a production that was revived in 1988. Also in 1986 English National Opera presented *Mikado* at the Coliseum in a production directed by Jonathan Miller and designed by Stefanos Lazardis and Sue Blane. It was set in a spa hotel in the 1920s, with the chorus, made up of waiters, maids, and schoolgirls, dressed strikingly in black and white. Eric Idle of *Monty Python* fame played Ko-Ko, Bonaventura Bottone was Nanki-Poo, and Lesley Garrett played Yum-Yum as a 'flapper'. An instant success, it was revived the following year with Bill Oddie as Ko-Ko and Alfred Marks as the Mikado. Since then it has been one of the mainstays of the ENO repertoire, revived around Christmas time on an almost annual basis. It has also travelled widely. As a co-production with Houston Grand Opera and Los Angeles Music Center Opera Association, it first went to the United States in 1987 with Donald Adams as the Mikado and Dudley Moore as Ko-Ko and has more recently been performed by New York City Opera (2001 and 2003). The Miller *Mikado* stands alongside Papp's *Pirates* as the most enduring G & S production of recent decades.

In Continental Europe, *Mikado* was performed in Danish at the Royal Theatre, Copenhagen, in 1980 and in German as *Der Mikado, oder Tumult in Titipu*, at the Zurich Schauspielhaus, Switzerland, in 1984. This latter production, which was screened on Swiss television on 1 January 1985, was set in a London brothel attended by the Prince of Wales (later Edward VII) and the Japanese ambassador and featured a female Mikado played by Eva Rieck, who also doubled as a nude Queen Victoria in a new prose prologue and epilogue written by the translator, Dieter Bachman. The *Mikado* centenary in 1985 raised hopes that there might be a number of other productions in German-speaking countries where the opera had once been very popular, but these did not materialize, for reasons adduced by Horst Statkus, director of the theatres in Basle: 'A threefold translation—England in a Japanese guise played in German—makes it almost incomprehensible to us today. Gilbert is one of the wittiest librettists. To carry humour over into another country, another language, is difficult enough. Wit, however, gets irredeemably lost. . . . For Gilbert and Sullivan, including *The Mikado*, I see no real chance of "naturalization" to our clime'.[6] Elsewhere in Europe, however, there was more enthusiasm for *Mikado* productions. In 1986 a Catalonian version, in which a cast of twelve provided chorus as well as principals, opened in Barcelona, toured Spain, and was recorded. The same year saw the world premiere of a Gaelic version in Galway, Ireland. In 1988 the Odessa Theatre of Musical Comedy staged a Russian version and in 1991 *Mikado* was performed in French by Toulon Opera.

In Australia Victoria State Opera performed *Iolanthe* in Melbourne in 1982 and toured *Pinafore* with Paul Eddington of BBC's *Yes, Minister* as Sir Joseph Porter in 1987. The newly formed Australian Opera entered the G & S repertoire in 1985 with *Trial by Jury* and *Mikado* directed by Christopher Renshaw and conducted by Richard Bonynge. The *Mikado* production was taken up by Opera Pacific, Los Angeles, in 1997 and the State Opera of South Australia in 1999. Australian Opera's 1989 *Gondoliers*, directed by Brian Macdonald, was successfully revived in 1990, 1994, and 2000.

In the United States, New York City Opera and Chicago Lyric Opera both unveiled new *Mikado* productions in 1983. The Chicago production, directed by Peter Sellars, who had previously had Don Giovanni shooting dope and dining on Big Macs, was especially innovative. During the overture young ladies dressed as Northwest Orient Airline stewardesses stood on stage and among the audience rhythmically miming the familiar airline safety drill with seat belts, oxygen masks, and lifebelts. The action was set in a corporate Japanese boardroom with flashing signs advertising Sony, Canon, Toshiba, Fuji, and Coca-Cola. 'If You Want to Know Who We Are' was sung by a chorus of executive clones made up in identical black business suits, dark glasses, and black toupees. Nanki-Poo was transformed into a rocker with a red guitar, Yum-Yum became a teenybopper in a flared short skirt and visor cap, and Donald Adams arrived on stage as the Mikado in a Datsun. In Canada, the Stratford Festival in Ontario continued to provide innovative and imaginative productions throughout the 1980s under the direction of Brian Macdonald, with orchestrations by Berthold Carrière, Eric Donkin in the patter roles, and Richard McMillan in the bass-baritone parts. The 1984 *Gondoliers* won plaudits for a staging of the Cachucha involving the cast dancing with dummies as partners and in the same year the Stratford *Mikado* came to London's Old Vic.

Before leaving the 1980s mention must be made of the complete cycle of operas broadcast on Sunday lunchtimes on BBC Radio 2 during 1989. Recorded over a five-year period, with Barry Wordsworth, Ashley Lawrence, and Charles Mackerras conducting, they differed from the 1966 broadcasts in having songs and dialogue performed by the same people. The cast list included John Fryatt, Leslie Fyson, Derek Hammond-Stroud, Marilyn Hill Smith, and Gillian Knight, and several lost songs were restored. Informative interval talks by David Mackie included re-creations of other lost material, and there was much disappointment among G & S fans that the recordings were not issued on CD.

The early 1990s saw one of the most bizarre and controversial stagings of a Gilbert and Sullivan opera in the United Kingdom with English National Opera's 1992 production of *Princess Ida*. A strong cast was led by Rosemary Joshua as Ida, Anne Collins as Lady Blanche, Richard Van Allan as Hildebrand, and Nickolas Grace and Richard Suart alternating as Gama. Jane Glover conducted from a new score based on Sullivan's autograph edition. Director Ken Russell and designer James Merifield gave the opera a contemporary setting, with act 1 taking place in the grounds of Buck'n'Yen Palace, a theme park created by selling off Buckingham Palace to the Americans and Japanese, and acts 2 and 3 set, unaccountably, in the Tower of London. Hildebrand was based on Prince Charles, Hilarion on Prince William, Gama turned into a Sushi-king who made his first entrance on a swishing-tailed goldfish burger, and the female students of Castle Adamant were kitted out in Madonna-style pointed breast-plates. The critics were virtually unanimous in their condemnation. John Higgins described it in the *Times* as 'a gaudy, vulgar hog, grunting loudly and incessantly for attention', the *Telegraph*'s Robert Henderson as 'a lethal cocktail of the boring and banal', and Max Loppert in the *Financial Times* as 'a heedlessly energetic blending of the crass, the coarse and the witless'.[7]

Several leading Gilbert and Sullivan aficionados, by contrast, rather liked Russell's idiosyncratic treatment of one of the least-performed Savoy operas. Brian Jones, editor of the *Gilbert Society Journal*, enthused that 'of all the professional productions I have seen in the last ten years, this is the one I have most enjoyed. . . . Of all the modern stagings, this one has the greatest sympathy for Gilbert's stagecraft'; Stephen Turnbull, secretary of the Sullivan Society, found some inspired touches and felt that 'for all its gimmickry and garishness, I found Ken Russell's stage business less intrusive on the music than that of Jonathan Miller for the *Mikado*'.[8] However, the generally hostile reception scuppered plans to keep *Ida* in the ENO repertoire and to record the production.

In much more traditional mould, Welsh National Opera presented a splendidly sung and staged *Yeomen* in its 1994–95 season. Conducted by Charles Mackerras with a cast led by Richard Suart, Donald Adams, and Donald Maxwell, it was performed in April 1995 at the Royal Opera House, Covent Garden, so far the only production of a Savoy opera in that venue. It was recorded together with *Trial by Jury*, taking its place as one of the finest recent CD versions of G & S alongside earlier Welsh National Opera recordings under Mackerras's baton of *Mikado, Pinafore,* and *Pirates*. Another fine recording of *Yeomen*, with edited dialogue and featuring Bryn Terfel as Shadbolt and Thomas Allen as Jack Point with the Academy and Choir of St. Martin's in the Field conducted by Sir Neville Marriner, was issued in 1993.

A production of *Trial by Jury* in Bow Street Magistrates' Court in Central London in 1993 gave another G & S opera an authentic setting. Directed by Stephen Barlow as part of the Covent Garden Festival, it returned to the same venue on a virtually annual basis through the 1990s. In 2000 *Trial* received forty-three performances, with up to four on each day of the festival. It has also been staged on several occasions in a courtroom at St. George's Hall, Liverpool, by Opera Piccola and in the Richard J. Daley Courthouse in downtown Chicago in 1998 by a cast made up entirely of active members of the legal community in Chicago, accompanied by the Chicago Bar Association Symphony Orchestra.

The welcome revival of professional productions in Continental Europe continued through the 1990s. *Mikado* was performed in Italian in Palermo, Sicily, in 1991; *Gondoliers* in English at La Fenice, Venice, in 1993; and Danish versions of both operas were put on by Danish National Opera. *Die Piraten von Penzance* was staged in Austria and Germany in 1993 and *Der Mikado, oder Tumult in Titipu* in Munich, Basle, Zurich and Giessen, near Frankfurt, in 1995. A Russian version of *Trial by Jury* was premiered in St. Petersburg and received a concert performance in Moscow in 1996. The same year saw two significant G & S productions on German radio, with Südwestfunk broadcasting the WNO *Yeomen of the Guard* and Saarländische Rundfunk presenting a 150-minute programme on the Savoy operas—signs, perhaps, that the resistance noted in the 1980s to G & S in German was breaking down.

In the United States, the 1990s and early 2000s were a period of rather mixed fortunes for G & S. Several major opera companies continued to keep it in their repertoire and present new productions of the most popular works. New York City Opera staged a new *Pinafore* in 1996 and Santa Fé Opera presented *Pirates* in 2002. Glimmerglass continued to show a strong commitment to G & S, performing *Mikado* in 1991, *Iolanthe* in 1994, *Yeomen* in 1995, and *Patience* in 2004. Southeastern Savoyards, however, found that an exclusive diet of G & S was leading to a situation where, in musical director J. Lynn Thompson's words, 'at some performances there were more people on stage than in the audience' and re-formed as the Atlanta Lyric Theatre to perform musicals and operetta but still retain one G & S production per year. Ohio Light Opera, which had earlier moved in a similar direction, made notable complete recordings of *Ida* (1999) and *Utopia Limited* (2002) and fulfilled its promise to perform the entire Savoy canon with the *Grand Duke* in 2003.

In Canada Brian Macdonald's productions at Stratford continued to win plaudits from the critics and draw bigger audiences than the Shakespeare performances for which the festival was famed. His 1992 *Pinafore* had no overture but instead a few opening bars led into interpolated dialogue explaining that the crew were awaking in their hammocks and preparing for the morning's ablutions. This provided the opportunity for one sailor to bare his bottom and Ralph to sing 'A Maiden Fair to See' stripped to the waist. Sir Joseph descended in a hot air balloon and his sisters, cousins, and aunts came on in colourful boats on wheels resembling fairground dodgems. 'When I Was a Lad' was enlivened by a naughty sea gull and a large octopus which appeared from the orchestra pit. Macdonald's 1994 *Pirates* featured a stodgy British company being employed to make a Hollywood movie of the opera in the 1920s. An interpolated prologue introduced Heinrich Von Schtompinc, the sadistic film director who managed to persuade the members of the company to play their roles in a more athletic, responsive, and sexy manner for the cameras. This device provided the opportunity for plenty of mutual incomprehension between the British singers and the Hollywood crew. When one of the understudies complains, 'I haven't done Nanki-Poo in a fortnight', the cameraman suggests 'you might want to try the prunes in our canteen'. Most critics felt this was rather striving for effect, the *Toronto Globe and Mail* concluding that 'over all, the G & S musical is clearly better than the Hollywood bits grafted on to it. . . . The Stratford creative team has gone to a lot of trouble to fix something that wasn't broken; and if they didn't quite break it, they certainly haven't improved it'.[9] Macdonald's 1995 *Gondoliers* was shown on German television.

In Australia Stuart Maunder directed a lavish *Iolanthe* with tap-dancing fairies for Victoria State Opera in 1991, and the same company performed *Ruddigore* in 1995. In 1999 Opera Australia, the result of a merger between Victoria State Opera and Australian Opera, staged the *Gondoliers* and in 2002 it revived Maunder's *Iolanthe*. Professional G & S reached Malaysia in 1996 with three fully staged performances of *Mikado* in Penang featuring a mixture of local and British professional soloists in Chinese Opera costumes and an amateur chorus and orchestra. Richard Suart played Ko-Ko and Michael Ducarel the Mikado of Penang.

In Britain, there were several positive developments in the later 1990s. A concert version of *Gondoliers* in 1997 constituted the first complete performance of a Savoy opera at a Promenade concert since *Patience* in 1976. More important, three new professional companies dedicated to performing G & S emerged, one by design and the other two by accident. The Gilbert and Sullivan Opera Company was formed in 1997 as part of the Buxton G & S Festival with the specific purpose of performing the Savoy operas and nothing but them (see page 193). Opera della Luna and the revived Carl Rosa Opera were both originally set up primarily to perform other things but found themselves majoring in G & S, al-

most despite themselves and virtually to the exclusion of their intended repertoire, because it sold tickets. In their very different ways they are now providing
the most dynamic and exciting professional performances of G & S in Britain.

Opera della Luna was set up in 1994 by Jeff Clarke, who had worked with
Scottish Opera and subsequently in musical theatre, where he found that
trained actors brought a very different approach from those trained as singers:

> Actors will come in on first day knowing nothing and that's good be-
> cause you work it out and discuss it together, whereas a singer will know
> everything and have decided what the part is about—they just want to
> know where the spot light is. I found working with actors very exciting and
> because of the growth of musical theatre training in drama colleges it
> seemed to me there were more and more actors who were capable of tack-
> ling operatic roles and certainly Gilbert and Sullivan roles.[10]

Clarke founded Opera della Luna as a small ensemble company of actor-
singers to perform the kinds of works which singers usually shy away from doing,
like operas with dialogue such as Haydn's comic operas and lesser-known operettas. He began with a revival of Offenbach's *Robinson Crusoe* but it lost
£7000. In an effort to recoup this, he turned to the trusted milch-cow of G & S
and devised an unorthodox scaled-down version of *Pirates* in 1995. Since then,
Gilbert and Sullivan has been Opera della Luna's mainstay and although he
does not want it to be thought of as a company that performs only the Savoy
operas, he concedes that they have made its reputation and are what the audience wants. He also owns up to having a G & S past himself, having played Jack
Point and directed the *Mikado* while a student at St. Andrews University.

Parson's Pirates, which remains one of the key items in the Opera della Luna
repertoire, is set in the hall of the parish church of St. Michael's Under Ware,
where the vicar, the Reverend Arthur Bender, is putting on *The Pirates of
Penzance* to raise money for church funds. His cast consists of the two churchwardens, Mr. Prickett and Mr. Prendergast; Tracey, a punkish girl who does
amazing things with chewing gum; an un-named local youth who is recruited
to play Frederic; and Mrs. Goodbody, a lady who is into alternative spirituality
and dabbles in Tarot cards and tantric therapies. The music is supplied by
Mr. Clerkenwell, the church organist. The first act is devoted to casting and rehearsing the show and is full of double entendres worthy of the 'Carry On' films
of the 1960s such as 'Mr. Clerkenwell's organ is going flat'. There is a high camp
quotient and a considerable amount of audience participation. At one point the
two churchwardens each take half of the audience and get them singing 'tit' and
'willow' in rapid succession, letting the vicar indulge in another round of double

FIGURE 4.3 The Reverend Bender puts Tracy through her paces. Richard Gauntlett and Fiona O'Neill in the first performance of *The Parson's Pirates*, 1995 *(Christine Walford/ Opera della Luna)*

entendres: 'If you don't join in, I'll make you all stand up and you can show us your willows'. The second half consists of a truncated performance of *Pirates*, with the six performers doubling up as pirates, daughters, police persons, and principals with lots of cross-dressing and a good deal more camp. The whole show cost just £250 to stage—a programme note reads 'costumes by Sue Ryder'—and is enormous fun.

In 1997 Clarke added two more G & S–related works to the company's repertoire. *The Ghosts of Ruddigore* is based on an idea from *The Rocky Horror Show*. Amanda Goodheart and Kevin Murgatroyd, stalwarts of their local G & S society, are on their way down to Cornwall to try and find Rederring when their car breaks down and they have to abandon it. A band of ageing professional bridesmaids appear through the fog and Kevin and Amanda find themselves caught up in the terrifying antics of mad maidens, wicked baronets, and ghostly ancestors. The reduced version of *Pinafore* was first devised for the cruise liner QE2, which demands that on-board entertainments last no longer than an hour. The band members are on stage dressed as sailors, the ship is built during

FIGURE 4.4 Gay Soper, John Griffiths, and Martin George as the three ghostly brides-maids in Opera della Luna's *The Ghosts of Ruddigore*, 1997 *(Stephen Wright)*

the overture, and the company come on as sailors, gradually disappearing and reappearing as the various individual characters. In 1998 *Mikado* was added to the repertoire, set in Ko-Ko's tailor's shop and with the three little maids in Versace dresses.

Opera della Luna's scaled-down productions are performed by an ensemble of six or seven actor-singers and a similar-sized band. Removing the chorus gives the shows a completely new dimension and emphasizes their intimacy. Clarke reckons that this treatment is only feasible for some of the operas and would not work for *Iolanthe* or *Patience*: 'I don't think I want to start with 20 love sick maidens and they are all in the wings'. While he frequently uses words like 'modernise' and 'looking to the future' when describing his approach, he also insists: 'my raison d'étre is not to re-write the pieces but to do them with the resources we have'. The chorus-free approach appeals to the performers. Martin George says that he has always felt when watching traditional G & S 'that the chorus is a huge distraction from what the actual story is because there's always thirty people on stage regardless of what is happening. I've always had a difficulty with that. It's not naturalistic. Taking out the chorus modernizes it and makes it more accessible'. Rebecca Knight agrees: 'from an actor's point of view there is so much more you can extract out of a scene when it is so reliant on such a small team. There's so much more scope for pulling that stuff out and giving it a new life than there is in a straight production'. She says that compared to working with Opera della Luna, doing G & S for more traditional companies is 'like being in a strait-jacket. I will be expected to slip into doing what the person before did. This is the way it's done. You do this hand movement for these particular words. As a singer-actor you want to know the reason why you have to put your hand down there every time you sing 'He Was a Little Boy' in *Patience* or whatever. OK I'm singing it but why do I have to do that just because it's the tradition'.

Because of its size, Opera della Luna, which regularly does twelve-week tours, is able to perform in small venues which do not usually host opera companies. Clarke is particularly pleased with the response in places where there is no tradition of G & S performances and Rebecca Knight agrees: 'If Gilbert and Sullivan is to continue, we should be appealing to the people in Milton Keynes, not in the kinds of places where people know it already and they are all of an age. We need to appeal to young people and to those who aren't already converted'. This certainly seems to be happening on the evidence of the many highly enthusiastic letters that the company has received. A delighted parent wrote from Huddersfield to say that she had taken her six-year-old son to see *The Ghosts of Ruddigore*, 'hoping that he'd be able to sit through the performance and at least enjoy some of it'. She reported: 'You have made a small convert to G & S. He absolutely loved it and laughed his head off! He talked about it for days afterwards'. Another mother took her eleven-year-old son to *The Mikado* in Harlech, hoping he might be 'as inspired and enthralled by Gilbert and Sullivan as I was when I first went to see *The Pirates of Penzance* at a similar age. But could it compete with the TV programmes and computer games? No worries! Your production was brilliant!' Another satisfied customer who saw the *Mikado* in Basingstoke had never been to the opera before—'it was absolutely fantastic—I have never enjoyed a performance so much'.

Opera della Luna has achieved the rare feat of bringing in a new audience for G & S without alienating the old one. I watched *The Parson's Pirates*, with the ubiquitous and ever-fresh Richard Suart in the title role, and *The Mikado*, during the 2003 Buxton G & S Festival with the Opera House full of G & S aficionados, traditionalists, and D'Oyly Carte devotees. We were virtually all captivated by the freshness of the approach and the zest and vibrancy of the performances. A staging of the *Ghosts of Ruddigore* at the Bridewell Theatre, London, where the company had a month's residence in 2002, was lauded by the vice-president of the Gilbert and Sullivan Society and three past presidents of the New York Gilbert and Sullivan Society.

The other British company which has recently found itself concentrating largely on Gilbert and Sullivan could hardly be more different in history or approach. Originally founded in the United States in 1869 and established in

Britain in 1872, just three years before the D'Oyly Carte, Carl Rosa Opera established itself as a major touring company and was responsible for the first productions in English of such classics as *Aida*, *Cavalleria Rusticana*, and *The Flying Dutchman*. It finally ceased performing in 1959. The company's rebirth in the mid-1990s was the result of the vision and sheer brass neck of Peter Mulloy, an opera singer with drama training who cheekily used the name Carl Rosa for a production of *La Bohème* which he mounted in 1993 in his native Middlesbrough. He put all his money into forming a new opera company and in 1998 persuaded the Carl Rosa trustees to sign the name over to him so that he could legally register his title to it. Like Clarke, Mulloy did not originally envisage specializing or even majoring in G & S and intended rather to perform a broad repertoire of operetta and comic opera. He was, however, another long-term aficionado, having been taught singing as a boy by a former D'Oyly Carte principal, performed with the Rosedale Gilbert and Sullivan Society in Middlesbrough, and been captivated by the opening night of the 1977 D'Oyly Carte production of *Iolanthe* at the Sunderland Empire.

Carl Rosa came to perform G & S largely as a result of the chance discovery by Mulloy in the basement of a Middlesborough theatre of a pile of old D'Oyly Carte costumes used for the filming of the 1953 *Story of Gilbert and Sullivan*. He became fascinated with their designs, which went back to the original 1885 stage production. When he heard about the plans for *Topsy-Turvy*, he offered himself to Mike Leigh as design consultant on condition that he could have all the costumes and sets, based on the 1885 originals, which were being specially made for the film. The deal was done and they were duly used in his production of *Mikado* which opened at the Grand Opera House in Belfast on 14 September 1999. In 2000 *Yeomen* and *Iolanthe* were added to the Carl Rosa repertoire, and in 2001 he staged a production of *Pirates* which reintroduced many of the elements included in the 1879 version, notably the extended finale with its hymn to the nobility. The Carl Rosa *Mikado* toured Australia for four and a half months in 2001 and took over £5 million. *Gondoliers* was added to the repertoire in 2002; *Pinafore*, directed by Timothy West, in 2003; and in 2004 the company took *Mikado* to Rome for a week and toured *Pinafore* in Australia and New Zealand.

Carl Rosa has something of the feel of the old D'Oyly Carte. It tours a sixty-five-strong company, including a twenty-four-member chorus and twenty-four-piece orchestra. Although it has received small Arts Council grants, it operates largely without public subsidy and is run on a shoestring. The props are stored in Billingham-on-Teesside and the costumes in the basement of two adjoining Georgian houses in Shoreditch, East London, bought from the proceeds of the Australian tour. Mulloy and his wife, who is a singer with the company,

FIGURE 4.5 Donald
Maxwell in the title role
in Carl Rosa's *Mikado*
(*Carl Rosa Opera*)

live upstairs and the company offices are on the ground floor, staffed by just three full-timers with bookings, marketing, and fund-raising handled by part-timers. Audiences at Carl Rosa performances are invited to make a donation to keep the company going. A note in the programme points out that £25 will cover the hire of six orchestral music stands or the laundering of the men's shirts and £50 will provide a year's supply of hairspray for a wig. Mulloy is reconciled to the fact that the Arts Council does not want to fund a light opera company and says he would rather stay independent. A natural entrepreneur and go-getter, he went to Wolverhampton as soon as news came through that D'Oyly Carte were ceasing productions in 2003 and 'bought everything you need to run a company from them—sets, wigs, wig blocks, clothes rails, washing machines, furniture—the whole lot'. Carl Rosa gives regular employment to soloists from both the old and new D'Oyly Carte companies, including Gillian Knight, Gareth Jones, Bruce Graham, Eric Roberts, and Simon Butteriss. It has achieved the touring ambitions that always eluded the new D'Oyly Carte. In 2004, in addition to the Australasian tour of *Pinafore*, the company laid plans to take *Pinafore* and *Mikado* to North America. Mulloy plans to tour Europe and introduce more Savoy operas into the company's repertoire, and he has the enthusiasm and the business acumen to pull this and more off.

In contrast to the new D'Oyly Carte, Carl Rosa has developed a distinct house style. This is largely thanks to Mulloy himself, who has the title of artistic director and keeps a tight control over all productions. In many ways it is a highly traditional style that flies in the face of the trend towards updated productions and performs the Savoy operas very much in period with sumptuous costumes and sets, beautifully lit and very well sung by trained operatic soloists and a superbly drilled chorus. In contrast to Opera della Luna, Carl Rosa tends to perform in large theatres and opera houses and unlike Jeff Clarke, Mulloy likes to use trained opera singers—'they can bring so much more to the work than those who have only done G & S'. He has strong views about how G & S is performed: 'I wrestle with performers who want to treat it like pantomime. Audiences for Gilbert and Sullivan should not be having belly laughs but just simmering and smiling throughout the piece because it's a wonderful insight into humanity and into the strange world in which we are living'. While he himself has a deep knowledge of and respect for Gilbert's prompt books, he does not believe in following them unless there is a very good reason for doing so and constantly wants to ask the question why a move is being done in a particular way.

> Our versions of G & S are not traditional, but they are totally committed to the honesty of Gilbert's intention and the honesty of Sullivan's intention. We try and make them as truthful as we possibly can. We try to adopt the period style in which they were presented and the flavour which they had and we try to honour that and present it to a modern audience.[11]

The complementary approaches of these two companies, with Opera della Luna providing a postmodern minimalist and irreverent approach to G & S and Carl Rosa a lavish elegance and big operatic sound, have made the dawning of the twenty-first century an exciting time for professional G & S performance in Britain. They are by no means the only signs of renaissance, nor the only players in the field. The Proms returned to G & S with a concert performance of *Iolanthe* in 2000 for which Ian Hislop supplied a witty narration. A new production of Papp's *Pirates* toured the United Kingdom in the autumn of 2001 and a largely traditional *Gondoliers*, directed by Martin Duncan, opened the 2003 Chichester Festival. The year 2003 brought a record crop of the outdoor productions of G & S that have now become a regular feature of the English summer, at venues including Grim's Dyke, Grange Park, near Northington in Hampshire, Gawsworth Hall near Macclesfield in Cheshire, the Minack Theatre in Cornwall, and both Holland Park and Regents Park in London. Also in 2003 the Lantern Theatre Company presented a 'Complete Works of Gilbert and Sullivan (Pruned)' in which a cast of two performed all fourteen operas in ninety minutes. Billed as 'a cabaret-style evening celebrating with affection the wit and tunefulness of a beloved British institution', it very much placed G & S in the category of the whimsical and quaint:

> When Lord Whittle accepts a challenge to perform the complete works of
> G & S he thinks he is extricating himself from an unfortunate predicament
> with a woman. However he gets more than he bargained for when it turns
> out he has just ninety minutes in which to do it. He fears all is lost—that
> is until his trusty and faithful butler comes to the rescue.[12]

The spread of G & S performances on the Continent has continued in the new century just begun. *Le Mikado* was staged in Rennes, France, in 2001. *Die Piraten von Penzance* played in the repertoire of the Wiener Volksoper in both 2002 and 2003 in a production where the policemen made their entrance clutching cans of lager and then retired to the back of the stage to urinate. *Trial by Jury* was performed in Estonia in 2002. In 2003 the Miller *Mikado* was given five performances in Teatro La Fenice, Venice, with British principals and conductor and Italian orchestra and chorus. For the most part, the opera was sung in English with Italian supertitles, but some Italian lines were interjected—the Mikado wished Ko-Ko, Pitti-Sing, and Pooh-Bah '*buon appetito*' after telling them that they would be boiled in oil after luncheon. The reaction of the Italian audience was ecstatic, as was the reception given to the Miller *Mikado* during a tour of twelve cities in the Netherlands in 2004.

Perhaps the most remarkable recent *Mikado* performances are those that have taken place in the town of Chichibu in Japan. This opera has long been suspect in Japanese eyes because it caricatures the sacred figure of the emperor. Although it reached Yokohama as early as 1887, nervous British diplomats insisted that the title be changed and several passages deleted, and the audience was limited to expatriates. A D'Oyly Carte touring company hoping to bring it to Japan in 1923 were rebuffed by the government, and although a Japanese opera company presented it to military audiences during the country's occupation between 1945 and 1952, it received a very lukewarm reception from locals. The production in Chichibu was the brain-child of Yasuichi Tsukagoshi, who felt that the town must have been the inspiration for Titipu. There had been a major peasant rebellion in Chichibu in 1884, news of which would certainly have reached Britain, and Gilbert might also have become aware of the town's name through the reputation of Chichibu silk which was exported to the United Kingdom throughout the nineteenth century. Tsukagoshi initially had some difficulty persuading the local authorities to support a staging of the *Mikado* but eventually in 2000 the municipal assembly agreed to a production to mark the fiftieth anniversary of the city's official inauguration. The opera was performed in 2001 in a Japanese translation by Toshinori Kiyoshima with a cast made up predominantly of professional singers from the prefecture, joined by local ballet and kabuki troops. It was so successful that it was repeated in 2003 with an additional performance being given in Tokyo.

The year 2003 also saw the first known professional performance of a Savoy opera in central Asia when *HMS Pinafore* was staged in the opera theatre at Samarkand in Uzbekistan. Local soloists were backed by the Silk Road Chamber Choir and the Uzbekistan National Symphony Orchestra. The performance was organized by the British ambassador, Craig Murray, a dedicated Savoyard, as part of a British Music Festival. This wonderful example of mildly eccentric enthusiasm provides a fitting conclusion to this chapter and an appropriate link to the next, which explores the extraordinary world of Gilbert and Sullivan fans.

FIVE

MASCULINE IN SEX WITH THE MORALS
OF A METHODIST: GILBERT AND SULLIVAN FANS

Like the sons of Gama Rex in *Princess Ida*, devotees of Gilbert and Sullivan are, on the whole, masculine in sex. The male bias is particularly evident among what might be called the 'inner brotherhood', that company of enthusiasts who border on the obsessive, collect G & S memorabilia, write books on the subject, know every nuance of every recording, and sit in theatres waiting for a wrong word in a patter song or a move which deviates from the D'Oyly Carte norm. But even in the wider circle of G & S fans, men predominate over women. The archetypal G & S fan is male, middle-aged, middle-class and of middle income. He is also quite likely to be a Methodist. I say this on the basis of hard statistical evidence, personal experience and observation, and as one who conforms to most of these categories himself.

First, the statistics. I noted in the preface to my *Complete Annotated Gilbert and Sullivan* that among those who wrote to me following the publication of the original Penguin volumes, men outnumbered women by a ratio of thirty to one. I have also noticed when I do signings of my G & S books that about 75 percent of the sales are to men. Regular random sampling of Savoynet, the internet discussion forum dedicated to G & S, over the last six years reveals male contributors outnumbering females by an average ratio of nine to one. I have also counted attendance at fringe events at the Buxton G & S Festival and here men regularly outnumber women by three to one. Nearly all the books written about Gilbert and Sullivan are by male authors—Jane Stedman's biography of Gilbert is a rare exception (and she was a Methodist, so she at least conforms to one of my categories!). Men dominate the major appreciation societies, especially in the United Kingdom. The W. S. Gilbert Society has an all-male committee and the Sullivan Society has one woman on its seven-strong committee. The national Gilbert and Sullivan Society is similarly male-dominated, as are most of its provincial branches, with Manchester a rare exception in having a female, Jean Dufty, as secretary (although it does have a male, middle-aged Methodist, David Walton, as chairman). This is in marked contrast to the gender balance in appreciation societies covering other areas of classical and popular music, where women often predominate. Turning from statistical evidence to personal experience, I am struck by the fact that nearly all the G & S fans whom I know are male and that those of my friends who strongly dislike Gilbert and Sullivan are all female.

There are many reasons why Gilbert and Sullivan should appeal more to men than to women. The first is Gilbert's own very definite misogyny. This is well brought out in *Topsy-Turvy* in the portrayal of his almost nonexistent relationship with his wife, Lucy. Gilbert was, in the words of Margot Peters, 'a classic manly man, mixing with the "strong set" at testimonial dinners, in London clubs and in summer barracks as an officer in the Royal Aberdeenshire Highlanders. He sublimated his sexual drive: though he escorted attractive women, a squeeze in a hansom cab seemed to pacify him'.[1] He had an essentially male sense of humour, strong on irony and intellectual word tricks. He felt much easier writing about male friendship than about romantic or physical love between the sexes. Some of the most moving and memorable passages in his dialogue are on the theme of male bonding. Perhaps the supreme example is the exchange in the second act of *Iolanthe* between Tolloller and Mountararat about their fondness for each other during which Phyllis is entirely ignored. Mountararat's line 'Not even love should rank above true friendship's name' is a powerful testimony to the supremacy of same-sex friendship over romantic love. In *Ruddigore* Robin Oakapple and Dick Dauntless bond together and in *The Gondoliers* Marco and Giuseppe, acting and speaking 'as one individual' are in many ways much more of an 'item' than either is with his respective wife. There are virtually no comparable scenes of female bonding—perhaps the nearest is when Lady Blanche and Melissa sing 'Now Wouldn't You Like to Rule the Roost' in *Princess Ida*, but the atmosphere here is more calculating and competitive.

There is a distinct lack of real emotional involvement and development in the Savoy operas. The wife of one of the members of the 'inner brotherhood' has remarked to me that 'Gilbert and Sullivan appeals to men because it doesn't really engage with the emotions. It is all on an intellectual or a silly level—the characters don't really engage with each other emotionally. I think many women find this frustrating but it is where many men are'. Although there is sentiment in the Savoy operas, they eschew the emotionalism and romantic passion of many operettas and musicals. As Jeff Clarke of Opera della Luna says, 'they have an appeal to male audiences that other operettas—all that gushing Viennese stuff—don't have'. He himself was introduced to G & S by his grandparents, both of whom were fans, but he recalls that whereas both of them would take him to the Savoy operas, 'it would be grandma on her own who would take me to *The Sound of Music* or *The Song of Norway*—grandpa wouldn't come to something as emotional as that'.[2]

Then there is the fact that the male characters in the operas are much more appealing, interesting, and attractive figures than the women. The principal female parts are either somewhat anodyne and one-dimensional soprano heroines or spinster battle-axes. There is, indeed, a good deal of masculinity in these latter figures, and also a good deal of tragedy as Susannah Herbert observes:

> They aren't just desperate. They are Terrifyingly Desperate. You don't see these dames propped up in a Notting Hill wine bar, Silk Cut in one hand, glass of Chardonnay in the other. No, they may be hungry for a man—any man, actually, but they're beyond the reach of aerobics classes, hatha yoga or hormone replacement therapy. At the very best they are old and plain, at the worst they are old and ugly. And these are the qualities that are supposed to make them 'funny'.
>
> Women who love a good hum as well as the next man are presented with a dilemma here. We may clap until our hands are sore, we may thumb our noses as the nay-sayers, we may belt out those show stopping numbers in the bath—but Gilbert makes it so hard for us. We aren't blushing damsels and we aren't man-eating battleaxes. We aren't particularly politically correct. We're just wondering where we fit in—and how.[3]

It is not just that Gilbert makes the male parts much more attractive than the female ones. Sullivan also gives them much better and more stirring tunes. Female members of amateur operatic societies (who here are in the majority—that is another story which will be covered in the next chapter) constantly express the wish that they could sing the songs written for the male parts. Increasingly, because of the shortage of men, this is now happening and they experience something of the star quality and the bonding that goes with the male roles. Louise Crane, who has sung with a number of opera companies, is struck by the fact that 'the old D'Oyly Carte stars who are idolized are all male. In opera the diva is the star but in G & S it is the men. And I can understand why—I would much rather be a peer than a fairy'.[4] Men have much more fun than women in G & S productions, both on stage and off it, where an almost military or boarding-school type of camaraderie encourages (and is encouraged by) the placing of a barrel of beer in the male dressing room or the passing round of a hip flask before curtain-up.

Sullivan reinforces this male appeal by drawing so heavily in his music on the influence of the military parade ground and the Anglican choral tradition. He was, of course, steeped in both these worlds in his boyhood, being the son of an army bandsman and spending his formative years as a chorister in the Chapel Royal. Many of his choruses and melodies for the Savoy operas exude a robust militarism, and others have a churchy feel with their anthemlike structure and four-part harmonies. It is a masculine kind of church music—the sort that one finds in public school chapels and in the hearty singing of Methodists.

The great majority of Gilbert and Sullivan's male, middle-class, and middle-aged fans gained their love of the Savoy operas in their youth. Many were first initiated by their fathers. In the fifty or more interviews that I have conducted for this book, I have encountered only two fans who came to G & S via their mothers. Sometimes the key influence was an uncle or grandparent, but by far the most common introduction was through a father singing, humming, or playing extracts from the operas or taking a child to see a performance. This has also been the means of provoking a lifelong aversion to G & S among several females of my acquaintance. One still recalls her father taking her regularly to see the D'Oyly Carte in the 1960s and singing along to the peers' chorus to her acute embarrassment. She has detested Gilbert and Sullivan ever since.

Being taken to a performance of the old D'Oyly Carte company is one of the most often-cited formative experiences by fans on both sides of the Atlantic. It goes a long way towards explaining the devotion felt by so many towards the company. Bruce Graham, now principal bass with Carl Rosa, was eleven when he saw *Iolanthe* done by the company in Edinburgh. He was immediately hooked and after singing G & S at school and with amateur societies, eventually forsook his civil service job to join the old company in its last years. Richard Baker was the same age when he first saw the D'Oyly Carte—'we queued up for the gallery at Sadler's Wells Theatre and, thereafter, all our family were hooked completely. We went, week after week, to Saturday matinées whenever the D'Oyly Carte was in reach'.[5] Andrew Nicklin, now a leading G & S director and conductor, was sixteen when he had what he describes as his 'road to Damascus experience'. As a musically talented youngster, he had been recruited to sing Jack Point in a local amateur production of *Yeomen*. 'When I realized it was Gilbert and Sullivan,' he says, 'I nearly pulled out but an attractive girl in the chorus kept me in, as did the fact that the hall where we rehearsed and performed, the Denby pottery canteen, had a nine foot Steinway grand piano'. While rehearsing, the company went to see the D'Oyly Carte in Manchester with John Reed as Point. Nicklin describes this experience as 'one of the two or three occasions in my life when I was totally bowled over in the theatre'.[6]

It is striking how often fans describe their first encounter with D'Oyly Carte as a 'conversion' experience which they can date and recall as precisely as they might a classic religious awakening. Tim Hurst-Brown says of the performance of *Pinafore* to which he was taken on his twelfth birthday: 'The moment Isidore Godfrey entered the pit I was captivated, and a theatrical "happening" began which completely changed the course of my life. Following that *Pinafore*, I became a G & S freak and I couldn't get enough Savoy dope'.[7] David Walton was taken to his first D'Oyly Carte production when he was nine. He already knew the words and music of the Savoy operas by heart thanks to his parents' records but he was utterly transfixed by the live performance in what was his first 'proper' visit to the theatre: 'I was utterly lost in it as probably only a child can be, and my mother said afterwards that she had spent more time watching me than she had the stage'.[8] Ralph MacPhail Jr., leading North American G & S scholar and director, was over twenty and already steeped in G & S when he took his father, who had introduced him to the Savoy operas through singing in the car, to the opening night of the D'Oyly Carte's Washington season in 1966. He took his girlfriend to two further performances and reflects, 'that week changed my life and I haven't been the same since'.[9]

Recordings have been another key point of entry for many fans. Ralph MacPhail's earliest G & S memory is of children's cardboard 78 rpm records of *Mikado* and *Pinafore*. Later, as a student, he acquired a reel-to-reel tape recording of his college's production of *Mikado* and played it 'over and over again — so often, indeed, that it's a wonder my parents didn't kick me out of the house'. As a soldier in Vietnam, his G & S recordings were among his most treasured possessions and he took advantage of the free postal facilities to write hundreds of letters to dealers, with the result that by the end of his tour of duty his trunk was full of G & S memorabilia, the basis of his lifelong collection. Don Smith, another leading U.S. collector, was first hooked on G & S by the LP of Martyn Green singing the patter songs which his parents bought him when he was ten. 'Thereafter I haunted the public libraries to get libretti and more records'. This record also provided Andrew Crowther, leading Gilbert scholar, with his introduction to G & S at the age of thirteen. Dan Rothermel, longtime conductor of the Savoy Company of Philadelphia, was the same age when he borrowed an old D'Oyly Carte recording of *Trial by Jury* and 'played it morning, noon and night for a week'. Tony Rounsefell, chairman of the Cotswold Savoyards, was captivated by a performance of *Iolanthe* when he was fifteen. 'My father gave me the set of eleven LPs for Christmas and I drove the family mad constantly playing "With Strephon for Your Foe No Doubt!" '. David Lyall, conductor of the Edinburgh Gilbert and Sullivan Society, dates the beginning of his lifelong love affair with G & S to the discovery when he was thirteen of an old set of 78 rpm records of *The Mikado* in a cupboard in the music room at Leith Academy. Mel Moratti, a prominent New Zealand Savoyard, had his 'conversion' experience at the same age:

> I was browsing through a record store and saw the most wonderful record cover I had ever seen. It was 'The World of Gilbert and Sullivan' on Ace of Clubs. The cover consisted of some of Gilbert's drawings and sketches from the operettas. I had to have it. If I liked the outside so much then I knew I would love what was on the inside. Dad bought it for me. Soon 'The World of Gilbert and Sullivan' became the most played record in my (very small) collection. I knew all the songs off by heart and from those highlights my love grew as I slowly explored all the operas.[10]

Another common experience for middle-aged fans is exposure to G & S at school (and in the case of North Americans, summer camps—see page 150). For those of us who attended all-boys schools there is a familiar progression from singing the female parts when our voices were unbroken to taking on the more manly roles of policemen or pirates in our teens. Joseph Papp sang as one of the train of little ladies in his Brooklyn school. Simon Gallaher first got hooked on G & S at the age of twelve through singing Mabel in his Australian school production of *Pirates*. James Conroy-Ward, the last patter man in the old D'Oyly Carte company, played Katisha and Mad Margaret at Altrincham Grammar School. Martin George, a soloist with Opera della Luna, had a similar experience: 'I went to an all boys' grammar school where since the early 1900s there had been a tradition of doing G & S every year. It was an all-male world. The only occasional female we saw was the history teacher's wife who came to do the make-up'. He feels that the lack of emotional involvement makes G & S very suitable for single-sex schools. 'People come on and say 'I am in love with somebody' but you never see them falling in love. There's no development— which is why it's so suitable for boys' schools—you've got no love scenes. There's never that much snogging'.[11]

Like their first encounter with the D'Oyly Carte, the experience of performing G & S at school, especially in an all-boys school, is something that few people, even those who do not go on to become addicts, ever seem to forget. The British literary agent Giles Gordon played the Queen of the Fairies in a 1955 Edinburgh Academy production of *Iolanthe*. Twenty-five years later he spotted Gordon Honeycombe, who had played Private Willis and went on to become a well-known television newscaster, walking down Charing Cross Road in London. He sidled up to him and said 'Private Willis, how would you like to marry a fairy?'[12]

Richard Dimbleby, the great BBC commentator at state occasions, who loved playing Gilbert and Sullivan on the piano, made his stage debut as Ralph Rackstraw while a pupil at Mill Hill School. John Hanson, who did so much to revive and keep alive the operettas of Sigmund Romberg, made his first major stage appearance at the age of sixteen playing Strephon in a school production of *Iolanthe*, an experience which launched him on his professional singing career. Others first encountered G & S via the school orchestra pit rather than the stage. Richard Suart played the viola for a *Mikado* production in his first year at Sedbergh School. By his final year, he had graduated to singing the judge in *Trial*, with the headmaster's wife as the leader of the bridesmaids. Conductor and Sullivan scholar David Mackie was introduced to G & S in the third form at Greenock Academy when the school performed *Pinafore*. His voice was still breaking at the time so he helped as a rehearsal pianist and call boy for the stage manager.

For some it was the chance to meet girls that first led them to G & S. Stephen Turnbull, secretary of the Sullivan Society, came to it when his all-boys' grammar school in Hartlepool teamed up with a local girls school to do *Pirates*. He was sixteen and reckoned that auditioning for the show was as good a way as any to meet a girl. During a performance of *Trial by Jury* at Buxton in 2003 I found myself sitting next to Jo and Tim McGuire, and their three young children. They had come over from Manchester because it had been at a joint performance of *Trial* in 1977 by their respective single-sex Catholic schools that they had first met. Out of that single production came two marriages, including theirs, and five other relationships of rather shorter duration. Both were singing along throughout the performance and were word perfect despite the fact they hadn't seen the show for twenty-six years. 'I'm completely tone deaf', Tim told me, 'but I absolutely love it—and it was the only way to meet a girl'.

Of course, not everyone exposed to G & S at school has gone on to become a fan. For some the experience has had exactly the opposite effect. This was certainly the case for Sir Peter Medawar, the world-famous British scientist, awarded the Nobel Prize in 1960 for his work on immunology and organ transplantation. The chapter of his autobiography which describes his school days in Marlborough in the late 1920s and early 1930s has a two-page diatribe on what he calls (and the italics are his to give extra emphasis) '*The Peculiar Awfulness of Gilbert and Sullivan*'. He recalls singing Ko-Ko's little list song—'characteristically Gilbertian in its witless doggerel and gratuitous jibes at elderly spinsters' and notes that 'the song was well received, for W. S. Gilbert was the poet laureate of the class that the boys and their parents belonged to'. For him, 'Sullivan was a minor composer who wrote the musical equivalent of Gilbert's doggerel, and Gilbert was much the more offensive of the pair. He was a deep-dyed snob

FIGURE 5.1 AND 5.2 All boys together: 5.1. Yardley Court School production of *The Batsman's Bride*, 1961. The author is the cricketer second from left *(Author's collection)* 5.2. Yardley Court School production of *HMS Pinafore*, 1962 *(Author's collection)*

and he knew his audiences were too, so he wrote down to their weaknesses and took cruel advantage of some of their more disagreeable traits'. He particularly takes Gilbert to task for lampooning Victorian spinsters and seizing the chance in virtually all his operettas 'to raise a sneer about unmarried women' and describes him as 'a card-carrying Philistine who did much to create the widespread antipathy to any public display of high sensibility such as the aesthetes were wont to indulge in'. Indeed, Medawar seems to blame the Savoy operas for the general boorishness and philistinism of English public schools.[13]

His is an unusual and extreme reaction, however. Much more common in accounts of school days are affectionate memories of G & S productions and the teachers who inspired them. David Eden, author of books on Gilbert and Sullivan, was introduced to their work by a school production of *Pirates* in which the highlight for him was seeing the French master falling off a barrel. The teaching profession has produced a high quotient of G & S addicts. A splendid example is W. R .P. Thorne, a prep school master who relieved the tedium of his fire-watching duties during the Second World War by translating nine of the Savoy operas into Latin blank verse. It was another prep school master, Brian Chidell, who introduced Tim Rice to the intricacies and artistry of Gilbert's lyrics with such dramatic results for musical theatre in the later twentieth century. I myself was largely introduced to G & S by Raymond Reiss, whose annual productions at Yardley Court Preparatory School in Tonbridge remain one of my most powerful childhood memories. It was in his production of the G & S parody *The Batsman's Bride* that I first trod the boards in 1961. A breaking voice ruled me out of the following year's *Pinafore* but my brother donned skirt and headscarf to take his place among fellow male sisters, cousins, and aunts.

Dedicated schoolteachers have done much to foster a love and appreciation of G & S. Roger Wickson produced his first Savoy opera in 1965 as a young master at Brighton and Hove Grammar School and his last thirty-five years later as headmaster of King's School, Chester. In all four schools where he taught he either stepped into or created a Gilbert and Sullivan tradition and directed productions of the operas in which he had so much enjoyed performing during his own school days, when the principals of the D'Oyly Carte Opera Company and the Surrey and England cricketers were his heroes. Speaking shortly before his retirement, he gave a moving apologia for the G & S addicted schoolmaster:

> My career as a schoolmaster and headmaster is now coming to an end. I can truthfully say that I have enjoyed much happiness and little has brought me more happiness than my involvement with the Savoy operas. I am sure that my critics would say that headmasters should be doing something more serious than spending their time involving themselves

with such frivolities. To this I reply, 'Nonsense', and not 'precious nonsense' at that. We live in an absurdly bureaucratic age in which we are meant to deal with and respond to piles of 'official utterances'. All the more important to bring some fun and pleasure into life. Whatever my achievements and shortcomings are as a schoolmaster I am delighted to have had the opportunity to introduce hundreds of boys and girls to the 'laughing song and merry dance' of the Gilbert and Sullivan operas, so providing them with many a 'source of innocent merriment'. [14]

Other male-dominated professions which seem to have more than their share of G & S addicts are dentistry, accountancy, and law. Dentists found among the 'inner brotherhood' include Justin Bender, an expert on the G & S scene in Australia, Bob Tartell, co-founder, long-time president, and producer of the Gilbert & Sullivan Yiddish Light Opera Company, Tony Rounsefell, chairman of the Cotswold Savoyards, and John Cannon, archivist of the Gilbert and Sullivan Society and collector of G & S parodies. The accountants include Martin Haldane, former D'Oyly Carte trustee, and Peter Featherstone, mainstay of the Rose Hill Musical Society. Given Gilbert's own background and the prominent role that the legal profession and legal jokes have in his work, it is not surprising that the Savoy operas should have a particular appeal to lawyers. Legal practitioners found in the 'inner brotherhood' include Andrew Goodman, honorary vice-president of the Gilbert and Sullivan Society and author of *Gilbert and Sullivan's London*; the late Colin Prestige, the longest serving D'Oyly Carte trustee; Peter Bathurst, author of the standard guide to G & S for amateur performers; and A. J. Burgess, responsible for a massive tome on lawyers in the Savoy operas.

The clerical profession is another which is full of G & S aficionados. The Savoy operas have long had a strong following among the clergy of the Church of England. Robert Stopford, Bishop of London from 1961 to 1973, was chairman of the D'Oyly Carte Opera Trust from 1972 to 1976. Many a vicar has put on productions in his parish, like Canon Raymond Wilkinson, whose obituary in 1995 noted as a highlight of his first incumbency in Croxley Green 'Raymond's accomplished performance of *The Mikado*, in one of the Gilbert and Sullivan productions which he initiated wherever he ministered'. [15] The appeal of G & S to the clergy is well described by John Wall, vicar of Newbury, Berkshire, in his recollections of the University of York Gilbert and Sullivan Society in the early 1970s:

Just as some clergy go weak at the knees at the first toot of a steam train, so some of us still go misty-eyed (well, a bit) at the opening bars of *Iolanthe*. Indeed, the first time I wore clerical garb was when playing Dr Daly in

The Sorcerer. It's amazing the swirl you get with a five-pleater cassock, if you put your hips into it.

But the thought of one particular York production of *Ruddigore* is sobering: our beer-swilling, party-going director is now married to a rural dean. Dame Hannah is now in full-time Charismatic lay ministry. Two of us are ordained, and our somewhat louche Robin Oakapple is now a monk. Maybe Diocesan Directors of Ordinands should stop addressing Christian Unions, and start prowling round light-opera groups instead.[16]

There are strong G & S fans among the clergy of other denominations. Ian Taylor, longtime producer of the Edinburgh Gilbert and Sullivan Society and author of *The Gilbert and Sullivan Quiz Book* and *How to Produce Concert Versions of G & S*, is a Church of Scotland minister. At my own service of licensing into the ministry, he preached a sermon based on Jack Point's song 'Oh! A Private Buffoon', with its salutary reminder to all budding clergy that 'What is all right for B would quite scandalize C (for C is so very particular)'. Cardinal Cormac Murphy O'Connor, Archbishop of Westminster and head of the Roman Catholic Church in England and Wales, named 'A Wandering Minstrel, I' as one of his choices on *Desert Island Discs* in 2001. He sang the tenor leads in several of the Savoy operas when training for the priesthood at the English College in Rome and admits to still regularly singing Nanki-Poo's aria while in his country retreat.

The connection between Gilbert and Sullivan and the church is a strong and intriguing one. There is undoubtedly a much higher than average proportion of active churchgoers in G & S appreciation and amateur performing societies. The Savoy operas have long been seen as a wholesome and safe option for performance by church groups and on church premises, and several distinguished performers and lifelong fans first encountered them through this route. John Reed's first stage appearances were in socials at the Wesleyan Methodist Chapel in Darlington. Bernard Goss, membership secretary of the Gilbert and Sullivan Society, was intrigued as a fifteen-year-old schoolboy in Swansea by a poster for a concert performance of *Mikado* at a local church and was absolutely captivated by the three little maids. He immediately got involved with a local society doing the show and landed the part of Pooh-Bah.

The clearest connection between churchgoing and enjoying G & S is, I suppose, that both pursuits involve indulging in that activity which Mad Margaret saw as the ultimate sign of madness, singing choruses in public—and you cannot get much madder than singing 'jam' and 'bun' antiphonally across stage. This is perhaps one of the reasons that church services figure prominently at many G & S related events—they are a central feature of every Sullivan Society weekend conference and of the Buxton festival. A special choral evensong held in Birmingham Cathedral in 1992 to welcome the D'Oyly Carte company to the city included as the anthem the duet 'Although of Native Maids the Cream' from *Utopia*, 'which was observed to set at least one eminent ecclesiastical head nodding in time'. The 150th anniversary of Sullivan's birth in May 1992 was celebrated by a service in the Queen's Chapel of the Savoy attended by Princess Alice, Duchess of Gloucester, and a host of luminaries. The ecclesiastical establishment has always taken G & S more readily to its bosom than the arts or cultural establishment and perhaps recognizes its status as a semisacred institution. Its ritual quality and close affinity with matters ecclesiastical was well summed up by the music critic and devoted Savoyard Philip Hope-Wallace, who described himself as 'one who has been mentally and even physically singing the Savoy Operas man and boy, a lifetime, like the Psalms of David and *Hymns Ancient and Modern*, permanent factors in the computer of memory'.[17]

While in Britain the religious constituency to which G & S has appealed has been almost exclusively Christian, in the United States it has had a very significant Jewish following. Gilbert's wit and irony have a clear affinity with Jewish humour and it is not surprising to find so many Jewish fans and adaptations, like the highly successful Yiddish versions (see pages 172–73). In his recent history of the American musical, John Bush Jones points to the influence of the Savoy operas on the development of Yiddish theatre, citing particularly the 1984 award-winning off-Broadway show *Kuni-Leml*, 'which looks and sounds as if Gilbert and Sullivan could have written it if they were Jewish and lived a little further east'.[18] Michael Abrahams, who served as rabbi in a Philadelphia synagogue in the late 1980s, wrote commentaries on his sermons for the festival of Purim set to G & S patter songs, and Richard Shapp, for many years cantor in another Philadelphia synagogue, has also adapted patter songs for a Jewish audience, of which the favourite is 'A Rabbi's Lot Is Not a Happy One'.

Alongside the church and the law, the other professions mentioned by the Lord Chancellor in his *Iolanthe* patter song have also produced a good number of keen Savoyards. This is certainly true of the stage and the armed forces. General Sir Michael Walker, Britain's most senior soldier and the Chief of the General Staff, went to see the D'Oyly Carte doing *Pirates* at the Savoy Theatre in 2001 and found it a 'wonderful performance' save for the fact that the major general's uniform was incorrect. 'The badges of rank were those of a major in the first instance and later those of an altogether incorrect marriage of badges'. The very next evening Walker appeared at the theatre and presented Royce Mills, who was playing the role, with a set of authentic nineteenth-century major general's shoulder boards.[19]

This kind of attention to detail is characteristic of the members of the 'inner brotherhood' of male fans. It often goes with a concern for order and tidiness—

which is partly why I have sometimes been tempted to refer to G & S as opera for accountants—and takes us back to the comfort factor and the alternative world which provides an escape from the disorder and complexity of reality. It is surely no coincidence that enthusiasm for Gilbert and Sullivan often goes alongside an interest in steam trains, model railways, and cricket—three other male obsessions characterized by nostalgia, rules, and detail. When I suggested at a fringe meeting in Buxton that male G & S fans exhibit behavioural traits that border on the obsessional, with an unusually developed attention to relatively trivial detail, David Duffey, an advocate specializing in education law, suggested that many tend to have the obsessional characteristics of the Asperger's Syndrome end of the autistic spectrum. He is struck by the similarity between his autistic clients and many of those whom he meets in G & S circles in terms of the pursuit of the inconsequential, the preoccupation with minutiae, and the concentration on a limited field with reasonably secure boundaries. He also suggests that performing G & S, particularly in the precopyright days of prescribed 'traditional' business, would also appeal to autistic personalities, providing the security of familiar routines and clear boundaries. It makes one ask, with George Mikes: 'Are they—are *we*, because I belong to their rank—members of a cult or are we just enjoying ourselves as one would enjoy, say, *Fiddler on the Roof*? Are we in love with an art form or suffering from an infection?'[20]

Is there a certain kind of personality or mind to which G & S particularly appeals? It may be relevant here to notice another significant overlap, particularly evident among North American fans, between love of G& S and enthusiasm for the world of science fiction and fantasy. Isaac Asimov is the best known but by no means the only G & S enthusiast among science fiction writers. An active member of the New York Gilbert and Sullivan Society, he provided additional lyrics for a production of *Pinafore* performed by the Village Light Opera Group in 1989. G & S also has a particularly strong appeal to mathematicians. Tom Lehrer is an obvious example. Robin Wilson, head of the pure mathematics department at Britain's Open University, is a dedicated Savoyard, as are Henrik Eriksson, professor of mathematics at the Royal Institute of Technology in Stockholm, and his son, who is also an academic mathematician. For Eriksson, the appeal lies in the logical nature of Gilbert's mind and plots. In the United States, the Savoy operas also have a strong following among scientists. This is much less true in the United Kingdom, where they are more popular among those doing arts subjects at university (see pages 153–54). Indeed, it is noticeable that the two most antagonistic opinions towards G & S expressed in this book (those of Graham Hills quoted on page 19 and Peter Medawar on page 101) come from British scientists. Don Smith, himself a biochemist, reckons that in the

United States, by contrast, there are a high proportion of computer scientists and researchers and teachers in physics and chemistry, as well as mathematicians, among G & S fans. This hypothesis is borne out by the membership profile of both appreciation and performing societies in the Northeast and the Seattle area, where computer programmers and project engineers are especially well represented.

This brings us back to a difference between the North American and British approach to Gilbert and Sullivan which has already been noted. In the United States Gilbert and Sullivan is very much seen as an intellectual taste and its appreciation largely if not entirely confined to an upper middle class, college-educated élite. A U.S. marketing organization profiled the typical G & S fan in the late 1990s as being overeducated and in an academic-style job, especially computer related. The fan base in Britain is and has always been much broader. Alongside the upper- or upper-middle-class route into G & S via public school and the professions, there has been another well-trodden path taken by lower-middle-class fans who have come to it through grammar school and amateur operatic society. It is here that Methodism has played a significant role, with many amateur societies being historically tied to Methodist and other Nonconformist chapels. There is a significant geographical difference between the two groups of British fans—whereas those with a public school and Anglican background tend to be from South East England, those who have come via the grammar school and Methodist route are more likely to live in the Midlands and the North of England.

The provincial, Nonconformist, lower-middle-class devotees of G & S provided much of the fan base for the old D'Oyly Carte company and have also been the bedrock of both performing and appreciation societies. On the whole, they are not into 'high' culture, preferring brass bands to chamber music and Stainer's Crucifixion to Bach's St. John Passion and so confirming the snobbish prejudices of the metropolitan arts establishment about the low cultural status of Gilbert and Sullivan. They are marked in other ways by their Methodist background, being essentially modest, respectable, and sober. One of the volunteers who works behind the bar at the Buxton Opera House told me that while during the period of the main Buxton Festival, which features grand opera and 'serious' music, most of the interval requests are for wine and spirits, during the Gilbert and Sullivan festival the most popular items are coffee, soft drinks, and mineral water.

The most committed Savoyard among twentieth-century British prime ministers belonged firmly to this group. It is no coincidence that of the two postwar British prime ministers who came from the classic G & S recruiting ground of provincial middle-class Nonconformity it was Harold Wilson rather than Margaret Thatcher who became the great fan. Gender rather than political hue was the crucial factor. If anything, and as one might expect, Gilbert and Sullivan has generally appealed more to Conservative than to Labour politicians and voters, although there has long been a strong Savoyard tendency in the Liberal Party, currently represented most prominently by Simon Hughes (yet another who caught the bug playing female roles at his all-boys boarding school) and Jim Wallace, leader of the Scottish Liberal Democrats and deputy minister of the Scottish Executive, who played the patter roles as a boy at Annan Academy. Harold Wilson's passion for G & S may not have chimed in with his progressive political views, although it conformed with the fervent monarchism of this Labour left-winger. It did, however, fit perfectly with his background as a bright lad from West Yorkshire, who loved playing with Meccano and whose boyhood heroes were Sherlock Holmes and Robert Baden-Powell, founder of the Boy Scouts. His Congregationalist parents were both enthusiasts for what, in the words of his biographer, Philip Ziegler, 'they referred to as "G & S" as if an un-holy compound of gin and soda', and by the age of six young Harold was word-perfect in *Pirates*.

> Each year our chapel choir in the Colne Valley, near Huddersfield, at-tempted one of the Gilbert and Sullivan operas until, baulking at what we felt to be an extortionate royalty demand of two guineas, we disloyally presented the alien production *Floradora*. There were threats of the valley running with blood at our apostasy and soon we were back with the Masters. When we staged *HMS Pinafore* I was, at the age of ten, technically a principal—the result of W S Gilbert's quirkish decision to include the non-speaking, non-singing Midshipmite, Tom Tucker, in that enviable list. All I can remember from that production is being sent off the stage in disgrace during a per-formance for sucking a bulls-eye given to me by Little Buttercup.[21]

Harold Wilson saw his first D'Oyly Carte production at the Liverpool Empire in October 1933. He was taken there by a schoolmaster in order to see Henry Lyt-ton playing Jack Point in *Yeomen*. It was at a performance of the same opera in the Golder's Green Hippodrome, London, twenty-three years later that his son Robin fell in love with G & S. Harold Wilson's enthusiasm for the Savoy operas was often bracketed with his taste for tinned salmon and HP sauce. For his biographer, it was a mark of his 'committedly *petit bourgeois*' character. His obituary in the *Times* observed that 'he had few, if any, intellectual or cultural interests—except for a love of Gilbert and Sullivan'.[22] When he resigned the premiership in 1976, he invited Dame Bridget D'Oyly Carte and several leading figures from the company to a farewell party at Ten Downing Street and passed around slips of paper for guests to note down their three favourite operas. He was delighted to discover that both he and Dame Bridget chose the same trio: *Iolanthe*, *Pirates*, and *Yeomen*.

Aside from Harold Wilson, the most famous G & S fan of the twentieth century was surely Malcolm Sargent. He had a similar background as a talented provincial grammar school boy who came to G & S via his local amateur operatic society, although in his case Anglicanism rather than Nonconformity provided the religious background. Sargent represents another significant archetype among G & S fans—the musical lad for whom early exposure to the Savoy operas started a lifelong love of classical music, and in his case a professional musical career. Like so many others, he was first introduced to the Savoy operas by his father, who was head clerk of a coal merchant's firm in Stamford, Lincolnshire, and a church organist. At the age of eight he was beginning to play Sullivan tunes on the piano. Around the same age he became a programme seller for the Stamford Operatic Society. Earning two shillings a night, half paid as a fee and the other in penny tips, he invariably stayed for the performances in the Assembly Rooms, becoming increasingly captivated by the magic of what he heard and saw. At thirteen he was given a walk-on part in *The Mikado* as the Lord High Executioner's sword bearer. He enjoyed the experience so much, even though he had nothing to say or sing, that thereafter he attended every single one of the society's weekly rehearsals. At fourteen he was accompanying rehearsals of *Yeomen*. One foggy evening the conductor was unable to get through, and 'young Sargent' was called on to take up the baton. In the words of his biographer, Charles Reid:

> He conducted with a briskness and fluency that fell on him from nowhere, like a mantle. When he had to pull the players up he rapped the desk and told people three times his age to tighten their rhythm and shape their phrases. For two hours he was their leader, ageless in his authority. Laying down his stick at the finish he suddenly looked fourteen again. There was a lot of clapping and bravoing and shouts of 'Well done!' He was chaired downstairs and into the street.[23]

The up-and-coming musician allowed his passion for G & S to extend into his more serious endeavours. Deputising once at Peterborough Cathedral, where he was a pupil of the regular organist, he accompanied the Creed at morning service with harmonies and descant which were a direct transfer at slow tempo from the fairies' opening number in *Iolanthe*, 'Tripping Hither, Tripping Thither'. 'You see how it all fits', he would say years later while demonstrating on his grand piano; 'the modulations and tune go perfectly with every section of the Creed. I don't suppose the dear old Dean would have minded if he'd known'.[24]

His first experience of conducting a brass band was taking the Melton Mowbray Band through a *Mikado* selection. He subsequently transcribed both the *Iolanthe* and *Yeomen* overtures for brass band. In 1919, following war service and inspired by a visit of the D'Oyly Carte company to Leicester, he founded a Gilbert and Sullivan Society in Melton Mowbray where he was teaching at the local grammar school. As well as acting as its conductor and director, he also took over as conductor of the Stamford society. He continued running both societies, taking weekly rehearsals and conducting all their performances for the next ten years despite his burgeoning career and commitments as a conductor in London. From 1923 he also rehearsed and conducted a third amateur society in Winchester, over a hundred miles away.

Sargent's work with these three societies established his conducting credentials. He was always immaculately clad for performances in tails and white waistcoat with a flower in his buttonhole. In Reid's words: 'In a sense he *was* the Melton amateurs, he *was* the Stamford amateurs. He turned nobodies into somebodies, small talents into sizeable ones'. Not just content with conducting, he made himself responsible for every detail of acting, dancing, and grouping and personally took charge whenever there was a crisis.

> There was the night when Rose Maybud found herself unable to produce more than a squeak half-an-hour before curtain-up. One of her friends came panting with the news to Sargent. Near the Assembly Rooms was a public house. 'Get some port wine,' he instructed, 'and tell Helen' for that was Rose's real name, 'to gargle with it. She'd better not swallow any, of course!' The trouble had been nervous constriction of the throat. She soon got rid of it. People put this down to the port wine gargle and said how clever Malcolm was. They did not know that, after the gargle, he had told her he had a substitute ready in Leicester.[25]

In 1926 Sargent was engaged by Rupert D'Oyly Carte as musical director for his company's forthcoming London season. He conducted for the 1926–27 and 1929–30 seasons and frequently came back as guest conductor. Among his many achievements was to conduct in 1926 the first live radio broadcast of a Savoy opera. *The Mikado* went out in two half-hour relays to what the *Evening Standard* estimated was 'probably the largest audience that has ever heard anything at one time in the history of the world'. He established the annual G & S night at the Proms and conducted several notable recordings. Sargent belonged in the classic D'Oyly Carte tradition, emphasizing the importance of good diction, valuing the role of the chorus, and insisting that just as much as when conducting a Mozart opera, 'the Gilbert and Sullivan conductor must aim at clarity, shape and beauty'.[26] He greatly speeded up the pace of several numbers, arguing, with some evidence, that Sullivan had intended them to go much faster than they were often played, and loved encores, the more the better. Although he conducted much else in his distinguished career, the Savoy operas remained his greatest love, along with the great oratorios of the English choral tradition. He often said that the two Ms, *Mikado* and *Messiah* (in that order), had been the twin pillars of his career.

Several later twentieth-century conductors and composers similarly owe their love of music to youthful exposure to G & S. John Owen Edwards's first visit to the theatre was to see his father playing Samuel in an amateur production of *Pirates* at Grange-over-Sands in Cumbria. Among Michael Tippett's earliest experiences of performed music were Malcolm Sargent's productions at Stamford when Tippett was a pupil at the town's boarding school. Peter Maxwell Davies's visit at the age of four to an amateur production of *Gondoliers* at Salford Central Mission was especially formative. In the words of his biographer, Mike Seabrook:

> It proved to be what Max calls 'a great ear-opener'. In the first place it imbued him with what has turned out to be a lifelong fondness for Gilbert and Sullivan—a rare diversion into lighter music for Max, whose tastes otherwise tend to be serious, or highbrow, if the word can be used without any of the undertones of affectation normally associated with it. But the visit had other, far more momentous consequences: it was, in effect, the light on Max's personal road to Damascus. The morning after the performance Max's parents were astonished to discover that he could sing all the songs from the opera. It was the first real sign of his extraordinary musical sense, and as from that amateur and probably undistinguished performance of *The Gondoliers* there was never any doubt in Max's mind about what he was going to do with his life: he knew he was going to be not just a musician, but a composer.[27]

Peter Maxwell Davies is unusual in having had his G & S conversion experience so young. For most fans, it happened between the ages of eleven and fourteen. As Paul Kresh observes, analyzing the anatomy of the Gilbert and Sullivan addict, and making a rare nod to the existence of a female of the species:

> The first telltale hints of the G & S complaint generally show themselves in late childhood or early adolescence, with puberty a particularly vulnerable stage. The boy or girl may be introduced to the virus that carries the infection through some school production. Certain words may stick in the

young victim's head, going round and round, even though he or she may not entirely understand them, until, from this focus, they spread insidiously through the vulnerable, half-formed mind. 'Turbot is ambitious brill; Gild the farthing if you will' the poor innocent may take to singing softly to himself, no doubt in secret, and there is no turning back.[28]

Psychologists would doubtless make much of the fact that 'the G & S complaint' so often comes with the onset of adolescence and puberty. Is it in some sense a sex substitute? The possible Freudian or Oedipal overtones are not (thankfully) a subject on which I am competent to pronounce, but there is one aspect of the G & S phenomenon which does demand at least brief mention. This is the question as to whether it has a particular appeal to gays. At one point I contemplated devoting a separate chapter to this entitled 'The Gay Sally Lunn', 'It's a Queer World', or 'Then One of Us Will Be a Queen'. There is undoubtedly a considerable homosexual following for Gilbert and Sullivan, and particularly for performing it, but then so there is for musical theatre as a whole. Some critics have detected a more distinct gay element and even a gay bias in the operas themselves. Stan Wu feels that this has been brought out by Mark Savage's gay *Pinafore*:

> Those uptight, burly and very properly English Gilbert and Sullivan heroes of yore are favourites of true musical theatre fans (for which read: gay men) everywhere. Through countless productions of *The Pirates of Penzance* or *The Mikado* we have escaped into this semi-fantasy world of derring-do, witty lyrics and lush music. But what if there was something more to all these idealized male figures? Finally, someone has adapted a G & S musical to play off all of this long-simmering gay male consciousness, all the male bonding, averted glances and camp, to create this brilliant, deliciously entertaining gay reinvention.[29]

Is there something intrinsically gay in G & S? For a long time in the 1950s and 1960s there were rumours of a scandalous collaboration between the two entitled 'The Sod's Opera' which was supposedly locked away somewhere. I am 99.9 percent sure that it does not exist, and furthermore that it never did. The word 'camp' is often used about their work and its performance. It is a notoriously difficult phrase to define, although it usually has connotations of effeminacy. Its general sense is, I think, superbly summed up in a remark made by a member of the male chorus at the end of a performance of *The Sorcerer* in which I was involved: 'There was more mincing on the stage tonight than in Tesco's meat department'. If camp means somewhat mannered, exaggerated, and precious, then the Savoy operas do certainly lend themselves to this kind of treatment. Gays have contributed hugely to the performance of G & S at both amateur and professional level but I am not sure that they are disproportionately represented among its fans. All one can say is that if G & S stands accused of having a particular appeal to the autistic, accountants, and homosexuals, it is a remarkably wide-ranging phenomenon. It brings out the gay in all of us, in all senses of the word.

I am conscious that one possibly substantial section of the readership of this book may well by now be feeling pretty angry. Female fans of G & S, of whom there are not a few, will have struggled through this chapter with a mounting sense of frustration and exclusion. It is high time that I turned to them, minority though they are. There are some who have come to G & S through performing it in all-girls schools, like the contributor to the *Times* who recalled: 'When I was in the sixth form I played the part of a mezzo-soprano policeman in *The Pirates*. It was not a mixed school, and the tenor and bass parts were allocated according to size. At five foot eight, and well covered with puppy fat, I never got anywhere near a female part'.[30] It has, however, been much less common for all-girls schools to do G & S than all-boys schools and when they have tried it, the experience seems to have been less memorable and formative. Indeed, among the female G & S fans to whom I have spoken, more first encountered it through watching their brothers performing in all-boys productions. It is also striking how many share other interests which are usually perceived of as male such as cricket and steam railways.

I do not want to give the impression that females who like G & S are somehow strange or freakish. They are, in fact, generally less strange and certainly much less obsessive than the male members of the inner brotherhood. They are also a growing breed. This chapter has largely been about a dying or at least a doomed species—the middle-aged, middle-class males who have dominated the G & S 'fan club' for the last half-century or so. The world in which they grew up and which formed them, the world of the old D'Oyly Carte company and single-sex schools, has passed away. The future lies with those like the young female whose enthusiastic utterances end this book (see page 205). Men may be in the majority among those pestilential nuisances who write for autographs but they are in a distinct minority among those who sing choruses in public. When it comes to active performance of G & S, rather than just passive appreciation, the gender balance is reversed. Ladies, your chapter is about to come.

SIX

AMATEUR TENORS SING CHORUSES IN PUBLIC:
THE WORLD OF AMATEUR PERFORMANCE

Amateur performances are the backbone and bedrock of Gilbert and Sullivan's enduring popularity. They have been around for a long time—the first took place on 30 April 1879 when the Harmonists Choral Society performed *HMS Pinafore* in the Drill Hall, Kingston-Upon-Thames. Since then, church halls and schoolrooms across the English-speaking world have resounded on winter evenings to the strains of would-be pirates, policemen, fairies, and bridesmaids.

It is difficult to estimate how many amateur productions are mounted each year or how many societies are still exclusively dedicated to performing the Savoy operas. The G & S Archive on the internet lists 126 amateur groups in the United Kingdom ranging in order alphabetical, rather than categorical, from the Aberdeen Opera Company to the Zodiac Amateur Operatic Society in Frodsham, Cheshire. This list omits many societies and includes several, including the two just mentioned, whose repertoire is now much wider than the Savoy operas. The National Operatic and Dramatic Association (NODA), the coordinating body for amateur theatre in the United Kingdom, estimates that there may be as many as 200 societies in Britain still dedicated to an exclusive diet of G & S, although I suspect that the true figure is nearer 150. Many of the 2,000 or so more general operatic societies still perform G & S from time to time. My best estimate would be that, not counting performances by schools and colleges, there are around 200 amateur G & S productions a year in the United Kingdom, the great majority concentrated in the winter months and especially in February and March. Some run for two weeks or more and others for just a couple of nights, but overall there must be something like 1,000 actual amateur performances each year.

It is more difficult to estimate the extent of the amateur scene in the United States. In 1981 George Walker told me that he had been given a figure of 283 performing societies there but I cannot establish where he obtained it. The U.S. equivalent of NODA, the American Association of Community Theater, does not keep statistics and is unable to hazard even a rough guess as to the number of groups performing G & S. Many of the U.S. performing groups listed in the G & S Archive are professional. On the basis of his extensive contacts and research, Gayden Wren has identified 196 amateur societies in the United States performing the Savoy operas on an annual basis, of which at least eighty-seven are exclusively dedicated to G & S. There are also a number of other groups that perform them on an occasional basis.

I am well aware that the title of this chapter is in danger of breaking the trade descriptions act. The one commodity of which nearly all amateur societies are in desperately short supply is tenors. Men in general are scarce and it is becoming increasingly common for societies to intrude females into the male chorus, often to spectacular effect—in the 2003 production of *Pirates* by the St. Andrews Amateur Operatic Society, the quartet of tap-dancing policewomen stole the show. My research suggests that in most performing societies in the United Kingdom women outnumber men by a ratio of three to one. In the United States the gender balance is more even. Significantly, the majority of the females I have spoken to in amateur societies say that they are not particularly bothered as to whether it is Gilbert and Sullivan, Rodgers and Hammerstein, Lerner and Loewe, or whatever that they are performing, an attitude which would, of course, be regarded as heretical by the inner brotherhood of male Savoyards.

The appeal to women of performing in the Savoy operas has been the subject of serious academic analysis by Shani d'Cruz, a lecturer at Manchester Metropolitan University and keen amateur performer herself. Despite the fact that Gilbert's 'positive representations of femininity are predominantly youthful' and his portrayals of older women more negative, with 'origins in the grotesque, cross-dressed dame of burlesque', d'Cruz concludes on the basis of interview evidence that 'older women in particular, aided by the possibilities of moving between performing and social identities that this leisure activity encourages, have made empowering and selective imaginative appropriations from these gender ideals'.[1] She argues that the older women who predominate in amateur societies and enjoy playing fairies, young maidens, and bridesmaids, however incongruous this may look, are simultaneously making a stand against ageism, Gilbert's fixation with elderly, ugly daughters, and the modern obsession with youth and beauty. In her words:

> Operatic society identity has offered respectable, middle-class, sometimes
> conservative and often anti-feminist women the opportunity to play with

FIGURE 6.1 Making up for the missing men. Tap-dancing policewomen in St. Andrew's Amateur Operatic Society's *Pirates*, 2003 *(Arran Aird)*

and to satirise dominant constructions of femininity in ways which contained any risks to their reputations through the 'serious' leisure content.[2]

This emphasis on respectable, middle-class values has been a feature of amateur operatic societies since their Victorian origins. It was, indeed, Gilbert and Sullivan's operas, with their wholesome and family appeal, which really gave birth to the whole amateur operatic movement on both sides of the Atlantic. The official history of the movement in Britain notes:

> Relatively easy to stage with a good variety of parts, plenty of chorus work and box office appeal, they became instant favourites. *The Mikado, The Gondoliers, Iolanthe* and the rest of what are known collectively as the Savoy Operas provided the artistic springboards from which most amateur musical groups launched themselves, and indeed, many still do over a century later. No works have played a more important role in developing and sustaining the amateur movement and Gilbert and Sullivan remain the only artists to whose works numbers of societies are specifically designated.[3]

Several of the earliest amateur operatic societies formed in the United Kingdom are still going strong. Pride of place must go to the Glasgow Orpheus Club, which was formed in 1892, produced its first show (*Trial by Jury*) in 1893, and has mounted annual productions without interruption ever since. It remained almost exclusively dedicated to G & S until 2000, when it diversified into operetta and musicals. Other societies still going strong more than a century after their foundation, which have similarly extended their repertoire in recent years, include Settle (first production, *Pinafore*, in 1891), Sunderland (*Pinafore*, 1894), Bristol (*Sorcerer*, 1894), Stoke-on-Trent (*Patience*, 1896), Huddersfield (1897), and Hereford (*Sorcerer*, 1898).

Among U.K. societies performing nothing but the Savoy operas, Plymouth G & S Fellowship is one of the oldest. It was founded in 1923 by Horace Bickle, a local solicitor and G & S devotee. While in London studying for the Law Society intermediate exams, he found himself in the company of Henry Lytton and Darrell Fancourt, two stars of the D'Oyly Carte company:

> I happened to say that I thought our culture was being spoilt by Americanism which started with the coming of 'Alexander's Rag Time Band' and that our language was being debased. Then someone said that as they had no outstanding figures of their own, the Americans were importing Shakespeare, Dickens and Gilbert and Sullivan and treating them in a most undignified way by various alterations and that the love of altering things was spreading to this country. As a keen admirer of W. S. Gilbert, I joined in and said that if we were not careful the operas would be turned into musical comedy and all the lovely touches of humour would be lost and the whole thing brought down to the vulgar level of so-called American humour. Fancourt turned to Lytton and said, 'Harry, you will soon be dancing the Charleston instead of the Cachucha' and turning to me, said 'If you feel so strongly you should do something to keep the operas intact'.[4]

This exchange says much about the motives which lay behind the formation of G & S societies and which to some extent still drive them today. We are back once again to the sacred appeal of tradition and the fear that it is about to be sacrificed on the altar of modernity, or, even worse, Americanism.

Bickle duly returned to Plymouth and set up his G & S Fellowship, a name suggestive of a shared commitment to a quasi-religious purpose. He made clear that its chief object was to preserve the 'Savoy Tradition', something that he felt could not really be left to the current management of the D'Oyly Carte, 'judging by the awful mutilations of the last few productions I have seen'. This was not to be the last time that amateur societies would take upon themselves the guardianship of the holy grail when they felt even the blessed D'Oyly Carte were treating it with insufficient reverence and respect. Bickle envisaged fortnightly meetings to study Gilbert and Sullivan and annual performances of the operas, a model of combining appreciation and performance which has been followed more in the United States than the United Kingdom. The fellowship's first production, *The Mikado*, in 1924 nearly came unstuck for lack of a local amateur tenor capable of playing Nanki-Poo. Bickle was forced to hire a professional who had sung with both the D'Oyly Carte and Carl Rosa. The day before the dress rehearsal, however, a telegram arrived saying that he had injured his back and would be unable to appear. Bickle took the next train to London and went straight to the Savoy Hotel to see Rupert D'Oyly Carte: 'On hearing my trouble he said he had no spare tenors and when I suggested that perhaps we could borrow an understudy, he told me he did not keep understudies for **** amateurs'. D'Oyly Carte did, however, offer Bickle a free night's accommodation in the Savoy and even provided pyjamas—he had left Plymouth in such a hurry that he had forgotten to pack an overnight bag. The following day he was able to track down a professional tenor in London and booked him to start that night, responding to his protests that he had never acted with amateurs, 'well now is your chance and you might learn something'. Advised to keep his new star off spirits but to give him plenty of beer, Bickle telegraphed Plymouth to have a case of bitter installed in his dressing room and returned with him just in time for the first performance. Realising that his last-minute Nanki-Poo was not yet ready when the overture finished, he slipped a note to the conductor telling him to play it again.[5]

Since this rather fraught debut, the Plymouth G & S Fellowship has not missed a single year without staging at least one Savoy opera. Its eighty-four productions to date have included *Yeomen* performed in the Citadel on Plymouth Hoe and *Pinafore* performed on the warship *HMS Antelope*, which later went down in the Falklands War. It has presented updated versions—the 1984 *Pirates* was described by the octogenarian Bickle as 'very good musical comedy, but very bad Gilbert and Sullivan'—while maintaining the D'Oyly Carte connection. Its current director, Alan Spencer, is a former chorister with the old company.

The United States boasts an even more venerable body of amateur Savoyards. The Savoy Company of Philadelphia proudly claims to be the oldest amateur theatre company in the world continuously dedicated solely to the production of the works of Gilbert and Sullivan. It was founded in 1901 by Alfred Reginald Allen, a medical doctor concerned over the bizarre treatment that the Savoy operas were receiving in the United States. Like Bickle, he wanted to 'gather together a group of like-minded friends to perform the works in their "original" English manner'. The company treasures the letter sent by W. S. Gilbert to its president in 1904 in which he says: 'It is gratifying to know that the joint works of Sir Arthur Sullivan and myself are of sufficient interest to justify the promotion of an amateur company for the express purpose of interpreting them'.

The Savoy Company exemplifies many of the characteristics of the amateur G & S scene in the United States. The Anglophile streak evident in Allen's original mission statement persists—the main rehearsal venue is the Germantown Cricket Club and since 1985 every performance has been preceded by two verses of 'God Save the Queen'. It is only relatively recently that the company has shed its upper-class and high-society image. Until the 1960s membership was confined to those listed in the Philadelphia Social Register. Although the annual summer tennis parties have recently been replaced by a ten-pin bowling evening, and the adage 'Join the Savoy and meet a boy' is not bandied about quite as much as it used to be, there remains a strong social element to the company's activities. Its annual calendar of events begins in November with a recruitment party (often held at the Philadelphia Racquets Club) to which existing members bring along new recruits. Admissions teas for new members, of whom around twenty-five to thirty are recruited annually, follow in early January, although in another sign of the times the drink on offer at these occasions is now more likely to be beer, wine, or cocktails and membership is restricted to those over twenty-one because of the U.S. drinking laws and the generally convivial nature of the company's gatherings. Auditions for the annual show are held in late January—in keeping with the patriotic appeal of G & S, the standard audition piece is 'My Country 'Tis of Thee'—and are traditionally concluded with the president's dinner, a formal occasion for new members and cast, board of directors and advisory board, and production team.

Rehearsals begin in February, with singers rehearsing for two hours on Tuesday and Thursday evenings and backstage crew meeting every Wednesday evening and all day Saturday to build the set. The annual production is staged in May, with two performances in Philadelphia's magnificent 2,000-seater Academy of Music and two on the outdoor stage in Longwood Gardens, which has a similar audience capacity. The company is run as an extremely efficient business as well as a social club, with a ten-strong board of directors, a thirteen-member advisory board, and more than twenty committees. The 115 or so active members make a considerable financial commitment, each undertaking to sell $350 worth of tickets and $400 worth of advertising, as well as paying a $50 membership subscription. Another 300 or so members not actively participating in a production pay $25 a year. The annual budget is around $140,000, of which $100,000 goes to hiring the two production venues and $28,000 to paying the twenty-six-piece orchestra. A small honorarium is paid to the director, music director, designer, and choreographer, but all the performers are unpaid although many have professional musical training. The company regularly fields an eighty-strong chorus with up to twenty in each voice range (no problem with amateur tenors here), and the average age of those on stage is a youthful thirty-five.

The company is hugely and rightly proud of its history. It has published weighty annals with appendices listing 'Savoy marriages' between company members (one took place on stage after a dress rehearsal in 1995 with the ceremony performed by a judge who had been playing the Mikado) and second- and third-generation members—there are sixty of the former and fifteen of the latter. Famous past performers include Nelson Eddy, who sang Strephon in the 1920s and wrote a letter of advice to the soloist taking the same part thirty years later: 'I suggest to keep him gay, happy and care-free. . . . Dance with a sort of cute abandon. . . . Don't get too serious, even in the serious parts. Keep your tongue in your cheek'. There have been several remarkable examples of long service: John Thoms served as both stage and musical director from 1929 to 1969, the patter roles since 1951 have very largely been played by father and son Hastings and Sam Griffin, and Dan Rothermel has conducted every performance since 1981. There have also, inevitably, been changes over the last forty years. The shift of jobs out of town and tougher drinking-and-driving laws have made for much less socializing before and after shows. Older members look back fondly to the spaghetti dinners that preceded rehearsals and the hard-drinking sessions that followed them in the 1960s but concede that standards have improved in the new more sober atmosphere. As in many other U.S. societies, there are an increasing number of younger soloists who have come through music academies and use performing with amateurs as a stepping stone in their professional singing careers and fewer old stagers slotting into solo parts simply because they have always done so. Although lawyers and Presbyterians still predominate, there is also much more of an ethnic mix on stage than there used to be when the Savoy Company was a WASP (White Anglo-Saxon Protestant) preserve. The 2003 *Mikado* had an Indian Nanki-Poo, an African American Pish-Tush, and a Jewish Mikado.

Despite the more rigorous auditioning and serious atmosphere, the overall ethos remains one of fun and conviviality, as wonderfully expressed by the refrain sung to the tune of the closing bars of 'When Britain Really Ruled the Waves' at every company gathering: 'Let every heart be filled with joy and sing the praise of old Savoy'. Over the last ten years more than $150,000 has been raised for local charitable organizations and there is an imaginative schools program which involves distributing to local high schools a specially prepared teacher's lesson plan on the show being performed, together with free tickets and libretti.

British performing groups tend to be more sober and modest affairs, befitting their Nonconformist origins. One of the longest-surviving began in 1932 when the Sunday school choir of Rose Hill Methodist Church in Derby decided to extend their repertoire beyond the strictly sacred into the quasi-religious realms of G & S. Its opening production of *Trial by Jury* was staged in the Sunday school room to such acclaim that repeat performances were given at seven other churches in the town. Subsequent productions had to be moved to a nearby Temperance Hall when the town clerk pointed out that legal liability 'attaches in connection with any part of the church premises which are not *exclusively appropriated to public religious worship* and I think you will agree with me that it can hardly be said that, although it might be in aid of Church Funds, the presentation of the musical play *Mikado* can be deemed to come into this category'.[6] The performing group adopted its current name, Rose Hill Musical Society, in 1937 and has put on a G & S production every year since, except during the Second World War. The church link has continued throughout. When Rose Hill Methodist Church closed in 1989, over 80 percent of the society's members had personal associations with the church and the remainder were either associated with other churches or friends of members. The society is now associated with another Methodist church in Derby and its minister is the president.

Like the Savoy Company of Philadelphia, Rose Hill has inspired long and devoted service rivaling that found in the old D'Oyly Carte. Alan Stevens, the founder, directed every show from 1932 until 1976 and Douglas Milner, the church's organist and choirmaster, was music director from the outset until 1977. A more recent mainstay of the society, Peter Featherstone, discovered G & S when he was taken by his father to watch Rose Hill performances in the 1950s. He has been continuously involved since 1966, performing in all but two years and acting as treasurer since 1968. His wife, Margaret, who acts as subscription secretary, joined in 1967 and has missed only one show since then. Between them, the Featherstones have played over fifty principal roles and their son, John, is now following in their footsteps. The society prides itself on performing the less popular operas, subsidizing them out of the profits from the more popular shows. In the treasurer's words: 'We remain comfortably solvent because, for one thing, we jealously guard our amateur status. We pay for our orchestra and occasionally for a relief pianist, but nobody else receives a penny, not even for expenses'.[7]

A significant number of the amateur performing groups in the G & S heartland of Yorkshire and the East Midlands have similar Methodist origins. They include three of the four G & S societies in Sheffield (Intake Methodist Musical Society, Birley Carr Amateur Dramatic and Musical Society, and Meresbrook Methodist Music Society) and at least two of the six societies in West Yorkshire. Christchurch Gilbert and Sullivan Society in Leicester was founded in 1965 out of a one-off concert performance of *Iolanthe* to raise funds for the Methodist church. Although performances now take place in a community college rather than in the church, many of those involved in the society are still church members or adherents. Generally G & S in Retford, Nottinghamshire, which has been responsible for some high-quality productions of Sullivan's non-G & S operas, has a close connection with the Methodist church in the town. Several societies in other parts of Britain also have strong Methodist links. Trinity Gilbert and Sullivan Society in Chelmsford, Essex, was founded by members of the town's Trinity Methodist Church in 1965. There is also a strong Methodist element in the more recently formed Manx Gilbert and Sullivan Society, although it was surely not present at the initial meeting held in an office off the quay in Ramsey in 1987 where, according to the programme for the first production, 'some folk could not sing, others could not read music and there was no pianist'.

Methodism is not the only denomination to have spawned G & S performing groups in Britain. Haworth West Lane Baptist Society in Yorkshire began in 1948 with singers recruited entirely from the local Baptist chapel. Among societies associated with the United Reformed Church (formerly Presbyterian and Congregationalist) are Bingley in Yorkshire and St. Andrew's in Whitley Bay, near Newcastle, founded in 1952 on the initiative of a church elder to provide a church-based organization in which men, women, and young people could all participate. There are also a number of societies linked to Anglican churches. The reviewer of *Topsy-Turvy* for the *Church Times* reflected that 'there was a time when to belong to the Church of England and to Gilbert and Sullivan societies felt like one and the same thing' and wrote that the film had transported him back to a 1950s childhood 'that was about worship in church and G & S at St. Gabriel's Amateur Operatic Society in the hall'.[8] The Abbots Langley Gilbert and Sullivan Society started life in 1950 when a new vicar coaxed members of the parish church choir into performing *The Mikado*. The society's current principal patter man, Brian Andrews, is a canon at St. Alban's Cathedral. The Dagger Lane Operatic Society in Hull owes its origins to the custom of members of the town's Holy Trinity Church choir meeting after choir practice to sing Gilbert and Sullivan. In 1982 they staged *Trial by Jury* and have put on an annual G & S performance ever since. The clergy provide a good number of enthusiastic amateur performers as well as fans of G & S. One of the most sought after, because he is that rare commodity, an amateur tenor, is Tony Luke, vicar of St. Edmunds, Allenton, and warden of readers for the Diocese of Derby who regularly sings the tenor leads with Rose Hill and also happens to be married to the daughter of the Methodist minister who is the society's president.

I do not want to give the impression that every amateur G & S society in Britain is teeming with born-again Christians but it is a fact that there are a considerably higher than average number of churchgoers among amateur G & S performers, as well as among fans, doubtless for the same reasons. The crossover with singing in church choirs is particularly striking, if hardly surprising. For many societies now the main ecclesiastical link is with the church halls that provide cheap and convenient rehearsal venues. For the more dedicated amateur performers, of course, G & S has the status of a para-religion in itself. As the reviewer of a recent amateur *Mikado* in Edinburgh put it: 'There's nothing quite as devotional in the world of theatre as the effervescent enthusiasm of a Gilbert and Sullivan Society member for the work of the Victorian duo'.[9]

Fewer North American performing societies have church origins but several do maintain strong denominational links, with Methodism again predominating. The Sudbury Savoyards, one of a number of groups in the Greater Boston area, rehearse in the hall of the Sudbury United Methodist Church and store their costumes and props in the church basement. The minister of the church is a performing member and all proceeds from productions are donated to the church's committee for the relief of world hunger. It performs an opera every spring in the 900-seat auditorium of the local high school, with up to sixty-five people on stage, thirty in the orchestra pit, and another sixty involved backstage or front of house. It prides itself on having no auditions for the chorus and in being 'a 100% volunteer organization with none of the 150 or so people involved in each production receiving any financial compensation'. There are also Methodist churches in the United States which regularly put on G & S shows. I was delighted to discover on a recent visit to Lubbock, Texas, that the First United Methodist Church there was mounting a semistaged performance of *Pinafore* in August 2004 to celebrate the arrival of a new British organist and salute 'British friends who have greatly influenced Lubbock's musical scene'. Village Light Opera in New York is one of several performing groups with Presbyterian links. Its newsletter regularly quotes bons mots from sermons by the pastor of the city's First Presbyterian Church, such as his question to the choir: 'How many altos does it take to change a light bulb?' and the answer, 'Four, one to climb the ladder and change the bulb, and the other three to complain that it is too high!'[10]

Jewish interest in Gilbert and Sullivan in the United States extends to performance as well as appreciation. A 1995 staging of *Pirates* by Beth Shalom Synagogue in Philadelphia is one of several recent synagogue-based productions. The Gilbert and Sullivan Yiddish Light Opera Company of Long Island, founded in 1984 as an offshoot of the Gilbert and Sullivan Light Opera Company of Long Island, has performed *Der Yiddisher Mikado, Der Yiddisher Pinafore*, and *Di Yam Gazlonim* (*Pirates* set on the coast of Israel) not just in New York but as far afield as Florida, Toronto, and London. Its versions of *Mikado* and *Pinafore* have also been recorded on CD. Not all the members of the company, who range professionally from dentists to cantors, are Jewish but they share a commitment to the survival of Yiddish and choose to perform the Savoy operas rather than genuine Yiddish material 'because they love Gilbert and Sullivan. Furthermore down-to-earth Yiddishkeit stands out all the more vividly against such a genteel, Victorian ever-so-English background'.[11]

One of the biggest and most successful U.S. performing societies began in 1954 as an offshoot of an Episcopal Church choir in Seattle. John Andrews, the organist and choirmaster who had previously directed G & S productions in an all-girls school in New England, combined his own choir members with those from a neighbouring Lutheran church to form the Parish Gilbert and Sullivan Society. In the opening production of *Mikado* the following year, Ko-Ko was played by the Episcopal chaplain at the University of Washington and the local diocesan bishop had a walk-on part as umbrella bearer to the Mikado. Andrews intended that profits from the shows should be ploughed back into future productions but the church vestry decided it had a right to them and voted to use the proceeds from *Pirates* in 1956 to buy new choir robes. A rather acrimonious parting of church and society followed, leading to the incorporation of Seattle Gilbert and Sullivan Society as a non-profit-making and non-church-affiliated society in 1957. The society now has an annual budget of over $250,000, half of which goes to renting the theatre in which it performs over four weekends every July, and a membership of nearly 1,000. It has its own 7,000-square-foot rehearsal facility with space for set construction and costume storage. Each production involves a cast of around forty and a twenty-six-piece orchestra and is seen by nearly 10,000 people. In its fifty-year history the society has staged all the Savoy operas at least twice and some as many as seven times, as well as making audio and video recordings which have been shown on local public television stations. Fifty-three members have performed in all thirteen Savoy operas. Despite its considerable financial resources, the society, which has a large contingent of Boeing and Microsoft employees in its ranks, prides itself on its amateur status and the fact that it has never paid a performer anything. Several of its soloists cross over from Seattle Opera and other professional companies for the fun of doing an amateur G & S production.

Both the Seattle and Philadelphia societies operate on a scale unimaginable to even the biggest British societies. This is evident from their programmes, which resemble paperback books in size and standard of production. Each Seattle programme comes complete with a separate thirty-two-page booklet printed on high-quality art paper containing the complete libretto of the show, full glossary, and photographs of original D'Oyly Carte stars and of previous productions. The back page is devoted to an appeal for members and sponsors with a reminder that 'all monetary contributions by members are tax deductible' and that 'our volunteers at the members' table in the front lobby are eager to sign you up. They can accept personal checks, VISA or MasterCard (or even cash!) and will give you an instant tax receipt'. Alistair Donkin, who regularly directs another big U.S. group, the Houston G & S Society, observes: 'There aren't as many societies in the States as in Britain. So the standard is much better. If I want ten tenors in the chorus, I get ten tenors and not one tenor and nine baritones with aspirations above their station. Their theatres are much bigger too, and of course their budgets. Houston will happily spend $250,000 on one show'.[12] Most North American performing groups cover far wider geographical areas than their British equivalents and have a larger pool of talent to call on as a result. Seattle had a hundred people auditioning for the chorus of its 2001 *Pinafore*. Most British societies would be lucky to see a third of that number.

The beneficial effects of having a sizeable catchment area to draw from are evident in the case of the Lamplighters in San Francisco, who are the main West Coast performers of G & S. Founded in 1952 as an exclusively G & S company, they now put on two Savoy operas and one non–G & S show each year. Their budget per production is upwards of $300,000, with director, musical director, choreographer, designer, and orchestra all being paid. While none of those who perform on stage are paid, they are increasingly made up of full-time students in music colleges and conservatoires and aspiring professional singers. As a result, the average age of performers is just twenty-five.

Jane Hammett, the Lamplighters' director, who herself grew up with and sang with the company before turning professional, sees a big difference between U.S. and British amateur productions in terms of staging and choreography:

> Our productions are very traditional and very detailed. They also tend to be very dense. We have much more movement going on in them, especially in the chorus. I guess this may come from the influence and mindset of the American musical. We do not go in for static choruses. We treat them as individuals each with a point of view and a different character. Our choreographer encourages them to come up with a character. They engage in meditation as to where their inner person is. It's all very Californian.[13]

She also notes a different approach to rehearsing on either side of the Atlantic: 'We rehearse more intensively for a shorter period. My impression is that many British societies rehearse once a week for up to six months. That makes it hard to remember the dance routines. Lamplighters rehearses for just seven to eight weeks, but within that period we will be rehearsing Thursday, Friday, Saturday, and Sunday for three hours or so each day'.

There are almost certainly two other reasons that the dance routines in British amateur shows are rather less spectacular than their American counterparts. The average age of those performing on stage is considerably higher and the average budget much lower. Edinburgh, one of the bigger G & S societies, spends just over £40,000 on a production, less than a quarter of the Lamplighters' budget, nearly half of which goes on hiring the theatre where they perform and the rest on orchestra, costumes, and props. There are now a small number of British societies emerging which are more similar to the big American groups in taking performers from a wider geographical area and recruiting younger professionally trained singers. One such is South Anglia, started by Derek Collins in 1977, which has made something of a speciality of taking the Savoy operas to foreign parts and boasts that it has sung G & S in Italian, Portuguese, and Welsh. It was going to present *Iolanthe* in Slovenian in Bled in 1991 but the civil war broke out four days before the seventy-strong cast were due to go out there. Also in this category are Derby and Trent, both of which are very much the creation of Andrew Nicklin and are regular award winners at the Buxton G & S Festival. Trent is unusual in British terms in casting by invitation only and using semiprofessional singers but it still operates with a fraction of the budget of the big American societies.

Just as there are areas of Great Britain with a particularly rich culture of amateur G & S performance, such as Yorkshire and the East Midlands, performing societies in the United States tend also to be concentrated in certain regions. Overall, there are far more located east of the Mississippi (157) than west of it (39). The biggest concentration by far is in New England (47 performing groups) followed by the central eastern states (40) and the midwest (35). The states with the largest number of performing societies are New York (24), Massachusetts (23), California (18), Pennsylvania (12), and Virginia (11). This heavy bias towards the northeast may have something to do with climate. The G & S Society of Hancock, Maine, was founded in 1976 in response to four irresistible forces, one of which is 'the length of the Maine winters'. But almost certainly more important is the general cultural atmosphere in this most anglophile and 'preppy' corner of the country. If Nonconformist chapels have been among the main nurseries of G & S companies in Britain, institutions of higher education have played a similar role in the United States. Two of the five main performing groups in the Philadelphia area began as university societies. The Penn Singers still retain their strong link with the University of Pennsylvania, and the Gilbert and Sullivan Society of Chester County, formed in 1987 as the result of a collaboration between local residents and students in the music department of West Chester University, holds its rehearsals and performances on the university campus. As well as an annual G & S production, the society also performs

Trial by Jury every December in the Chester County Courthouse as part of the 'old fashioned Christmas in West Chester' experience. In the south, Houston Gilbert and Sullivan Society was founded in 1952 by the head of the University of Texas's music department and performed initially in the campus auditorium.

The academic bias already noted among G & S fans in the United States is also evident in the membership of amateur performing groups where there is a heavy concentration of lawyers, scientists, and university teachers. British societies, while similarly well supplied with lawyers, tend to have a smaller quotient of boffins and academics. Rose Hill's recent soloists have included the Midland Region winner of 'Britain's Favourite Plumber' award and a stylist in a hairdressing salon. The star parts in a recent *Mikado* production by the Savoy Singers of Camberley, a leading society in Southeast England, went to an insurance broker, a listings officer at a magistrates court, a librarian, a solicitor, a primary school teacher, and two local bank officials. Analysing the mid-twentieth-century membership profile of another major Surrey society, Godalming (founded in 1924–25), Shani d'Cruz found it to be essentially lower-middle-class and rooted in the local trade and business community. She also saw it as mirroring the D'Oyly Carte's strict moral code, pointing out that as late as 1960 members could bring their spouses or fiancés as guests to social events, but no one else. Overall, she concluded that:

> Throughout the (twentieth) century, the social profile of amateur operatic societies has been predominantly white and lower middle class: principally traders, white-collar workers and professionals. Societies have acted as nodal points in over-lapping sets of people's social and leisure networks, particularly those of neighbourhood, friendship and family.[14]

This family aspect is still strongly evident in performing societies on both sides of the Atlantic. They may have different social and intellectual profiles but they have fulfilled similar roles as marrying and dating agencies. Seattle is typical of U.S. societies in having spawned a good number of marriages—for one couple it all started at a cast party after *Ruddigore* and for another 'our first date was to a G & S sing-along and we had so much fun singing together that we just thought we would stick together'.[15] This aspect of the British amateur G & S scene also struck a somewhat bemused reporter sent to write about the Edinburgh Society: 'It seems if you are not the son or daughter of a G & S member, then you are probably the wife or husband of one, and if you are not that, you probably soon will be.'[16]

Among families bitten by the G & S bug few have a more impressive tally of performances between them than the Savournins of Sheffield. John senior just leads the way with sixty, his wife, Judy, comes a close second with fifty-five, daughter Jo so far has twenty-six, and son John junior, twenty-two. On several occasions all four have been involved in the same show. John senior and Judy have played alongside each other, as the Mikado and Katisha, Sir Marmaduke and Lady Sangazure, and twice as the Duke and Duchess of Plaza-Toro. A somewhat rare breed in British G & S circles in being an engineer, John first encountered Gilbert and Sullivan in 1965 when as a student at Sheffield University, he responded to a somewhat desperate appeal at the end of a maths lecture for male chorus members for a production of *Pirates*. Judy had her initiation the same year when she played the Fairy Queen at school. She subsequently auditioned for the D'Oyly Carte but decided to turn down a professional singing career in favour of looking after the family. Jo first trod the boards as an eight-year-old daughter in *Pirates* and John junior made his debut at nine as a drummer boy in *The Gondoliers*. He is now studying opera at Trinity College of Music and Jo still regularly performs with Sheffield societies.

The tradition of amateur performance is not just confined to the United Kingdom and the United States. In Australia and New Zealand, where there are at least twenty-three performing societies, to quote Stuart Maunder: 'The G & S phenomenon has been part of the basic language of performing for more than a century. People sing the numbers in competitions, musical societies stage the pieces all the time. The idea that a successful performance of "something from G&S" is within reach of those who want to achieve it is very powerful in the Australian psyche'.[17] Mel Moratti's website of 'productions down under' listed fifteen amateur productions over the summer of 2003, including a *Hot Mikado* from North Shore Music Theatre in Auckland, *Iolanthe* from both the Queensland Musical Theatre and the Gilbert and Sullivan Society of Victoria, *Gondoliers* from the Ignatians Musical Society in Brisbane, *Sorcerer* from the Rockdale Opera Company in New South Wales, *Mikado* from the Gilbert and Sullivan Society of South Australia in Adelaide, and *Yeomen* from the Gilbert and Sullivan Society of Victoria in Melbourne. The Gilbert and Sullivan Society of Western Australia mounts two full-scale productions per year. The society in Dunedin, New Zealand, embarked in 2002 on an ambitious project to stage all thirteen surviving Savoy operas over a twelve-year time-frame.

In Canada there are at least thirty-seven amateur groups regularly performing G & S. The biggest is probably the Gilbert and Sullivan Society of Winnipeg, with nearly 500 members, and the most innovative the North Toronto Players, who have a reputation for irreverent productions. Their 1991 *Mikado* was subtitled 'Look Ma . . . no fans!' and set in the Chicago of Al Capone. The Mikado became the Crime Lord of the Chicago South Side, Katisha an ageing moll, and Ko-Ko the manager of the 'Flash in Japan' restaurant, while Nanki-Poo was disguised as the lead singer of an all-girl band, 'The Wandering Minstrels'. New characters introduced included Mai-Wee, a tall waiter, and Koo-Chi-Koo, a fan dancer. In setting out his reasons for abandoning the traditional Japanese setting, the director, John Huston, observed that 'although very intelligent people are prepared to accept *Hamlet* set outside of Denmark they will balk at *The Mikado* set abroad from Japan'. This he blamed on the long and lingering hold of the D'Oyly Carte tradition:

> Too often, tradition is invoked as a creative 'cop out' or, even worse, the original intention behind the traditional business is lost and so the performer becomes a mere automaton, and the performance itself, dull. When this happens it can give not only traditional performances but Gilbert and Sullivan opera in general a reputation for stodginess.
>
> Do 'classics' really need to be preserved in aspic in order to be appreciated? Surely the sign of a classic work of art is its timelessness. Beethoven's 9th Symphony, Bizet's *Carmen* and Tchaikovsky's *Swan Lake* can stand on their own without the services of would-be protectors. Like *The Mikado*, these works are not delicate hot-house plants but hardy perennials. That they are susceptible to fresh interpretation through the years, and that each new generation will find new appeal in them, is one of the reasons behind their status as classics.[18]

The main society in South Africa was set up in Cape Town in 1947 by Edie West, whose husband, Jack, played the patter roles. Lorna Hanson, its honorary life president, says that there used to be two shows a year 'in the days when women didn't work and Mrs. West and her chums would meet at each other's homes to spend the day sewing costumes'.[19] For the last five years it has done one show annually, alternating G & S and a musical. The musicals make more money and subsidise the G & S. The society does a twenty-four-performance three-week run in a 600-seat theatre and has black and Afrikaner, as well as white, performers. As one might expect, G & S tends to flourish in places where there is a sizeable British expat community. The Brussels Society began in 1975 when thirty-five people met on a wet February evening in the basement of the city's Anglican church. It has since extended its repertoire beyond G & S and changed its name to the Brussels Light Opera Company, but the Savoy operas are still a major feature of its programme. Its founder, Peter Barton-Jones, who worked for the European Commission, had been John Reed's dresser and bought several of the old D'Oyly Carte costumes when they were auctioned off. Rome Savoyards were founded in 1980, and a group of British residents in France staged

Pinafore in a chateau in Jonzac in March 2002. As a concession to the locals, the costume designer gave the sailors striped Breton T-shirts and there was one Frenchman in the male chorus but otherwise it was an entirely British affair.

There have also been amateur performances further afield. In 1983 the British military team in Nigeria staged *Mikado* in Kaduna, the former capital of Northern Nigeria, with an Irish Ko-Ko, a Belgian Nanki-Poo, a German Yum-Yum, an American Peep-Bo, and the Nigerian minister of culture in the audience. A production of *Pirates* the following year featured a real-life colonel as the Major General and an RAF group captain as the Sergeant of Police. The programme contained translations of the plot into French, German, and Hausa, the local African language. Sadly, a military coup shortly afterwards put an end to these 'colonial fripperies'.[20] *Pinafore* was performed for four nights in 1997 in the gardens of the British Embassy in Jeddah, with the commercial secretary as the musical director. Jerusalem has a thriving society founded in 1984 by Robert Binder, who had first encountered G & S in 1958 as a student in a U.S. summer camp where a Hebrew version of *Pirates* was performed. He was particularly amused that in the paradox trio, the translators, being unable to find a Hebrew word for 'paradox' had rendered it 'zug barvazim', which means 'a pair of ducks'. In 2003 the Jerusalem Society mounted a full-scale production of *Mikado* with a cast of over thirty and sponsorship from the Jerusalem Municipality. Topical references included allusions to 'the Israeli motorist' and the schoolgirls' obis were decorated with the Jaffa oranges logo.

Performing societies are, of course, notorious for long-standing rivalries and jealousies. If they are a natural home for egotists and prima donnas, however, there is also huge camaraderie and cooperation, with performers teaching their partners the dance steps, adjusting one another's costumes, and covering for missed cues or wrong lines. There is, indeed, a good deal of selflessness as well as self-discipline involved in performing G & S well. This is particularly true in the chorus, and it is here also that much of the real fun of amateur performance lies, as expressed in this parody from the late David Dew's operetta 'On Song and Story', written to mark the fortieth anniversary of the Oundle Gilbert and Sullivan Players in 1998:

> If you want to know who we are
> We're a chorus of G and S.
> Though we're never the ones who star,
> We are serious nonetheless.
> We're covered in greasy paint,
> The lighting may make us faint,
> We caper without complaint. Ah! [21]

Amateur G & S choruses, especially male choruses, delight in recounting stories of mishaps with helmets, swords, and truncheons. The reminiscences of David Butcher, who describes himself as a 'dodgy tenor' (what other kind is there?), of the perils of playing a heavy dragoon in the 1982 production of *Patience* by the New Rosemere AOS in Bolton are typical:

> Our stage costumes of white trousers were in fact elasticated leggings as worn by gymnasts. As we strutted on stage at the dress rehearsal we thought that we looked like the cat's whiskers. Our appearance did not, however, have the desired effect on our audience which consisted mainly of the ladies' chorus. The love-sick maidens forgot their genteel acting personas and raised the roof with howls of laughter. We subsequently learned that the stage lighting had penetrated the white trousers and highlighted, in some detail, our 'undercarriages'. Needless to say, jockstraps and tight underwear were the order of the day for subsequent appearances of the 33rd Dragoon Guards. It certainly made for some grins from the ladies in the orchestra at the Duke's line 'I have a great gift to bestow'.[22]

For the outsider, it is all quite baffling. Vicky Allan, the reporter sent by *Scotland on Sunday* to write a profile of the membership of the Edinburgh G & S Society, had a distinct idea what she would find: 'I could have drawn a photofit: white, middle-class, middle-aged, slightly overweight with an anorakishly extensive knowledge of the life and times of Gilbert and Sullivan'. What she encountered when she dropped in at a rehearsal confirmed all her worst suspicions—'a bunch of doctors, lawyers and chartered accountants lumbering about the stage in ill-fitting sailor costumes, crashing into each other . . . there was more tripping than there was skipping—and if it wasn't for the fact that the bodies hurtling around the room were, on the whole, far from youthful, you would think that here in the middle of it all was a teacher scrabbling for control and there, in the corner, a couple of classroom assistants gossiping, while all around a playground of children shouted and ran'. She had been warned by her mother, who had done a few stints in a G & S chorus, that 'it's like caravanning or sailing, dear. A world of its own. Not everyone can understand it, but those who do really get into it'. When the discussion in the pub afterwards turned to the exact dimensions of the rigging of the Victory, however, she confessed, 'I felt my eyelids start to droop. I began to wonder if I was cut out for this G & S business. Even watching it is exhausting'.[23]

The atmosphere of performing with an amateur society is wonderfully captured in Peter Bathurst's book *Here's a Pretty Mess*. The author, a Sussex solici-

tor who has sung with ten different societies, lists the particular perils and
quirks of amateur productions as follows:

> The cut and thrust of principal auditions; misbehaving props; collapsing
> scenery; ill-fitting costume and ill-applied make-up; restless and somnolent
> spectators; ill-chosen ad-libs; sudden attacks of stage amnesia; hurriedly-
> planned curtain calls; interminable thank-you speeches; chaotic band calls;
> tenors who are less than competent at hitting the high notes; unsubtle
> fishing for compliments; over-optimistic rehearsal schedules and dance
> routines and officious rehearsal hall caretakers.

Bathurst tackles many issues that will sound familiar to seasoned amateur
performers, such as the difficulty of finding rehearsal pianists, the almost invariably depressing atmosphere of the places where auditions are held, 'which
exude the congeniality of the waiting room of a dentist who has never heard of
local anaesthetics, and boast a temperature resembling either that of a kitchen
in a Calcutta curry house during a heat wave or a Reykjavik bus shelter during
a blizzard', and the best way to improvise props such as truncheons before the
real things arrive shortly before the performance date. He has a salutary warning to young performers, 'young in this context meaning under 40', about the
older, almost invariably female, members who will 'take them in hand' and in-
sist on 'three evening tuition sessions in a suburban bungalow' and wonderfully
sums up the feeling of letdown once a show has ended:

> After several weeks in which anything seems preferable to the prospect
> of rushing the evening meal and braving snow, hail, wind and storm to be
> bawled at by a temperamental producer, the amateur performer will feel a
> curious sense of emptiness as he helps to dismantle the set. No longer is he
> a Venetian gondolier, a lofty peer or a smart dragoon guard, but Mr. Smith
> of 12 Apple Tree Gardens with nothing more to look forward to on the
> Monday except a bulging in-tray, two basketsful of ironing, and a trip to
> Sainsbury's Homebase to buy a sack of tiling grout.[24]

The world of amateur G & S performance sustains a number of wonderfully
arcane small businesses. There are a handful of theatrical costumiers who make
their living primarily by hiring out complete sets of costumes for the Savoy operas. A rummage in the pockets of a policeman's tunic can often unearth the de-
tritus of *Pirates* productions up and down the country over the previous year or
more. There is even a specialist G & S props company set up by Ben and Margaret Chamley, a West Yorkshire couple, whose experience illustrates how in-

volvement in amateur performance can end up taking over one's life. Ben was introduced to the Savoy operas while training to be a public health inspector in Bradford. He was working in the local abattoir with the city's chief inspector of meat, who was the leading light in the local Baptist Chapel G & S society. 'As we went round inspecting carcasses he used to sing snatches of G & S. One day he turned to me and said that the Society were short of male chorus for their next production of *Pirates*. With the exams for my diploma in meat hygiene coming up, I thought it might be as well to keep in with him, so I volunteered and I've been hooked ever since'. Ben went on to perform with the West Yorkshire Savoyards. His wife, Margaret, started her backstage career running the raffle but quickly graduated to making the tea. 'If you're doing the raffle, you spend the show out in the foyer guarding the whisky and don't hear anything. Making the tea is better because you can at least watch things'. She was eventually promoted to the dizzy heights of props mistress and that is how the business of collecting props started. Years of rummaging at car boot sales and in antique shops has led to the accumulation of an unrivalled collection of props for every Savoy opera, which are now hired out in a business run from the former rectory in Halifax which also serves as headquarters of the Buxton G & S Festival. [25]

Although the line is becoming increasingly blurred in the big American societies and some of the bigger British ones, there is still an essential difference in ethos between amateur and professional companies. In the words of Betty Moat, longtime president of the Godalming Operatic Society: 'Members of an amateur society are not there to earn their living; they are there for pleasure, relaxation and to enjoy the show'.[26] This aspect does have its down side. Amateurs can lack the discipline of professionals, and there is often more enjoyment for those on stage than for the audience, particularly when things are slipshod and underrehearsed. David Turner, who has adjudicated hundreds of amateur G & S productions, believes that ultimately they do lack something:

> Of course amateurs bring an enthusiasm. But whereas a pro will always be searching to extend the role, an amateur will reach a level and stick there. Once they get to the performing level, they never take it any further. I think the original success of the Savoy Operas and the way they were presented may well be the amateur's downfall. What Gilbert and Sullivan created was a musical repertory company. They wrote parts for certain types and of course what happens in an amateur company is that you have the huge great big contralto, you have the rather fey tenor and so on and if you are playing only G & S then people tend to fall into a slot and maybe because of this their performing powers become narrower. I think that's why amateur companies flourish with G & S because they know exactly what is expected of them.[27]

I have to say that I have seen several amateur performances which have had more zest, commitment, and enthusiasm than professional G & S productions. Yes, the fairies may be a little on the elderly side and the sailors not quite in step with each other, but there is something very moving and uplifting about seeing people who are not trained singers or dancers put their hearts and souls into a production. There is also the thrill of seeing the lady who works in the chemist's or the man from the bank in a completely different and unexpected role.

Amateur societies are often praised (or criticized) for being wedded to G & S 'tradition'. Long after the expiry of copyright, many retained their close relationship with the old D'Oyly Carte company and continued to treat it as a model for their productions. This relationship was kept going after its demise by the many former D'Oyly Carte choristers and principals who went on to direct amateur companies. Several still do today. Amateur societies are hugely proud of their D'Oyly Carte links. Godalming boasts that over the years it has been directed by Clara Dow, Leo Sheffield, Billy Morgan, Leonard Osborn, Meston Reid, and Cynthia Morey. Ex–D'Oyly Carte artistes naturally bring into their productions many of the moves and bits of business which they themselves learned. Alistair Donkin reckons that about 50 percent of the blocking for the amateur shows that he directs is very similar if not identical to that for the

FIGURE 6.2 Tripping hither. Alistair Donkin puts amateur fairies through their paces for the 1996 Buxton Festival production of *Iolanthe* (*Rodney Leach*)

D'Oyly Carte productions in which he himself took part. When directors do want to change things, there is often fierce resistance from the amateur performers who want to keep traditional moves and business. Donkin regards himself as a traditionalist, defining this as 'representing Gilbert's words and Sullivan's music clearly and cleanly, but using modern theatrical techniques to update the productions, not just keeping them as museum pieces'. He would love to put on a rock version of *Ruddigore* set in the 1960s in the style of a Hammer horror movie 'but none of my amateur societies have let me do it yet because they are more traditionalist than I am'.[28]

The attachment of amateur societies to tradition in the face of new producers wanting to update things is the subject of a wonderful parody by Norman Leonard:

We are the very model of a G & S Society,
Inheriting traditions of theatrical propriety.
We'd like to think that D'Oyly Carte, if he were looking down on us,
Would certainly approve our style and have no cause to frown on us.
But winds of change are blowing through our musical community,
From which not even G & S can dare to claim immunity;
We've got a new producer now who wants to change things drastically,
And some of us have welcomed him less than enthusiastically.
He says, 'Your style's outmoded—I see I must correct a lot'.
The man has obviously been influenced by Brecht a lot.

He's revamped all the songs and claims he's substituted better words,
And to our consternation stuck in several four letter words.
He'd like to do *The Gondoliers* on ice in Wembley Stadium
And *Patience* with a topless chorus line at the Palladium,
He's ruled out *The Mikado* on the grounds that it is racial,
(It's making fun of differences linguistical and facial),
He plans a new production of another Savoy hardy'un,
The *Yeomen of the Guard* will now become *The Avant-Gardian*.
Poor *Princess Ida*'s been demoted from the aristocracy
She's now just plain 'Ms Ida' in the interests of democracy.

He's redone *Trial by Jury*, made it spicier and fancier,
The jury now gets nobbled by a Tokyo financier.
We ask him 'What about the *Pirates*, *Iolanthe* and *Ruddigore*?
The new man shook his head and said 'No way. Not any bloody more'.
In short, the situation's now becoming quite Gilbertian,

Though if you dare to hint as much, the look you get's a dirty'un.
Dismissing cavalierly all the repertoire encompasses,
With minimum delay he's caused a maximum of rumpuses.
He is the very pattern of those modern impresarios
And we can only hold our breath and wait and to see how far he goes.

Ian Taylor, who has written thoughtfully on this subject, has strong views on amateur performers' particular attachment to G & S 'tradition' based on his own extensive experience of directing them. He is in no doubt of their key role: 'It is the amateur societies who have maintained the appreciation of "G & S" throughout the length and breadth of the land. On them falls the responsibility of supplying continued lifeblood to keep the operas as living theatrical entities, not museum pieces to be admired by steadily ageing, and so diminishing, audiences'. He has little sympathy with those who extol the 'G & S tradition':

The phrase has no fixed definition: its meaning is made manifest only in presentations dedicated to its cult. In all too many cases the 'tradition' is used as a cloak to conceal lack of inventiveness in both producer and player. In a belief that they are offering the works as conceived by Gilbert, they perpetuate stage techniques and 'business' long outmoded in the modern theatrical world the application of which does nothing but alienate an increasingly large section of the audiences whose knowledge, appreciation and sophistication of visual theatre has been increased immensely by television.

Anyone with an artistic feeling cringes with embarrassment when the ladies' chorus, with right index fingers raised, beat time one in the bar in 'How beautifully blue the sky'. It is an action smacking of the well-meaning but talentless spinster's production of kindergarten playlets of 30 or 40 years ago.

For Taylor, 'the true Gilbertian tradition is that of taste and refinement, coupled with sensibility and sensitivity towards text and situation, plus a forward looking and inventive mind'.[29]

There is surely room for both traditional and updated productions in amateur as much as in professional G & S performance. Some of the most old-fashioned productions I have seen have been done by amateurs (and not necessarily the worse for that), as well as some of the most innovative and modern. Southampton, a noticeably young society by British standards, with many members drawn from the university, does some excellent updated versions with minimal changes of wording and scenery. In their 2001 Starship Pinafore the opening chorus began 'We Cruise the Galaxy', Buttercup was 'beamed up' rather than welcomed on board, and the bosun sang of Ralph, 'he is a Starfleet man'. Their 2003 *Princess Ida* was set in the 1960s with Hilarion, Florian, and Cyril as teddy boys and Arac, Gurion, and Scythion as bikers, serenading 'the brrrm, brrrm, brrrm of the Harley Davidson' in their song 'We Are Bikers Three'. By contrast, the nearby society just along the coast in more sedate Bournemouth specializes in superbly crafted traditional productions with beautiful period costumes and scenery. Each has its own integrity and both seem to me equally valid interpretations of the genius of G & S.

In general, amateur performers in the United States are more reverential of and wedded to traditional productions à la D'Oyly Carte than those in Britain. In Alistair Donkin's opinion, 'this goes back to the fact that they have no history in America. When they come here they see our history, our traditions, our monuments and they are in awe of them. If they can import any, like Gilbert and Sullivan, they treat it as opera in a foreign language and they listen to the words'. Whereas most British performers will happily play the Savoy operas with regional accents, North Americans nearly always adopt cut-glass Queen's English voices. It is interesting that American societies manage to combine a more traditional approach to G & S with much younger performers than are generally found in the United Kingdom. For Roberta Morrell, who has directed several amateur groups in the States, their secret lies in viewing the Savoy operas as 'an opportunity to have great fun on the stage; an attitude that should be emulated by amateur groups in Great Britain which struggle for survival, unable to replace their ageing membership with fresh young performers'. She concludes: 'It is ironical that the future of such a quintessentially English institution as Gilbert and Sullivan should be in safer hands in the United States than in its homeland.'[30]

Whether G & S is, indeed, in safer hands in the United States or in the United Kingdom, there is a growing concern among Savoyards on both sides of the Atlantic that it is not being performed as much by amateurs as it once was. One measure of this is the number of societies who have moved from concentrating exclusively on the Savoy operas to making them just an occasional part of their repertoire. This has been a clear trend over the last four decades. Village Light Opera in New York, which dates from 1935, first ventured beyond G & S in 1971. Aberdeen Opera Company concentrated solely on G & S from its foundation in 1940 until 1966, since when it has performed a Savoy Opera roughly every four years. Oxford Operatic Society performed twenty-four Gilbert and Sullivan operas in its first twenty-five years, from 1946 to 1971, but just twelve in its next twenty-five years, from 1972 to 1997. The decision by the Glasgow Orpheus Club to end more than a century of almost exclusive dedication to the Savoy operas in 2000 was prompted by the 'bald economic fact' that of the four popular operas it performed in a row in the late 1990s, only *Mikado* made a profit. According to Vice-President Walter Paul there were other factors as well:

> We found that our Club membership was dwindling; the days when people joined a society and remained faithful to that society whatever show was performed, seem to have long since passed, and as in life in general, we are now faced with a slightly selfish attitude where members join for the show and not for the Club. And so, after much debate, The Orpheus Club changed policy in 2000 and attempted an Offenbach—making a gigantic loss, it must be said! However, our membership increased, and we now find, after only 4 years, that there is no interest whatsoever from the majority of our members to perform a Gilbert and Sullivan opera as our main production.[31]

Another apparent indicator of the waning appeal of the Savoy operas among amateur groups in Britain is the poor take-up of G & S performance classes at recent NODA summer schools. The association has now abandoned its attempts to encourage and tutor its members in this particular branch of the amateur operatic repertoire. The switch away from Gilbert and Sullivan towards musicals on the part of amateur societies is variously put down to the decline in the tradition of choral singing (more marked in Britain than the United States), the fact that schools have largely abandoned the Savoy operas, and the general sense that they are showing their age and no longer enthuse either audiences or performers as they once did.

In fact, it is by no means clear that there has been a serious decline in the level of amateur performances of G & S over the last forty years. There is no statistical information available on which to make an authoritative assessment of the position in the United States, although virtually all observers are agreed that there has been a clear downward trend in the number of amateur performances. By going through old NODA yearbooks and newsletters, it is possible to add up figures which give at least a rough guide as to the number of productions and also the 'market share' of G & S within the total spectrum of amateur operatic performance in Britain. My research comes up with the following findings in respect of the first year of each of the last five decades:

Year	Total productions	G & S productions	% share
1961	996	167	16.7
1971	866	178	20.5
1981	803	123	15.3
1991	725	117	16.1
2001	942	173	19.1

These figures do not suggest that there has been any significant decline in either the overall number of amateur G & S productions or the G & S 'market share'. Indeed, the figures for 2001 are higher in both respects than those for 1961. It is also noteworthy that in all of these years at least one Savoy opera was among the top five most-performed shows in Britain:

> 1961: 1 *Merry Widow* (45), 2 *Mikado* (32), 3 *Carousel* and *South Pacific* (28), 4 *White Horse Inn* (24)
>
> 1971: 1 *Sound of Music* (34), 2 *Merry Widow* (31), 3 *My Fair Lady* (29), 4 = *Gondoliers* and *Mikado* (25)
>
> 1981: 1 *Fiddler on the Roof* and *Merry Widow* (28), 3 = *Mikado*, *Gondoliers* and *The King and I* (24)
>
> 1991: 1 = *Carousel* and *South Pacific* (26), 2 *Oklahoma!* (22), 3 *Brigadoon* (21), 4 *Pirates* (19 performances, including six of the Papp version)
>
> 2001: 1 *Oklahoma!* (45), 2 *Fiddler on the Roof* (36), 3 *Mikado* (33, including five of the *Hot Mikado*), 4 *Me and My Girl* (29), 5 *South Pacific* (27).

Since 2002 NODA has moved to a new way of recording productions by means of a computer database. This gives lower overall figures for Gilbert and Sullivan performances than in 2001—138 out of a total of 1,335 productions in 2002, and 142 out of 1,367 in 2003—and a considerably lower 'market share' of just over 10 percent. This latter figure is almost certainly considerably depressed in these recent statistics because they include many nonmusical plays which were not included in the earlier compilations, but it does look as though the 2001 figures may well represent an exceptionally good year for G & S. Other recent research that I have undertaken suggests that performances of the Savoy operas now make up around 15 percent of all amateur operatic society productions, very much as they have over the last twenty-five years or so. Of the thirty-three amateur operatic society productions notified to NODA Scotland between June 2003 and March 2004, for example, five (15.15%) are of G & S. I think this is probably a reasonably accurate reflection of the overall situation in the United Kingdom today, where roughly one in every six amateur operatic society productions involves a Savoy opera.

The figures also suggest that there is no out-and-out favourite among the operas in terms of amateur performance. This is confirmed by statistics compiled annually by the D'Oyly Carte with respect to the hire of band parts and scores. *The Mikado* is fairly regularly the most requested—it was in 2003—but other recent years have seen *Pirates* and *Gondoliers* coming out on top. *Pinafore* and *Iolanthe* are also consistently popular. Once again, there are no comparable statistics available in the United States, but it is fair to assume that the '*Piramikafore*' trinity dominates the amateur as well as the professional scene there. *Gondoliers* is noticeably less popular in the States. As Dan Rothermel observes, 'Brits like it because it isn't British, and that's exactly why Americans don't like it'.[32]

There are frequent lamentations that both audiences and performers are getting older. Many U.S. amateur societies were founded shortly after World War II by GIs returning from Britain where they had picked up the G & S bug—two of the major performing groups in the greater New York area, Troupers Light Opera (1947) and the G & S Light Opera Company of Long Island (1954), originated in this way. Now celebrating their fiftieth birthdays, they find themselves with a youthful membership but an ever more greying audience. Describing the audiences for local productions in which he has been involved, Paul Cohen from Fairfield, Connecticut, says: 'You can count the coaches from the retirement homes rolling up'.[33] The age factor makes David Turner pessimistic about the future of the amateur operatic scene in Britain: 'I have to say that in twenty years I can see none of this existing. The people who are the driving forces in the societies are now all over fifty, maybe over sixty. It's not just true of musical theatre, it's there in the Women's Institute and the parochial church council and everything. People are not willing to give their time. Most societies are run by people who have done it for a very long time'.[34]

This seems to me an unduly pessimistic assessment. It is certainly true that the average age of amateur G & S performers in Britain is considerably higher than in the United States and in this respect, as in others, the future of G & S perhaps looks less secure in their own homeland than across the Atlantic. A number of the smaller British societies are facing a crisis in terms of failure to recruit new and younger blood. But this is by no means a universal state of affairs. At a late stage of my research for this book, I was delighted to receive this e-mail message from Sarah Olney, chairman of the Grosvenor Light Opera, which dates from 1949 and has become the leading amateur G & S performing group in London:

> The company has changed a good deal in the last fifty years, and what is most notable about the current membership is that in complete contrast to most G&S societies, the majority of our membership is under 35 (I'm only 26 myself). We still rehearse and perform in central London and our members are mostly young people working in the city of London. Our productions tend to be a little more anarchic than most—our members are not as precious about their Gilbert and Sullivan as other performers I have met—nobody remembers the days when the D'Oyly Carte sent a representative to all the shows to check that the movements were being done properly. However, we know of all these things and have an understanding

of the traditions thanks to a large body of former members who keep in touch and help us maintain the link with the past.[35]

Perhaps the most heartening sign for the future of amateur performance of Gilbert and Sullivan is its very buoyant state in many educational institutions. It is time to turn our attention to national schools, ladies' seminaries, and colleges of useful knowledge.

~

IN THIS COLLEGE, USEFUL KNOWLEDGE:
G & S IN SCHOOLS AND UNIVERSITIES

Gilbert and Sullivan has always had a particular appeal to young people. Gilbert himself produced children's versions of the operas, and performing editions for unbroken voices have long been used in schools. As with amateur productions, school performances almost certainly reached their peak in the 1950s and 1960s. Although there has been a marked decline since then, the appeal of G & S among the young is still evident in institutions ranging from British universities to North American summer camps.

A glance through a back copy of the *Savoyard* provides a good indication of the number and flavour of school productions in their heyday. The June 1966 issue lists over thirty, with six alone among secondary schools in a relatively small area of the West of Scotland—Marr College, Troon, Coatbridge High School, Greenock Academy, Kilmarnock Academy, Lenzie Academy, and the Albert Secondary School in Glasgow. It also includes an article by John Murphy, a music teacher in Cardiff, proposing G & S as the answer to 'the school music crisis' and 'the difficulty of finding suitable music with which to counter the appeal of "pop" music for children':

The school choir works for the simple reason that those children who genuinely love singing herd *together* and enjoy it *together*. So the *common* project is the answer—prepared by all, enjoyed by all, and sacrificed for by all; and in the Savoy operas, the timeless G & S light operas, performed in the impeccable tradition of the D'Oyly Carte Opera Company, that ideal solution lies. For this is a project that crowns a whole year's preparation; that can embrace every single child in the school in *some* capacity or another; and one that gives all that music was ever meant to give—enjoyment, satisfaction, and fulfilment.

I have held a chorus of eighty children together with anything from six to eight hours' rehearsal a week for a solid twelve-month, and I know what I am talking about. I have found my salvation, my alternative to 'beat'. This is the only right road to follow, at these difficult musical crossroads we face in our secondary schools.[1]

This splendid piece of evangelism for G & S in schools is full of good advice. Murphy recommends starting with *Pinafore*, using the arrangement published by Cramer where the chorus numbers are in simple three-part SSA harmony. Pupils can then graduate to *Iolanthe* and a 'versatile school with one or two responsible senior pupils' might even have a shot at *Ruddigore*. Precise instructions are laid down with regard to rehearsals—one and a half hours twice weekly after school with an additional weekly rehearsal during the month before the production—and chorus size, which should be as large as possible, eighty not being unusual in the author's own productions.

You do not need eighty born choristers. You need eighty people who enjoy the hard work involved, a percentage of whom can hold their different musical lines as they carry out their varying 'business' on stage; and it is your job to blend them into a chorus. Remember, principals cannot 'carry' an entire production, and the success, or otherwise, of the chorus makes or breaks your production. So choose well your principals, but be perpetually grateful that the chorus has chosen you.[2]

Murphy has no doubt as to the style of production suitable for schools:

Although the copyright of the Savoy operas expired at the end of 1961, the only right way to produce them is in the Savoy traditions, as laid out in the detailed libretti supplied by Bridget D'Oyly Carte Ltd.

Never neglect an opportunity to see the D'Oyly Carte Opera Company perform, if you are fortunate enough to be given it, and organise a school outing for those faithful members of your cast. To miss this experience would be well-nigh criminal![3]

The most vital imperative is to keep alive the flame of enthusiasm:

You may never know in the full the harvest that came from your sowing. But this I promise you! You *will* see teenagers who have regained their musical senses and are prepared to admit that there are other things in life bar the music of their normal world; properly balanced youngsters, who have their rightful pleasures still but know and love something better—and *are* better, in themselves and in their strengthened community spirit, for it.[4]

Coming at the height of the swinging sixties and Beatlemania, this stirring paean to the educative properties of the Savoy operas reads now like a gallant rearguard action to defend the stern moral fibre and community spirit of a vanishing age. It is precisely the atmosphere in which I came to what Noel Coward referred to as 'the healthy clean-limbed but melodious high jinks of Gilbert and Sullivan' in the early 1960s. In my Kent preparatory school the operas were performed annually in the gymnasium where we also gathered for morning assembly based on readings from the Authorized Version of the Bible and the Book of Common Prayer and weekly physical education classes under the tutelage of an ex-RSM from the Royal Marines. Gilbert and Sullivan was a central part of a traditional, all-male schooling based on muscular Christianity, learning Latin verbs, and not doing anything naughty behind the bike sheds.

But already the hold of G & S in schools was being challenged. Other more up-to-date and even more specifically uplifting Christian cantatas and musicals were appearing, like *Jonah-Mann Jazz* and *Captain Noah and His Floating Zoo.* Then in 1968 a prep school in London performed a work specially written for it by two young men starting out in their careers in musical theatre. *Joseph and the Amazing Technicolor Dreamcoat* had many affinities with the Savoy operas in its brilliant rhyming schemes and musical pastiche, not surprisingly when they had been such a model for its lyricist, Tim Rice. A reviewer of the show perceptively noted: 'For lack of anything else, Gilbert and Sullivan has long been the staple fare for school musical performances. Here is something with which they can more readily identify, and which should be widely peformed.'[5] During the 1970s schools increasingly abandoned *Pirates* and *Pinafore* in favour of *Joseph* and other racier musicals like *Guys and Dolls.* Gilbert and Sullivan in schools was also hit by the general move away from singing and choral training in favour of instrumental and keyboard skills, and, in the state sector particularly, the growing reluctance on the part of staff to devote their time to extracurricular activities and the increasing pressure on both teachers' and pupils' time.

There were committed teachers like Roger Wickson who kept the G & S flag flying through the 1980s and 1990s. His moving apologia for doing the Savoy operas in schools, delivered at the end of his long teaching career in 1999, echoes many of the points made by John Murphy twenty-five years earlier in setting out why 'it is worth spending a great deal of time and energy—often to exhaustion point—producing works that some would regard as archaic and others as musically, dramatically, and intellectually beneath contempt'.[6] Confessing to being an 'unashamed traditionalist', Wickson talks in terms of perpetuating the English cultural tradition and compares G & S to the Authorized Version of the Bible, the Book of Common Prayer, and the treasury of English hymnody. He believes that the Savoy operas are particularly well suited for school production: 'They are sufficiently demanding to present the most talented youngsters with a real challenge without being so difficult that the less talented find that insuperable difficulties meet them at every turn. . . . The principal parts lack emotional complexity and intensity so they can be acted convincingly by inexperienced and unsophisticated youngsters. Nevertheless they are not without pathos or poignancy and boys and girls can handle these effectively.' For him, as for John Murphy, they also serve a deeper educational purpose:

> For a schoolmaster perhaps the greatest attraction of the operas is that they involve large numbers of boys and girls and they depend on teamwork and discipline. Up to sixty boys and girls are required on stage and a good number in the orchestra. Then there are set builders and painters, stage crew and lighting and sound technicians, make-up teams and front-of-house assistants. All in all more than a hundred pupils will be involved in some way in a production.
>
> On stage there are no real star parts, no one character dominates the show, success depends on the contribution of everyone. Many of the most successful numbers are duets, trios and quartets.
>
> Above all, it is the importance of the chorus that makes the operas so worthwhile. Few stage works give the chorus such importance and prominence and in few is the chorus so important to the development of the action. For this reason girls and boys of all sorts want to take part in them. I could have had girls' choruses of forty or more had there been room for them, and I have not had difficulty in recruiting men's choruses of twenty or so, nearly all sixth formers. There is a real element of prestige attached to taking part in the operas. There have always been scholars, cricketers, footballers and oarsmen in the cast as well as serious musicians and indeed boys who play no other part in school life at all.

Wickson is right to make much of the educative aspects of the discipline, precision, and teamwork required in putting on a good G & S performance, but he also underlines the great sense of achievement and satisfaction that comes from gradually building something together, concluding on a personal note that 'by producing Gilbert and Sullivan I have developed my relationship with my pupils very positively. It has always been a matter of delight, indeed pride, to watch the enjoyment and friendship develop.'

Sadly, there are fewer teachers around now with that kind of burning passion for G & S. Indeed, for a long time many in both music and drama departments have been decidedly sniffy about the Savoy operas, sharing the familiar prejudice against them. This has been true in the United States as well as in Britain— Richard Shapp, a longtime fan and currently development director of the Philadelphia Chamber Orchestra, was sad to find that G & S was 'beneath the aesthetic dignity' of his high school teachers in the 1960s although the music master grudgingly gave him permission to miss classes in order to go to D'Oyly Carte performances—but it has almost certainly been more pronounced in the United Kingdom. Susan Elkin, a teacher turned educational journalist, regularly bangs the drum for doing G & S in schools, arguing that they are an 'unsung educational resource' from which teenagers can learn about music, production, teamwork, language, and Victorian social history. Yet her experience confirms the prejudice against them in many educational circles:

In my own 31 years at the chalk face in a very wide variety of schools, I have never taught in a school which has even contemplated putting on a G & S production. 'Too dated', people say. 'Too difficult' say others, 'too obscure, or too highbrow'. 'The parents wouldn't like it and wouldn't come'. Or worst of all 'We have to do something accessible these days'. That word 'accessible' is high on my list of education weasel words. Making things 'accessible' is usually synonymous with 'dumbing down' or fobbing young people off with the banal.[7]

In fact, there are still schools of all kinds on both sides of the Atlantic regularly performing Gilbert and Sullivan. Susan Elkin herself has written enthusiastically about the annual productions put on by a grant-maintained comprehensive school in New Cross, South London, as a postexam project with just two to three weeks of intensive rehearsal and has quoted the director of music, John Skinner, as saying that his pupils love singing in four-part harmony and also appreciate learning to sing from the diaphragm 'without microphones stuck under their noses'.[8] Holy Cross, a Roman Catholic sixth-form college in Bury, Lancashire, regularly performs G & S. Another faith-based school with a strong community ethos in the same part of England has probably done more than any other educational establishment to promote the Savoy operas among young people in recent years. St. Mary's Catholic High School, a 1,700-pupil comprehensive school in Astley, near Manchester, put on a large-scale production of a G & S opera every year but one between 1988 and 2002, with around seventy-five fourteen- to eighteen-year-olds in the cast, of whom at least thirty-five were boys. Andrea Atherton, the head of music and drama, is an unrepentant enthusiast for putting on the Savoy operas at school :

> Our students require more than unison singing and banal scripts. In G & S there is a challenge for all. At the end of it students have extended their skill base and had fun in the process. They learn more about music from G & S than anything else because it teaches ensemble and part-singing and it has substantial chorus work that is invaluable when you are trying to involve as many students as possible. There are also major character roles that are usually taken by the more experienced performers which offer real challenges in their speech patterns, interpretation and their relationships with the audience.[9]

In her view 'Gilbert is really the forerunner of the absurdist theatre of the twentieth century rather than a representative figure of his own time. That's why I can't understand people who want to see his work frozen in the time of the nineteenth century'. The St. Mary's productions, which have regularly won awards at the Buxton G & S Festival, eschew the old D'Oyly Carte style in favour of updated settings. *Mikado* was transferred to a Nissan car plant in Sunderland to show the Japanese takeover of British industry; *Iolanthe* was performed on roller skates with an Alice in Wonderland theme; and *Yeomen* was set in Blackpool Tower, *Gondoliers* in modern Venice, and *Ruddigore* in 1930s Hollywood. There was huge demand to be in the productions, which had to be limited to those in year ten and above, and students happily came in for four to five weeks in the holidays, rehearsing from ten until four every day. St. Mary's students enthuse about the satisfaction and community spirit engendered by performing G & S and also about its own intrinsic appeal: 'There's something special about it. The music is so happy and there's so much you can do with it'. Two former pupils have won Oxbridge choral scholarships largely on the strength of the musical skills that the productions have given them.

Yet it has not all been plain sailing and Andrea Atherton is not sure that the school, which forsook G & S in 2003 to stage *Les Misérables*, will return to the Savoy operas. She says that students inspired by the productions have tried to join university or adult societies when they leave school but 'tend not to stay as they find them rather dull and often very ageist and patronising'. She also admits to being worn down by the 'unpleasantness and negative reactions' with which the productions have been greeted by hard-core traditionalists at Buxton. Funding is an ever-more difficult problem, 'as is finding time in an increasingly stressful school schedule. . . . If we had been supported more by outside agencies we could have shown the way as to how G & S can be fun and challenging and a real boon for children to be "stretched" in a musical and dramatic way'.[10]

There have, in fact, been several initiatives to try to encourage G & S appreciation and performance in schools. Both the old and new D'Oyly Carte companies ran educational programmes as, more recently, has Carl Rosa. Ian Smith, founder of the Buxton G & S Festival, which has featured an annual children's production since 1996, has tried to reach out to schools with schemes to provide volunteer directors and other support but these have been hampered by lack of funding and lack of take-up from schools. I suspect that trying from the outside to 'push' G & S in schools is not going to achieve very much. It may be better to recognize and welcome the fact that so many schools are now performing musicals and accept that this may be the route through which pupils will come to an appreciation of the Savoy operas later in life. A more successful way to stimulate interest in G & S among young people is through youth performing groups set up under the auspices of amateur societies. The Plymouth G & S Fellowship has the Young Savoyards, a training group for twelve- to sixteen-year-olds. The Gilbert and Sullivan Youth Theatre in Sheffield puts on an annual show and also trains performers for the annual youth production at Buxton. It currently has over thirty performing members aged between eight and eighteen, with girls outnumbering boys by a ratio of four to one.

The situation in the United States is much the same as it is in Britain. In Ralph MacPhail's words, 'Until the mid-1950s most high schools did G & S. Then along came *My Fair Lady* and *Brigadoon* and other musicals and they gradually displaced G & S. It's very rare to see high school productions now'.[11] Yet there are still teachers dedicated to performing the Savoy operas. One such is Pamela Leighton-Bilik, who teaches drama and voice at Hoover Middle School, in Potomac, near Washington, D.C. A veteran member of the Washington Savoyards, she planned to audition for the old D'Oyly Carte company when she was nineteen but an IRA bomb scare on the day of the audition put her off. Her school productions regularly involve 120 or more students—the 1996 *Gondoliers* had a 125-strong cast, eighty-five of whom were girls. They are very much seen as a huge community activity and no one is turned away. One of those taking part in a recent show said, 'I like doing Gilbert and Sullivan. It's a little bit of extra theatre education because no one else knows it'. Bilik, who also regularly directs the youth production at Buxton, sees G & S as a huge antidote to the troubled times in which we live and hopes that young people performing it will learn the lesson that 'if the world gets dark and things get bad, they can go do a show and lose themselves in it'. She is careful not to refer to it as operetta, 'or, heaven forbid, as light opera but as a musical which makes it more palatable because kids are familiar with that term' and, when pressed by her colleagues as to whether it is not too difficult for children, robustly retorts: 'By and large I would say kids get it better and get it faster than adults do'.[12]

Dan Rothermel, music director with the Savoy Company of Philadelphia, has directed school productions in the city and proudly told me that his 2001 *Pinafore* at Radnor High School featured an Asian Captain Corcoran, an African American Josephine, and an Indian boatswain singing 'He Is an Englishman'. A number of youth choirs across the United States also have G & S in their repertoire. In 1996 the Simona Valley Children's Chorale from California flew 6,000 miles to Buxton to perform *Gondoliers* with a cast of seventy-three seven- to fourteen-year-olds, of whom sixty were girls. When I asked why so few boys were involved, the responses were 'they don't think it's cool' and 'they can't sing and they don't like dressing up'. The chorale's director cuts out the love duets 'because a tenor and a soprano usually sing them but we've got two sopranos and they are a little bit self-conscious. We also find that these are the boring bits for the children.'[13] As in Britain, there are also educational outreach programmes run by amateur and professional companies. Albert Bergeret says that *Pinafore* goes down particularly well in the New York public schools visited by the New York Gilbert and Sullivan Players:

> I make a two minute speech in which I say it's sort of like the Titanic but we promise you the Pinafore won't sink and then I say it's rather like if some black comedian's son was dating one of the Bush twins—that's what Ralph and Josephine is all about. And whenever you see the guy with the eye-patch, boo![14]

Summer camps have traditionally introduced many North Americans to Gilbert and Sullivan and several are continuing to fulfill this function today. Camp Tecumseh in New Hampshire conforms to the British prep and public school tradition in being all-male. It has done a G & S production every year since 1930, with around seventy boys rehearsing for six weeks for the end-of-camp show in the 'Opera House'. The website notes that 'only the bravest of Tecumseh campers' audition for the female leads and the accompanying photograph of a recent *Pinafore* production certainly suggests that most boys prefer not to cross-dress and retain their own gender on stage. The coeducational Interlochen Arts Camp in Michigan has an equally long tradition of putting on annual G & S shows, with anything up to 200 high school students aged between fourteen and eighteen giving two performances in a 5,000-seater outside auditorium. For over fifty years they have been directed by Clarence 'Dude' Stephenson, who believes in doing the lesser-known works as well as the popu-

FIGURE 7.1 Summer camp Savoyards. The all-male cast of the Camp Tecumseh *Pinafore*, 1999 *(Mark Luff/Camp Tecumseh)*

lar ones—the 2004 production was *Ruddigore*. Since 2003 the Lamplighters and San Francisco Conservatory of Music have cosponsored a G & S summer camp in which around twenty-five ten- to eighteen-year-olds in the San Francisco and Bay areas rehearse and perform a Savoy opera under the direction of Jane Hammett.

Before we leave the school-age scene, it is pleasing to note that the new enthusiasm for G & S in Continental Europe has spawned at least one recent youth production. Pupils of a gymnasium in Parsberg, Bavaria, put on *The Mikado* in 2001 and recorded a CD of the show with both German and English lyrics.

If fewer schools are now performing G & S, the level of interest in universities, certainly in Britain, is as high as it has ever been. There are around twenty university performing societies in the United Kingdom specializing entirely in the Savoy operas and several others which regularly perform them as part of a wider repertoire. As one might expect, Oxford and Cambridge lead the way. The Oxford University Gilbert and Sullivan Society puts on three productions a year (two concert versions and one fully staged show) and every other year it holds a complete sing-through of the entire canon, which usually takes around twenty-seven hours without a break. A recent such marathon included a gender-reversed *Pinafore* to accommodate the girls' criticism that the boys got all the good parts. The society's secretary is entitled the Public Exploder; its treasurer, the Grand Inquisitor; and other committee members are Lords High Everything Else, Flowers of Progress, or Ghostly Ancestors. The website emphasizes that the works are 'enjoyed rather than studied' and 'horseplay is encouraged but not obligatory'. The society did labour for many years under the nickname 'the gays and spuds society' and its officers admit that 'getting a male chorus is difficult. We have to scour the University to get the numbers up' but they also report that 'there seems to be something of a revival on at the moment'.[15] Oxford is the only university society to have appeared at the Buxton

Festival and it has been a notable training ground for promising young singers—Ben Withington-Smith, who did six shows in his first two years as a student; David Menezes, who went to Oxford largely because of its G & S Society; and his sister, Elizabeth Menezes, have all gone on to sing professionally with the D'Oyly Carte and Carl Rosa.

The Cambridge Society conforms to a more common pattern among university groups in mounting one fully staged production and one non-auditioned semi-staged concert performance per year. Since 1974 it has also presented a one-week production every summer in the open-air Minack Theatre in Cornwall. Its website proclaims (quite justifiably) that:

> Joining the CU G & S Society is possibly the single most significant event that you can perform in your entire life. On a par with such life-changing experiences as birth, death and finals. No one experiences the marvellous works of Sir William Schwenck Gilbert and Sir Arthur Seymour Sullivan unaffected.

Some of the longest-lived societies are associated with the so-called red-brick universities—Manchester's was founded in 1951 and Newcastle's the following year—but several newer universities also have thriving societies, like Exeter (founded in 1968) and York (1972), which celebrated its thirtieth birthday with a sing-along *Mary Poppins*. Other English universities with dedicated G & S societies include Bradford, Hull, Lancaster, Nottingham, Southampton, and Surrey. King's College, London, has one of the most recent, founded in 1987. All four of the ancient Scottish universities have thriving performing groups. Edinburgh University Savoy Opera Group, founded in 1962, made a hit at 2003 Edinburgh Festival fringe with 'Murder at the Savoy, a late night comic murder mystery musical in which 'Agatha Christie meets Gilbert and Sullivan' and is in the enviable position of being able to coax plenty of men on to the stage—its 2004 *Pirates* had a male chorus of eighteen. Aberdeen University Gilbert and Sullivan Society was founded in 1976 as 'a more accessible alternative' to the operatic society. Within seven years the operatic society had folded and all its members joined the G & S group. Its 2002 *Hot Mikado*, the society's first departure from traditional productions, was also its most successful show in terms of ticket sales and critical acclaim. St. Andrews University Gilbert and Sullivan Society, founded in 1972, recruited 137 members at the societies' fair at the opening of the academic year 2003–4 and is the richest student society in the university, thanks to sell-out shows which are popular with townspeople as well as students. Students also enthusiastically join the local amateur operatic society for its ventures into G & S. Indeed, the university rector, Clement Freud, look-

FIGURE 7.2 Student G & S. Marco (Bill Calderhead) and Giuseppi (Alex Bradford) do their ironing on the famous Old Course with the Duke of Plaza-Toro (Robert Brignall) looking on in a publicity shot for the St. Andrews University G & S Society *Gondoliers*, 2004 *(George Hollis)*

ing for an event which would unite town and gown, suggested a competitive Gilbert and Sullivan sing-along.

A survey which I carried out of those attending the first meeting of the St. Andrews society in the 2003–4 academic year gives some insight into the background and profile of students interested in performing G & S today. Females outnumbered males by a ratio of three to one, much as they do in most amateur societies. Sixty-eight percent came from the United Kingdom, 16 percent from the United States and 14 percent from elsewhere (South Africa, Canada, Australia, Germany, and Cyprus). Sixty-two percent had encountered or experienced G & S before coming to the university and joining the society, with significantly more North American (85%) than British (60%) students falling into this category. Of those who were already familiar with it, 50 percent had been introduced through their parents, 42 percent through school, and 8 percent by other means (two through the film *Topsy-Turvy* and two through thrilling to Sideshow Bob's rendition of *HMS Pinafore* on *The Simpsons*!). When asked to highlight words which summed up G & S, two-thirds opted for 'fun' and 40 percent characterized it as 'very British' (with one Scot changing this to 'very English'). The great majority of the students were reading arts subjects, with modern languages, international relations, and history as the most popular

subject choices. The Harvard graduate who directed the society's 2003 production of *Sorcerer* identified this as one of the biggest differences between the student G & S scene in the United Kingdom and the United States when I shared
the survey findings with him. In American college societies, he said, there would
be a much higher proportion, and possibly even a preponderance, of science
students, and especially of those majoring in computer science, physics, and
mathematics.

If this survey is representative, it indicates both that schools are still a significant point of entry into G & S (although I suspect that universities are increasingly taking over this role) and that what most attracts students about the Savoy
operas is the 'fun' factor. This latter aspect is summed up in a recent recruiting
poster for the St. Andrews society which reads: 'G & S—what does it mean to
you? Groovy Shows, Great Socialising, Glitter & Sparkle'. It stands alongside the
continuing appeal of G & S to those of a religious and churchgoing disposition.
There is a noticeable overlap at St. Andrews University between membership of
the G & S society and of the chapel choir. The 'godly' bias of those drawn towards performing G & S was brought home to me when I watched a student
production of Sondheim's *Company* in 2001. Several of the cast had also been in
Iolanthe the previous semester, but the Sondheim show was almost entirely
missing the substantial chapel choir element which had featured prominently
in the G & S production—within the peers' chorus alone we had members of
the Christian Union, High Anglicans, Evangelical Baptists, and liberal Presbyterians. I don't want to give the impression that the G & S society is a holy
huddle—far from it, there is plenty of drinking after rehearsals but there is a
sense of camaraderie and a lack of the cliquishness and prima-donna attitudes
that are found in other student performing societies. A recent graduate who has
worked as stage manager for numerous student shows in St. Andrews tells me
that the G & S Society are easily the nicest to work with. Perhaps the 'divine
emollient' qualities of Gilbert and Sullivan do rub off on those who perform
their works!

The strong bonding experience that comes out of performing G & S is certainly found in university societies. It comes partly of those strange warm-up
routines with which student directors seem to be particularly enamoured
(much more so than their adult counterparts in my experience). In the case of
the North American director of the 2003 St. Andrews *Sorcerer* these consisted of
endless repetitions of the phrases 'I'm the best darned mother pheasant plucker
in this whole darned mother pheasant plucking town', 'I know I need unique
New York', and 'I am the visible personification of absolute perfection'. The
British student who directed the following year's *Gondoliers* preferred to get
everyone to do a Freddie Mercury impression and alternately sing 'Popocat-

apetal' and 'Copper Bottomed Kettle' down the scale before reminding the cast that the key to effective performance of G & S is shameless overacting. Student productions also reinforce the centrality of the chorus in G & S. The St. Andrews society has a tradition of a ballot at the end of each show to determine the sexiest male and female performer (after the *Sorcerer* this was changed to 'comeliest'). The voting is restricted to members of the male and female chorus, reinforcing their role as both the key observers and arbiters of each show and carriers of the society's tradition.

Those involved in performing G & S in universities do have to put up with occasional jibes from their contemporaries and it is sometimes difficult to persuade fellow students to come to the shows. The reviewer of a recent Cambridge University production of *Pinafore*, transferred to a cruise liner in the postwar era and with an entirely new libretto by Professor Michael Irwin of the University of Kent, noted that 'the speed with which they rose for the National Anthem bore witness to the age of the audience' and wondered why so few students came to see it.[16] Reviews of G & S productions in student newspapers generally begin with a statement of dread and low expectation based on 'childhood memories of Gilbert and Sullivan consisting entirely of very poor Sunday School renditions to a less than impressed crowd of sleeping pensioners and devout parents' but then often develop into a confession that the experience was much less ghastly than expected and sometimes even report conversion to the genre through the sheer vivacity and exuberance of the performance.

There are at least eighteen college and university societies in the United States exclusively or primarily performing G & S. As one might expect, the majority are located in the northeast. Harvard-Radcliffe and the Massachusetts Institute of Technology mount two productions a year and Boston Academy of Music, the University of Michigan, and the Penn Singers at the University of Pennsylvania each do an annual production. Several student performing groups in this area have recently disbanded, however, including those at Columbia and Boston Universities; the G & S Society at Yale, which was founded in the mid-1980s, is struggling with only around thirty-five members and a lack of money. Its president for the academic year 2003–4, Danielle Ryan, told me that she felt its best hope of survival lay in merging with the much bigger university opera company. A music major who came to G & S through performing *Iolanthe* in 2000 at the Interlochen Summer Camp, she herself finds that 'as a singer it is a lot of fun with good music vocally and ideal for a young voice and as a director you can have a lot of fun with it'. However, it does not seem to have huge performing appeal in Yale, which has played safe by sticking to playing '*Piramikafore*' and *Iolanthe* in rotation and manages to field only a relatively small chorus of three men and five women to each part.[17]

There are still a number of smaller liberal arts colleges regularly performing G & S. Oberlin College in Ohio leads the way, with a lively and long-established group of Gilbert and Sullivan Players who mount annual productions with twenty to thirty students in the cast and a further ten in the orchestra. Set up in 1950, the group has twice been brought back to life after going into abeyance, thanks largely to the efforts of Gayden Wren, who came to Oberlin as a student in 1979 largely because of its G & S credentials and has directed several productions. The 2003–2004 president, Alex Shepherd, reports a recent dramatic increase in student participation while admitting that 'we accept anyone who shows up to audition, although our leads are nearly all opera majors from our Conservatory. The student body loves us and we always sell out performances but the college administration/higher-ups couldn't care less if we existed'.[18]

The United States leads the way in the teaching and performance of G & S among students studying performing arts. In British universities and colleges G & S is almost entirely an extracurricular activity and it is noticeably absent from the curriculum in the growing number of courses and modules on performing arts. Christopher Browne broke this taboo when he put on *Pirates* with his BTech Performing Arts students at Huddersfield College. He says that they appreciated the part-singing as a change from the usual diet of *Grease* and *Fame* but confirms that G & S is seen as far too bourgeois and old-fashioned to feature in this booming part of the higher and further education sector. In the United States, by contrast, Gilbert and Sullivan is regularly taught in colleges in the context of theatre studies and performing arts courses. One consequence of this is that it is seen as a proper subject for academic study (see page 180). Another is the number of professional as well as amateur performing societies that owe their origins to and retain close connections with institutions of higher education. Perhaps the leading example is Ohio Light Opera, founded in 1979 by the College of Wooster, which still 'owns and operates' the company. Its first artistic director, James Stuart, had previously been coming to the college to perform G & S with his own troupe from Kent State University. It is also not unusual for professional performing groups to be resident on campuses. Huntington Theatre Company, resident at Boston University, for example, performed seasons of *Iolanthe*, *Pinafore*, and *Mikado* in the 1990s.

On neither side of the Atlantic, however, is much Gilbert and Sullivan done in specialist music academies and colleges. Peter Mulloy's experience while a student of opera at the Guildhall School of Music in London is typical: 'I was told to be an opera singer you mustn't do Gilbert and Sullivan. It's beneath you. And so I didn't for a few years but then I thought this is nonsense. It's actually not very easy to do and it's very witty and sophisticated so I got back into everything that I'd missed at college.'[19] Richard Shapp encountered the same élitist prejudice while studying singing at Temple University College of Music in Philadelphia, although he did manage to intrude two G & S songs into his graduation recital—'I felt two out of twenty-five would not cause too much upset'. Philip Sokolov, who is training to be an opera singer at San Francisco Conservatory and sings with the Lamplighters, is amazed that G & S is not made much more use of in training singers: 'It is hard to find material better suited to developing the human voice. You can't damage your voice with Sullivan but you can grow and train your voice with it. Yet it is hardly sung at all in American music schools and colleges—there is lots of foreign language stuff and plenty of Purcell and Handel, but no Gilbert and Sullivan'.[20] In the United States, at least, the neglect of Sullivan on the part of those teaching and studying singing does not extend to instrumental studies. John Schuesselin, assistant professor of trumpet at the University of Michigan, recently completed a doctorate at Louisiana State University on ' the use of the cornet in the operettas of Gilbert and Sullivan'. It is difficult to conceive of a similar study being undertaken in the United Kingdom. British music colleges remain infected with the long-standing prejudice against Sullivan although there are some signs of a change in attitude. British Youth Opera, founded in 1987 to enable the United Kingdom's best young singers to work in a professional company on stage, performed *Gondoliers* in 1997 and *The Yeomen of the Guard* in 2001.

If up-and-coming singers are not being exposed to G & S at music college, there are at least opportunities in the United States for them to perform it on a professional basis in their summer vacations. College Light Opera was set up in 1969 to play an annual summer season of musicals and operettas on Cape Cod, Massachusetts. It recruits its thirty-two singers and eighteen orchestral players almost entirely from those studying in music colleges and academies. Over the last thirty-five years it has performed all the Savoy operas. Ohio Light Opera is similarly focused on providing opportunities for performance for emerging young professional singers and instrumentalists. HWS/Rembiko, a Los Angeles–based project, brings conservatory and music students to the Edinburgh Festival. In 2002 they performed *The Pirates of Penzance County*, in which the pirates were all former executives of Enron and other failed businesses who ended the show doing fealty to George Bush, and in 2003 *The Mikado County USA*, with three little maids from Harvard Business School.

There is also an increasing recognition of the educative and community building potential of G & S among those of more mature years. Courses devoted to studying and singing G & S have been among the most popular elements of the Elderhostel movement in the United States. One of the first, held at an Episcopal camp and conference center at Ivoryton, Connecticut, in 1987, involved fifty senior citizens rehearsing and performing a fully costumed

Pinafore in just two weeks under the direction of Robert Cumming. The format switched in 1991 to one-week camps with workshops, lectures, videos, discussions, quizzes, and rehearsals for a final night concert involving extracts from a particular opera. The 2004 Elderhostel catalogue lists eight G & S courses in centers as far afield as Vermont, Colorado, New Hampshire, and Georgia. Since 1996 Ralph MacPhail and Deborah Lyon have run two week-long courses every summer at Ivoryton—one for newcomers which concentrates on the '*Pi-ramikafore*' trinity and another for old hands which features the lesser known operas. Both attract many people in their seventies and eighties and one lady in her mid-nineties who travels from California to Connecticut every year to sing soprano principal roles. One of the highlights of each week is 'The Great Elder-hostel Song Parody Contest', where participants work on producing a parody of a particular song—which leads us nicely to the subject of the next chapter.

EIGHT

◇

THINGS ARE SELDOM WHAT THEY SEEM: PARODIES, SPOOFS, AND SPIN-OFFS

Few works in the English language have been more parodied than the songs of Gilbert and Sullivan. There are several reasons for this. Because they are word-led and so teeming with wit and clever rhyming structures, they lend themselves to adaptation for all sorts of purposes and occasions. The songs are eminently singable and memorable—especially the patter songs—providing a wonderful framework on which to hang new lyrics appropriate to all sorts of subjects and occasions. They are also ubiquitous and widely known and recognized, having entered deep into the folk consciousness of English-speaking peoples in a way that has also been true of hymns, the only other literary genre which has been parodied on anything like the same scale. But whereas it is now rare to hear parodies of hymns—this particular art having reached its apogee in the trenches of the First World War—it is still common to come across politicians, journalists, and satirists rewriting the words of 'When I Was a Lad' or 'I've Got a Little List'. In this respect, as in so many others, the works of Gilbert and Sullivan have long outlasted those of their contemporaries and continue to provide inspiration and to influence new creative activity well over a century after they were written.

It helps, of course, that they are out of copyright. But even during their lifetime, parodies of Gilbert and Sullivan abounded, with Prime Minister William Ewart Gladstone being a favourite subject:

> A grand and verbose old man,
> A spout-as-he-goes old man,
> A highly sophistical,
> Non-atheistical,
> 'Come under my gamp' old man.

When a government committee interviewed the director of the British Museum in 1904 and asked him to describe his duties he did so in the form of an adaptation of 'Rising Early in the Morning' from *The Gondoliers*. I am not sure how many 'official utterances' since then have been made in similar form but G & S parodies have regularly enlivened political speeches and satirical journalism throughout the twentieth century.

John Cannon, a retired dentist from Sussex, has been collecting G & S parodies since the late 1960s and almost certainly has the largest collection in the world. His eight bulging and ever-expanding ring folders represent the tip of a gigantic iceberg but provide a useful guide as to the nature and extent of this particular aspect of the Gilbert and Sullivan phenomenon. Certain songs have particularly lent themselves to parodying. There are forty-nine versions of 'When a Felon's Not Engaged in His Employment' in John Cannon's collection, forty-eight of 'When I Was a Lad I Served a Term', thirty-two of 'Tit Willow', and twenty-eight of 'When You're Lying Awake with a Dismal Headache'. The most parodied songs are Ko-Ko's 'Little List', with 104 appearances, and 'I Am the Very Model of a Modern Major-General', with 130. There is a long tradition of updating 'The Little List' for stage performances of *The Mikado* and it was just about the only song that the old D'Oyly Carte management allowed to be changed. There is a learned article, if not a doctoral thesis, to be written just about the terms that have been substituted for 'the lady novelist' over the years—indeed, someone has probably done it. One of the more dedicated of the 'inner brotherhood' wrote following the publication of my *Complete Annotated Gilbert and Sullivan* to tell me that John Reed used the term 'referendumist' on 1 April 1975 and that Peter Pratt sang 'devolutionist' in a live broadcast performance from the Royal Albert Hall on 2 December 1978. More recent substitutions include 'the Karaokeist', 'the teenage vocalist', and the 'Cherie socialist'. Richard Suart has engaged in more substantial reworkings of the list to include

> All those who take their hols in gites and think it rather chic
> To drive at over ninety in their Vorsprung durch Technik . . .
>
> And TV screen evangelists who preach from morn till night,
> Who when the camera's off them bed everything in sight.

Among other miscreants singled out in parodies in the Cannon collection are 'the people who with Christmas cards send sheets of family news' (Rachael Keegan, 1996), 'private fitness coaches who develop people's pecs' (Faye Greensburg), 'the people who in parking lots can't park in just one space' (Ed Glazier for Stanford Savoyards, 1998), and 'the telemarket salesman always calling when you dine' (Sandy Rovner, 1998).

The Major-General's song has been adapted to apply, among many other categories, to the modern scientologist, modern Unitarian, Microsoft executive, Luddite on the internet, paediatric specialist, trendy faux bisexual, stuffy modern physicist, and 'girl picked up by Dr. Who'. Tom Lehrer set the entire table of chemical elements (or at least all those of which news had come to Harvard) to its tune and in 1977 the *New England Journal of Medicine* did the same with the pharmacological formulary, beginning 'There's Aldomet and Atronid and Antivert and Atarax'. Humphrey Carpenter adapted it for his rather dismissive review of Michael Finch's 1993 biography of Gilbert and Sullivan:

> I am the very model of an up-to-date biographer,
> I put a life on paper with the speed of a stenographer,
> My writing has the polish of a Hollywood scenario,
> With minimum research, just from the sources secondary-oh.
> I've never once reflected on my subject's ideology,
> I really can't be bothered over motive or psychology.
> I like the exclamation mark; my manner is declarative—
> It's easier to write that way than bother with the narrative.
> In short, though I've the patience of a Polaroid photographer,
> I am the very model of an up-to-date biographer.[1]

Several of the best parodies of this song relate to the more obsessive breed of G & S fans. Robin Beaumont's version for Savoynet members begins:

> I am the true embodiment of modern Savoy Nettering
> I follow G & S to Buxton, Inverness or Kettering.

Andrew Crowther catches the pedantic tendency with his:

> I am the very model of a G & S enthusiast,
> I know their famous heroines, both puritan and floozy-assed:
> When people say that *Trial by Jury* was their debut opera,
> I quickly educate them on the facts that are more properer.
> Although my vocal range is best described as one-note baritone
> And all my vocal efforts murder melody and harry tone,
> When I hear someone singing 'Little Buttercup' I criticize
> And point out all their errors—even those of itty-bitty size.

There is also this splendid definition of a patter song from Arthur Robinson:

> A patter song is something of incredible velocity
> Considered by some singers an unspeakable atrocity.
> The singer fills his lungs with air as far as they are fillable
> Then rattles off a string of rhymes, each one a polysyllable.

The affection felt by many Savoyards for the old D'Oyly Carte has expressed itself in several parodies of which perhaps the best is Jim Linwood's catalogue of the contents of the company's props baskets:

> If you want a receipt for that G & S mystery,
>   Known to the world as a D'Oyly Carte prop,
> Take all the remarkable oddments in history,
>   List them in verse and sing till you drop.
>
> The cloak used by Corcoran, hiding at dead of night,
>   Seeking to thwart the two lovers' escape—
> The 'cat' which he wielded when they sought to wed at night—
>   Ambrose's book of joke, jesting and jape—
> A philtre-filled teapot which fuddled the villagers—
>   Blindfold for Elsie when wed in The Tower—
> Dark lanterns doled out to piratical pillagers—
>   Bell which tolled twelve to mark Fairfax's hour—
> Three spare ladies' gowns, as discovered by Florian,
> Coins to bribe Pooh-Bah, his family's historian,
> Night wear for Stanley, exhorting each constable,
> 'Cello for Jane, future Duchess of Dunstable,
>   Willis' rifle, and also his wings,
>   Motley collection of very odd things.
>   Add to this list more knick-knacks miscellaneous,
>   All very vital—though most seem extraneous,
>   Brolly, a poignard, the list never stops
>   Of the items you find in the D'Oyly Carte props.
>
> If you want a receipt for that property catalogue
>   Buy all the remnants from country house sales,
> Write down what you've bought in a tongue twisting patter log,
>   Setting by Sullivan—that never fails.

A rope for sad Nanki-Poo, feeling obsessional,
   Seeking to bring a swift end to his life—
A large bunch of keys for a jailer professional—
   Raffle book tickets to choose Bunthorne's wife—
The teacups they use for the picnic at Ploverleigh—
   Union flag waved by p'licemen, when beat,
A mirror for Yum-Yum who saw she looked love-ly,
   Sausage rolls Ludwig and friends had to eat.
Uniforms bright that Jane said stood out garishly,
Chancellor's wig as he pattered nightmarishly
Telling the world he was cold as an icicle,
Loud suit of dittoes and Daly's old bicycle,
   Spinning wheel, Edwin's and Nanki's guitars,
   Case found by Blanche—which was full of cigars.
      Add to this list more knick-knacks miscellaneous,
      All very vital, though most seem extraneous,
      Flageolets, truncheons—the list never stops
      Of the items you find in the D'Oyly Carte props.

It is not surprising that G & S parodies have appealed to satirists and comedians. *Mad* magazine has published at least two cartoon features on U.S. politicians using adaptations of well-known Savoy songs—'a Day with JFK' in 1961 and 'White House Follies' in 1972. The American comedian Allan Sherman wrote and performed numerous parodies, including 'When I Was a Lad I Went to Yale', as did the British comedians Frank Muir and Dennis Norden ('A bus inspector I / And wise to all the fiddles') and Ronnie Corbett and Ronnie Barker ('Take a pair of bloodshot eyes / and a nose that's round and red / and a pair of loose false teeth'). Musicians have also been much given to parodying songs from the Savoy operas. In 1970 a distinguished group of singers, including Peter Pears, Norma Burrows, and John Carol Case, recorded a skit on the little list 'They Never Will B.Mus'. Written by Philip Cramer, it includes among those who will not graduate with a music degree 'the pianist who practises with doors all open wide' and 'the soprano with arpeggios that no one can abide'.[2] Andrew Davis, principal conductor of the BBC Symphony Orchestra, rounded off his speeches on the last night of the 1992 and 2000 Promenade concerts with parodies of the Major-General's song, concluding on the latter occasion with the couplet:

And yet I have been very glad, and here is no duplicity,
To play a part in quintessential British eccentricity.

At a dinner held in Cardiff in 2000 to celebrate Sir Charles Mackerras's fifty-year association with Welsh National Opera, three G & S parodies were sung by Richard Suart, including this fine one by Simon Rees:

> In enterprise of musical kind
> Where there's accelerando
> I lead my orchestra from behind
> To force a ritardando:
> For when my orchestra runs away
> There's none so hard to scare as
> That celebrated, cultivated, under-rated musico
> The great Sir Charles Mackerras![3]

As one might expect, there are a good number of parodies with an ecclesiastical flavour. Some of the best are of Anglican/Episcopalian provenance, like these two of songs from *Pirates* which come, respectively, from St Mark's Episcopal Church, Altadena, California, and the Lent 1985 issue of the *Anglican Digest*:

> Although we seem irreverent, we are not devoid of feeling
> And ev'ry Sunday morning you will find us gladly kneeling.
> It is for truth we search and we expect one day to win it.
> For what, we ask, is Church without a touch of ritual in it?
> Hail, Liturgy, thou heav'n-born dove,
> Thou blessed structure from above.
> Hail, Prayerbook trebly eloquent,
> All hail, all hail, divine emollient!
>
> We are the very model of today's Episcopalian,
> We're broad and high and low and wide and somewhat Baccanalian.
> We're mystical, political, we're secular and clerical;
> We can be charismatic but we seldom get hysterical.
> We're traditional and modernist and socialist-monarchical;
> We're protestant and catholic but not too hierarchical;
> About ordaining women we are teeming with a lot of views
> As well as on the prayer book that our bishops say we gotta use.

Another parody of the Major-General's song from St. Mark's Church includes the wonderful line 'Religion, like suspenders, should be there but not detectable'. The author and scholar Vera Rich has supplied a Roman Catholic feminist version:

She is the very model of a modern mother-general,
She's into every current trend, both long-term and ephemeral,
She hates all sexist language, so cites heroines <u>her</u>-storical,
From Deborah to Germaine Greer in order categorical.
On female ordination she is utterly fanatical,
And longs to see her nuns arrayed in chasubles hieratical,
In letters to *The Tablet* on this theme she'll never miss a trick—
For privately she knows that she could well grace an archbishopric.

Liturgical up-dating is a task she tackles merrily,
Writes 'OK!' or 'I dig it!' for the biblical 'Yea, verily!'
With plainchant and polyphony alike she's never sympathized
(The music in her chapel is Japonically synthesized!)
On pilgrimage of protest she leads out her whole community
(Informing first the media of a photo-opportunity).
She has no use for Fatima, nor Lourdes amidst its smiling vales
But dreams about the golden years at Greenham and at
Fylingdales.[4]

In a rather different ecclesiastical context, G & S parodies have also been used at memorial services. At the service held in Westminster Abbey in March 2001 to commemorate the life of the great Kent and England cricketer Colin Cowdrey, Richard Suart was accompanied by the Abbey choir in Sir Tim Rice's adaptation of 'Behold the Lord High Executioner':

> Behold a cricketer most suitable
> As personage with noble rank and title,
> Whose sportsmanship is indisputable
> Which on and off the field is simply vital!
> Defer, defer, to a model English cricketer.[5]

Newspaper journalists and politicians regularly have recourse to rewriting Gilbert's lyrics to make a topical point. When the catering magnate Lord Forte tried to buy the Savoy Hotel in 1985, the *Financial Times* devoted a whole article to an extended G & S spoof which alluded to his humble origins:

> A caterer am I
> Not just with ice cream cafés,
> English, Welsh and Taffies,
> I tempt the world to buy.[6]

Versions of Ko-Ko's 'little list' song have featured in two recent British party political conferences, with Tory social security secretary Peter Lilley in 1992 at-
tacking benefit offenders, such as 'young ladies who get pregnant / just to join
the housing list / and dads who won't support the kids / of ladies they have
kissed' and Liberal Democrat leader Paddy Ashdown in 1998 naming those MPs
who could easily be dispensed with in a slimmed-down House of Commons. In
1996 Virginia Bottomley, heritage secretary in John Major's government, treated
delegates to the Conservative Party conference to this parody of 'When I Was a
Lad' directed at Tony Blair, the newly appointed leader of the Labour Party:

> As a boy he went to public school
> And he learned one very important rule
> If you say what people want to hear
> Your advancement soon will be very, very clear.
>
> He used that rule so ruthlesslee
> That now he is the ruler of the Labour Partee.
>
> In Islington some time he passed
> And adopted all the manners of the chattering class,
> He drank white wine and he acted cool
> And he sent his son to an opt-out school.
>
> He went in style to Tuscanee
> And now he is the ruler of the Labour Partee.[7]

Songs from the Savoy operas have long been adapted for use as advertising
jingles. Shortly after *The Mikado*'s first performance Lever Brothers' adverts featured a trio of Sunlight soap tablets singing 'Three little aids to health are we'.
In the 1950s Martyn Green recorded a series of radio commercials for Camp-
bell's soup based on the Major-General's song. They were apparently never
used, despite the catchy opening: 'Begin with oxtail, tasty beef, and then cream
of pota-ato, / And consommé of corn, Scotch broth, and onion, and tomato'. In
1962 all general practitioners on the medical register in the United Kingdom
were sent a booklet, *My Goodness! My Gilbert and Sullivan!*, promoting the
health-giving benefits of Guinness. It included nine parodies, of which the best
were the two from the *Mikado*, 'On a tree by a river a little Tou-can / Sang 'Guinness, my goodness, my Guinness!' and 'The Barley we plant in the Spring, Yum,
yum, / Breathes promise of liquor divine'. The advertisements also appeared in
Country Life magazine. D'Oyly Carte programmes in the late 1970s and early

1980s carried advertisements for North Thames Gas and Barclays Bank in the form of song parodies. Among Barclays' better offerings was:

> Three little maids from school are we,
> Barclays Bank will help all three,
> They give students banking free!
> Three little maids from school.
> Barclays welcomes either sex,
> Barclaycard guarantees our cheques
> Without we'd turn into nervous wrecks,
> Three little maids from school!

More recently, eagle-eared G & S aficionados have reported hearing 'When I Was a Lad' featured in a television commercial for Terry's Chocolate Orange and being hijacked to sell Coldseal Double Glazing:

> When I get home from another hard day,
> I like to relax in a special way.
> I take the paper and a cup of tea
> And I go and sit in my conservatory

In the United States, songs from the Savoy operas have been rewritten with the more exalted aim of stimulating patriotic and communal feeling. The substitution of 'Hail, hail, the gang's all here' for 'Come friends who plough the sea' is the best known example of this practice but it is not the most uplifting. That honour surely goes to these new lyrics by James Wilder for 'When Britain Really Ruled the Waves' written to be sung by Boy Scouts:

> For sacred law from east to west,
> Our banner bright shall wave.
> No base design shall flourish here
> Against the land we all revere
> Whose men are strong and brave.
> Hold steady, then, our flag shall stand
> For law and order on the land,
> In freedom's name our flag shall stand
> For law and order on the land.[8]

In a rather different vein, some American Episcopalians have been known to sing the *Stabat Mater* ('At the Cross Her Station Keeping') to the tune of 'My

Eyes Are Fully Open' from *Ruddigore,* which has also been pressed into service by Barbara Heroux of the Lamplighters for a trio for John the Baptist, Salome, and Herod. Participants in the 2004 Sullivan Society festival were treated to renditions of the hymn 'Abide with Me' to the tune of 'When I Was a Lad' and 'The King of Love My Shepherd Is' to 'In Enterprise of Martial Kind'. Richard Sturch, formerly vicar of Islip in Oxfordshire, has published a hymn set to the company promoter's song from *Utopia Limited,* 'Some Seven Men Form an Association'. It is not the most obvious number in the Savoy canon for congregational singing but the result is not without effect:

> Some think it won't be hard to follow Jesus,
> And stroll along through life without a care:
> And then they find a stretch that really teases
> And give up when they're only half-way there.
> It's silly not to do a calculation;
> Who wants to look a fool to every eye?
> But when God offers you an invitation
> It's sillier to let that chance go by!
> So determine not to shirk,
> And prepare yourself for work,
> For a golden opportunity's been given;
> It will cost you quite a lot—
> Maybe everything you've got—
> But you'll find that it's the only way to heaven! [9]

It is not just these parodies of individual songs still cropping up in the oddest places that prove the survival powers and durability of Gilbert and Sullivan. So, too, do the extraordinary range of treatments to which their works have been subjected. There is a long tradition of performing bizarre and heavily adapted versions of the Savoy operas—there was a cross-dressed *Pinafore* as early as 1888, and in 1939 New Yorkers had a choice of 'Swing', 'Hot', or 'Red' versions of the *Mikado*—but the last forty-five years have seen a mushrooming of these kinds of production.

Inevitably, the *Mikado* has been the most often subjected to makeover and reworking. The 1962 British film *The Cool Mikado,* directed by Michael Winner, was one of the first to take advantage of the ending of copyright. Set on a flight from Tokyo to the United States, its hero, Hank Mikado, the son of the chief justice of the high court in Illinois, has fled to Japan to escape the girl that his father wanted him to marry and fallen in love with Yum-Yum, a student at Tokyo Art School. The cast included Stubby Kaye, Frankie Howerd, Lionel Blair, Pete

Murray, and Tommy Cooper. Only nine songs from the original opera were used, including a 'Tit Willow Twist' played by the John Barry Seven. A *Black Mikado* was staged in London in 1975, with Michael Denison as the only white member of the cast. In the United States, the *Mod Mikado*, set in Ko-Ko's Topless Bar, was staged in Las Vegas in 1970, and the *Incommunicado Mikado* performed in California at the height of the Watergate scandal in 1973 featured Pat-Pat (Pat Nixon), Nanki-Poo III (John Dean III), Katartha (Martha Mitchell), and the Mikado (Richard Nixon).

The 1986 *Hot Mikado*, first performed at Ford's Theatre, Washington, had elements of the 1939 'hot' and 'swing' versions but was essentially a new show with Gilbert's book and lyrics heavily adapted by David Bell and the music transformed into 'the sweltering swingtime sound of jitterbug, jazz, blues, and Gospel' by Rob Bowman. Set in a 1940s American nightclub, the Mikado became a slick tap dancer from Harlem and the three little maids a take-off of the Andrews Sisters. The accompaniment was provided by a six-piece jazz band and the dialogue bore little relation to the original—Ko-Ko's remark to Yum-Yum about Katisha 'But my good girl, have you seen her? She's something appalling' becoming 'I could take her face, put it in dough and make gorilla cookies'. The *Washington Post* critic, noting that it made Papp's *Pirates* 'look like a piece of scholarship', hailed 'a show for those who've always thought Gilbert and Sullivan were too fussy and precious for their own good' but warned that 'Grandma may have trouble humming along'.[10] Revived in the United States in 1994 and 2002, the *Hot Mikado* came to London in 1995.

Among adaptations of the *Mikado* performed by professional companies in the United States in the 1990s, three in particular stand out for both inventiveness and outrageousness. Paper Mill Playhouse, a leading theatre in New Jersey, presented *Mikado Inc.*, set in the corporate headquarters of a Japanese high-tech company where Mr. Ko-ko is manager of personnel, Mr. Pooh-Bah, senior manager, and Mr. Pish-Tush, a management trainee. Frankie-Poo is a young rock star chosen to promote the company's new product line and Yum-Yum, Peep-Bo, and Pitti-Sing are three office temps. Ko-ko's song became 'I've Got a Floppy Disk' and the musical numbers included the Samurai Stomp and the Teahouse of the Sliding Screens. In 1993 Virginia Opera presented *The NOT Mikado*, a 'hip-hop opera' set in contemporary Japan and patterned on *Saturday Night Live*. 'A Wandering Minstrel' was sung on roller blades, 'Young Man, Despair' turned into a rhumba, 'To Sit in Solemn Silence' performed as a rap, and 'Tit Willow' rendered as a country and western number. The Mikado was made to look like Darth Vader and Katisha like Tina Turner, while Nanki-Poo became a studded-leather punk and Katisha a drag queen. Director Worth Gardner explained: 'G & S cries out for presentation in modern hip-hop style.

When I hear one of the patter songs, I think of Gilbert as one of the original rap artists'.[11] In 1996 Interact Theatre Company in Washington performed a slightly more orthodox *Mikado* set at the famous Scottish golfing hotel Gleneagles. The music was largely untouched but the story was changed to centre on the arrival in Titi-on-the-Poo of Nanki McPoo, a wandering minstrel and golf caddy, fleeing the advances of Caddysha. The Mikado became Queen Victoria and Ko-Ko a be-kilted candidate for the Scottish Labour Party. A production by Cleveland Lyric Opera in 2004 relocated the setting to Tudor England with the Mikado as Henry VIII, Katisha as Elizabeth I, and Pooh-Bah as Cardinal Wolsey. Among recent British adaptations is *Maid in Japan* (2000), which uses the classic songs to tell the story of the lives and loves of the workforce in an electronics components factory, and a production set in a northern working men's club and entirely rewritten by Gary Winn in Geordie dialect ('Three Bonny Lasses from the Toon Are We' is probably sufficient to convey the flavour), which won an Arts Council grant for its premiere in Durham in 2003.

HMS Pinafore has also had a long tradition of pirated and parodied versions. The American Negro Light Opera Association's *Tropical Pinafore* in 1940 was the first of several productions which have transferred the opera's location from Portsmouth to the Caribbean. A recent example is Interact Theater's 1995 staging which featured Buttercup peddling rum and gyrating dancers summoning up spirits. George Kaufman's 1945 *Hollywood Pinafore*, which made Sir Joseph Porter the head of Pinafore Pictures, Ralph Rackstraw an aspiring writer, Dick Live-Eye a theatrical agent, and Buttercup a gossip columnist called Louhedda Hopsons, was revived in London in 1998. *Pinafore* has frequently been rewritten to varying extents in the style of *Star Wars* and *Star Trek*. There were amateur productions of *HMS Trek-a-star* in the 1970s and in 1983 Bev Grant wrote a complete parody, *HMS DeathStar*, which opens with Darth Vader singing 'When I was a lad, I went to school / To a Jedi Master who I thought was cool'. Several more recent productions have been set on the *Starship Pinafore*. For a 1997 North Staffordshire production, director Chris Monk changed the setting to a fast-food restaurant where Sid Corcoran is undermanager and Dave Coleslaw a waiter and an inspection visit is being made by Sir Joseph Snorter, KFC, the Minister of Food. In 2004 the Watermill Theatre, Newbury, put on a swing version set on a troop ship in mid-Atlantic in 1944. Buttercup became a singing group called the Buttercup Sisters and Josephine was made the daughter of a British band leader worried about her desire to marry an American GI.

Also worthy of mention in the context of offbeat treatments of *Pinafore* is Michael Savage's hugely successful gay version, which opened in Los Angeles in September 2001, ran for nine months, and then went on to Chicago and New

York in 2003. It is the first overtly gay reworking of G & S and could be a sign of things to come. The music is left intact but the plot-line, lyrics, and dialogue are substantially changed. *Pinafore* is a ship in an alternative gay U.S. Navy created by a liberally inclined Democratic president. The entire cast is male, apart from Bitter Butterball, and the ship's company are all gay with the exception of Dick Dockstrap. Captain Cornikit dresses his transvestite son, Joseph, in drag to please Senator Barney Crank, secretary of the gay navy, who arrives on board with a trio of drag queens in tow. Joseph secretly loves Dockstrap, who believes him to be a girl. In the end everything is resolved with the revelation that the Captain and Dick were switched at birth and that the Captain is really hetero-sexual and Dick gay. I fear that most of the lyrics are rather too racy to quote in this book. A brief example will suffice:

> A gay male tar is a hunky stud,
> And he's open to new ideas.
> With his six-pack tight and trim
> From his hours at the gym
> There are none so hot as he.

Joseph Papp's influential makeover of *The Pirates of Penzance* and Opera della Luna's highly successful *Parson's Pirates* have already been discussed (pages 76, 86). There have also been more radical parodies and reworkings of *Pirates*. One of the more original, rendered in the style of Dr. Seuss, was written over the course of a few free nights in 1999 by Daniel Florip while an undergraduate at the University of Michigan in the hope of fostering a love for G & S among the younger generation. Jana Hollingsworth's *The Star Wars of Penzance* begins with the chorus: 'Zap, oh zap the rebel planet, / Zing, oh zing the asteroid'. In 1995 Troupers Light Opera Company performed *The Pirates of Pittsburgh* and in 1999 Virginia Opera presented a radically rewritten version directed by Worth Gardner and set in London in 1942 in the middle of the Blitz.

A substantial reworking of *The Gondoliers* by John Doyle opened at the Water-mill Theatre in Newbury in April 2001 and went on to play a brief season in the West End. Relocated to an Italian restaurant in London's Little Venice, it told the story of the son of an Italian Mafia boss betrothed as a baby to the daugh-ter of a Chicago gangster. Much of the dialogue was changed to produce new aphorisms such as 'life is like spaghetti—a complicated, mixed up tangle' and the lyrics came in for similar treatment with 'Dry Martini' being rhymed with 'Contadini'. The act 2 gavotte was turned into a tango, and Sullivan's tunes were crooned rather than sung by the eight actor-musicians who made up the band, as well as the chorus and principals, both singing and playing a variety of instruments on stage. The *Financial Times* praised it for being 'non-camp G & S' and the *Daily Telegraph* hailed 'a genuine reinvention of our beloved G & S' while warning that 'the Taliban tendency among G & S supporters will suffer apoplexy when they see this show'.[12] I am afraid I did and left in the interval asking 'why?'

Iolanthe has been relocated to Edinburgh and the new Scottish parliament by Aberdeen Opera Company and updated to cover another recent British political debate by the veteran satirist Ned Sherrin. His *Ratepayers' Iolanthe*, written with Alistair Beaton and staged in the Queen Elizabeth Hall, London, in 1984 was inspired by the Conservative Government's plan to abolish the Greater London Council (GLC). It featured a 'red' Strephon representing Ken Livingstone, the GLC leader, and a Queen of the Fairies who was imprisoned in the Tower by her chief minister, Margaret Thatcher. Sherrin, who was also responsible with Caryl Brahms for a substantially rewritten version of *Pinafore* at the Nottingham Playhouse in 1982, devised another G & S spoof in 1985 on the subject of the GLC's plight. The cast of the *Metropolitan Mikado* included Katisha, Countess of Grantham, based on Margaret Thatcher, Boy Ken, the former council leader now disguised as a wandering minstrel, and three little maids who were former page 3 pinups in the *Sun*.

Opera della Luna has given *Ruddigore* a substantial makeover (see page 87) and in 2003 Rug Opera produced a version in the style of the 'Carry On' films so popular in the 1960s. The setting is transferred from Cornwall to Essex so that Basingstoke becomes Basildon, Rose Maybud the ultimate Essex girl, and Dicky Dauntless a cruise liner entertainments officer. A British Telecom London Light Opera Group 1991 production relocated *The Sorcerer* among the oil barons of Dallas, with Marvin Pointdextre, Sapphire Sangazure, 'Deliverance' Daly, a Southern preacher, and 'J. R'. Wells. There have also been more composite parodies and pastiches taking in several operas, notably the eighty-minute animated film *Dick Deadeye* made in 1975 and featuring the cartoons of Ronald Searle. With characters, songs, and plotlines borrowed from eight Savoy operas, its plot centred on Dick Deadeye's quest to recover the 'Ultimate Secret', England's most important possession which has been stolen and is eventually revealed to be the maxim that 'it's love that makes the world go round'.

Among the most original and successful reworkings of the Savoy operas have been those performed by the G & S Yiddish Light Opera Company (see page 124). The first opera to be given a Yiddish makeover was *Pinafore* in 1952. Because there is no Yiddish word for 'pinafore', the translator Miriam Walowit went for the nearest equivalent and called it *Der Shirtz* (the apron). In the 1970s Al Grand, a New York schoolteacher, realized that there might be an audience for

Yiddish productions of the most popular Savoy operas and it is his versions of 'Piramikafore' that the Long Island-based company has been performing since the mid-1980s. In their *Pinafore*, the ship flies the Israeli flag and Buttercup becomes Kleyne Puterschisl selling her wares of bagels, knishes, and latkes (potato cakes). The romance between Labe (Ralph) and Rokhl (Josephine) seems doomed because of Labe's Gentile status but all is resolved when the boatswain reveals that 'Er Iz a Guter Yid'. The Yiddish version of *Pirates* is entitled *Di Yam Gazlonim* (the Robbers of the Sea) and tells of how Fayvl (Frederic) was apprenticed by a friend of his mother's to *gazlonim* (robbers) whom, with their beards and hats, she mistook for *rabonim* (rabbis). In *Der Yiddisher Mikado* Ko-Ko is an East Side tailor and Pooh-Bah becomes Shmir Mir ('Bribe me'). Reviewing a 2003 production of this work, the classical music writer Lawrence Johnson reflected that 'Gilbert and Sullivan's operettas are musical titanium, indestructible even when subject to a variety of spins, transcriptions, and cultural head-on collisions'.[13]

Alongside these and the many other 'head-on collisions' to which the Savoy operas have been subjected there have also been a plethora of classic works of English literature rewritten as if by Gilbert and Sullivan. Tom Aitken's *W. S. Gilbert Tries His Hand at Chaucer* includes 'I Am the Very Model of a Medieval Prioress' and a version of the little list for the Wife of Bath beginning 'As some day it may happen that a lover might be found'. Charles Dickens's *A Christmas Carol* has been reworked to include adaptations of G & S songs both by David Spicer in Australia and by Gayden Wren in the United States, in a version which begins 'On a street in December / a little old man / snapped 'Humbug, bah humbug, bah humbug'. Wren's version has so far received over 200 performances around the world, including one for UN peacekeeping troops in Macedonia in 1995. Among other David Spicer productions are a Savoy opera-style version of the legend of St. George and the Dragon set in the kingdom of Barataria, Gilbert's play *Foggerty's Fairy* set to Sullivan tunes, and a reconstruction of the original *Patience* with rival curates in place of poets. At least two attempts have been made to render *The Lord of the Rings* in G & S style—one begins with a chorus of hobbits singing 'If you want to know who we are / We are gentlemen of the shire' and introduces Gandalf as 'A wand'ring Wizard, I'. Nick Olcott managed to combine Gilbert and Sullivan with their great fictional contemporary in his 1997 play *Sherlock Holmes and the Case of the Purloined Detective*. The plot involves the great detective being brought in to investigate the pirated American version of *Patience* and provides an excuse for thirty songs from different Savoy operas to be sung, mostly straight but with occasional adaptation, as when Inspector Lestrade reflects that 'When an amateur detective steals the

fun / A policeman's lot is not a happy one'. Gilbert and Sullivan–themed pan-
tomimes include *The Sleeping Beauty of the Savoy,* by ex-D'Oyly Carters Cynthia Morey and John Fryatt (1979), and *Jack Point and the Beans Talk* (1982).
Even Shakespeare has not escaped. In 1998 *A Midsummer Night's Dream* was
rewritten in the style of a Savoy opera.

There have also been numerous plays about Gilbert and Sullivan that use
their songs and music. Perhaps the most successful is *Tarantara! Tarantara!,*
first performed in the Bristol Old Vic in 1975 and set backstage during rehearsals
at the Savoy Theatre in 1888. *The Savoyards,* a full-length comic opera by Donald Madgwick, uses music from the Savoy opera scores arranged by Stanford
Robinson. More bizarrely, a production by the Vienna Volksoper in 1983 featured Gilbert and Sullivan conversing with a drag Queen Victoria; and *William
Schwenck and Arthur Who?*— performed at the National Arts Centre, Ottawa,
in 1978, and subtitled 'What if G & S had written their works in the twentieth
century?'—turned John Wellington Wells into a drug dealer and the three little
maids into clones of the Andrews Sisters. *I Have a Song to Sing O,* a one-man
musical play about original D'Oyly Carte patter man George Grossmith written by Melvyn Morrow, was first performed by Anthony Warlow and has since
toured across Australia starring Dennis Olsen. In the United Kingdom Leon
Berger and Simon Butteriss have performed one-man shows based on Grossmith's life. In the United States Gayden Wren has recently written *Very Truly
Yours, Gilbert and Sullivan,* which uses songs from the operas, letters, and mem-
oirs to tell the story of their collaboration.

Pastiches of the Savoy operas written for performance by schools constitute
yet another fascinating subspecies in this wonderful world of G & S take-off and
parody. *The Batsman's Bride* was written by Percy Heywood and Donald Hughes,
respectively music master and headmaster of Rydal School in North Wales,
where it had its first performance in 1948. Broadcast on BBC Radio in 1975, it
has since been taken up by several amateur operatic societies and was recorded
on CD by the Manx Gilbert and Sullivan Society in 2003. It is set in the English
village of Cattlecud, where the captain of the local team, George Cowshott, is in
love with the daughter of the squire, Sir Roderick Celluloid, who wants her to
marry a member of the Marylebone Cricket Club (MCC). Cowshott plays such
a splendid innings for the village against a visiting MCC side that Celluloid is
happy to have him as a son-in-law. There are some wonderful pastiches of Savoy
songs, notably 'Sir Rupert Murgatroyd, His Leisure and His Riches' and 'When
Britain Really Ruled the Waves', and the whole piece is full of innocence and
charm and deserves much wider performance.

A more recent work for schools even more directly descended from the Savoy
operas is the splendid *Pinafore Pirates,* written in 1999 by Malcolm Sircom, who

FIGURE 8.1 Pinafore Pirates—the Major-General, Duke of Plaza-Toro, Mikado, Admiral, Iolanthe, and Princess Ida in the St. Katharine's School production, 2000 (*Author's collection*)

felt that with G & S being increasingly rarely attempted by schools, a modern humorous parody might fill the gap and introduce pupils to a flavour of their style. It introduces the character of Daisy Corcoran, daughter of the erstwhile *Pinafore* captain and his wife Buttercup, who sets out to thwart a band of female pirates on the island of Paragonia. She enlists a motley crew including the Mikado, the Sorcerer, the Major-General, the Admiral, the Duke of Plaza-Toro, and a team of British policemen who enter singing that 'full of British pride is the heart that beats inside every policeman's bullet proof vest'. Just about the only imported character not found in G & S is the pirates' Irish cook, Sam O'Nella, a role in which my son made his theatrical debut. The play ends with the pirates forsaking their evil ways in favour of protocol piracy, a new calling based on esteem and social rank, and singing a concluding hymn to the Savoy operas' powers of divine emollient:

> But how will you keep yourselves cheerful
> In the teeth of the fiercest hurricane?
> We'll all sing ourselves an earful
> Of songs by Gilbert and Sullivan.

There is another body of G & S pastiche which is designed not so much to pay tribute to the Victorian duo as to take them off and send them up. Into this category comes Tom Lehrer's Savoy-style version of *Clementine*, with its memorable line 'now a pestering sister's a festering blister'. Presented as the conclusion of a set of variations on the folk song, which also includes verses à la Mozart and Cole Porter, it is introduced by Lehrer's remark: 'one can always count on G & S for a rousing finale full of words and music and signifying nothing'. Michael Flanders and Donald Swann's 'In the D'Oyly Cart', written shortly before the expiry of the copyright, was similarly scathing. It caricatured the D'Oyly Carte style:

> Dear little town of Nanki-Poo,
> (Smile, turn, pace to the right)
> Canst thou believe my heart is true?
> (Terrible house tonight)

and looked forward to the time when:

> We'll buy back Covent Garden
> And have the operas re-written,
> With words by J. B. Priestley
> And new tunes by Benjy Britten![14]

The 1970s musical *Liza of Lambeth* included an even more unflattering pastiche patter song which began 'Nothing is duller than Gilbert and Sullivan' and ended with the line 'The Grand Duke makes me puke'.

The supreme example of this particular genre is Anna Russell's masterly 'Write Your Own Gilbert and Sullivan Opera', which the talented singer-comedienne wrote in her last year at boarding school and subsequently performed around the world. She introduced her one-woman performance by remarking that 'in practically every city or town regardless of the size there's always someone in the process of putting on a G & S opera, in which case it seems a pity that there aren't a few more of them'. Having studied the genre, she was confident that 'I have evolved a formula for writing your own G & S. It's a sort of vitamin pill that contains all the necessary ingredients'. She went on to list these key ingredients as follows:

> As you know you always have to start with a homogeneous chorus, homogeneous as in milk. All the characters are the same—all Japanese, all pirates or all something or other. . . .

> Always connected with these operations is the British piercing-type soprano. She is very sweet . . . .

> The man that she is in love with is, of course, the tenor. Now it is absolutely obligatory that the tenor sing an aria in 6:8 time, usually accompanying himself on the guitar or mandolin. . . .

> The man she is going to be made to marry is the little man who prances around and sings the patter song . . . .

Now the wedding guests are all assembled and to entertain them there comes on the madrigal . . . .

The knot is just about to be tied when who should come in but the large fat contralto with a voice like a foghorn that you have to have in these productions. She stops the wedding because she has a confession to make, assisted by the chorus.

The final chorus of Anna Russell's 'Do It Yourself' Savoy opera, which includes the obligatory saluting of the flag, provides a wonderful summation of the essential qualities that define the G & S phenomenon:

> You need a handsome young couple whose voices are supple
> And charming if just a bit sickly,
> A chorus to prance through the same kind of dance
> And do everything terribly quickly.
> You need a small skinny guy who's amazingly spry
> With a voice like a vegetable grater,
> A tremendous old crone with a strange vocal tone
> Like her mouth is all full of potater.
> These operas have got an identical plot, so the narrative doesn't much
>   matter
> But it's great to poke fun at most everyone with your typical topical
>   patter.[15]

The final category of 'precious nonsense' to mention in this chapter is the practice of setting Gilbert's words to familiar non-Sullivan tunes. A cabaret performance by the Stanford Savoyards at a G & S festival in Berkeley, California, in 1997 included 'Pour, O Pour the Pirate Sherry' to Beethoven's *Ode to Joy*, 'Poor Wandering One' to 'New York, New York', and 'When the Foeman Bares His Steel' to 'Doe, a Deer' from the *Sound of Music*. There are doubtless plenty of other possibilities but please, dear readers, keep them to yourselves. The last word should be given to the church and to a Gilbert and Sullivan grace composed by Michael Perry while archdeacon of Durham. It goes to show how G & S can be adapted for any purpose, sacred or profane:

> Thank you, Lord, that we are not like those who sip no sup and crave no crumb, or those who have to make do with skimmed milk masquerading as cream. Thank you for enabling us to accept refreshment at any hand, however lowly, and for being so fond of our dinner that we don't get any

thinner. Thank you for the rollicking bun and the not too French French bean. Thank you for life that is a pudding full of plums, but grant that our taste for drink may never be so combined with gout as to double us up for ever.[16]

Amen, and may Gilbert and Sullivan continue to provide innocent merriment, divine emollient, and general silliness for many, many years to come.

NINE

MAINTAINING WITH NO LITTLE HEAT
THEIR VARIOUS OPINIONS: G & S SCHOLARSHIP,
PARTISANSHIP, AND APPRECIATION

The last forty years have seen an explosion of serious and scholarly interest in the Savoy operas. This has been expressed in academic conferences, a number of significant books, and new scholarly editions of vocal and orchestral scores. Appreciation societies have stimulated interest in Gilbert and Sullivan and added considerably to the tally of publications and new recordings of their works. Detective work has led to the recovery of lost songs. Perhaps most intriguing and encouraging of all, Gilbert and Sullivan have found serious scholars as well as fans outside the English-speaking world.

Much of this academic work has made use of the major collections of Gilbert and Sullivan material now available to scholars. Probably the single most important is in the Pierpont Morgan Library in New York. It is based on the private collection of Reginald Allen, who deposited forty-eight packing cases of material in 1948 and became the first curator in 1972. On his retirement in 1981 he was succeeded by Fredric Woodbridge Wilson. The library has mounted important exhibitions, notably 'Gilbert and Sullivan—A Window on the Victorian World' in 1990. In 1996 Wilson moved to become curator of the Harvard Theatre Collection, which also has important G & S holdings, and staged a major exhibition with more than 200 items on display between November 2000 and April 2001. Sullivan's diaries are held by Yale University. Within Britain, the most important collections are the Gilbert papers in the British Library; the Sullivan archive at the Royal Academy of Music; the D'Oyly Carte collection in the Theatre Museum, Covent Garden; and the D'Oyly Carte company archives, which have had a rather turbulent time shuttling between the Savoy Theatre and various venues in South London but are now properly catalogued and cared for.

It is noticeable that most of the academic work on G & S has been done in the United States rather than in Britain. This reflects the greater seriousness with which the subject is regarded on that side of the Atlantic, as well as the greater resources available to scholars. There are a number of North American academics who have devoted a considerable part of their careers to studying Gilbert and Sullivan. Prominent among them are Ralph MacPhail, professor of theatre at Bridgewater College, Virginia, whose life's work has been annotating *The Mikado;* James Ellis, who collected all of Gilbert's Bab Ballads in a scholarly edition (Harvard University Press, 1970); and John Bush Jones, who established his academic reputation in the late 1960s and early 1970s while at the University of Kansas with a stream of scholarly articles and by editing *W. S. Gilbert: A Century of Scholarship and Commentary* (New York University Press, 1970). Most recent scholarly books on Gilbert and Sullivan have appeared under the imprint of U.S. publishers, even when their authors were British. The book that you are now reading is a case in point. Indeed, Oxford University Press U.S.A. has been responsible for the last three major works on the subject, Jane W. Stedman's biography of Gilbert (1996), Gayden Wren's *A Most Ingenious Paradox: The Art of Gilbert and Sullivan* (2001), and Michael Ainger's 'dual' biography (2002). It is also significant that all but one of the major academic conferences held on G & S in the last four decades have taken place in North America. Their venues have included Kansas (1970), Boston (1986), Toronto (1987), and West Chester University (1989). The only major British conference during this period was held at Leicester in 1988.

If anything, perhaps, North American scholars take G & S too seriously. Henry Williams pointed to this tendency in his reflections on the Kansas conference: 'The danger of all this is that when the academicians take over, the delight and enjoyment of the operas may be overwhelmed. Before one goes to see an opera in the near future it may be imperative to take a course in Gilbert's topical illusions'.[1] Highly learned articles on abstruse aspects of G & S can be found in North American academic journals across a wide range of disciplines. They range from studies of 'Ruthven Murgatroyd as Byronic Hero' in periodicals specializing in English literature to monographs on Gilbert's kidnapping and his use of fantasy in the *Journal of the American Psychoanalytic Association.*

In the United Kingdom, by contrast, there has been next to no serious academic study of G & S but rather a steady stream of illustrated books written for a general popular readership and a clutch of highly specialized publications by devoted amateurs written for fellow members of the inner brotherhood. Recent examples of this latter category include A. J. Burgess's 575-page work on *The Notary and Other Lawyers in Gilbert and Sullivan* (1997); Maurice Farrar's *The Gilbert and Sullivan Alphabet of Artistes,* which provides the performance record

of every single artiste who sang with the D'Oyly Carte Opera Company between 1875 and 1982; and Paul Ernill's *Alphabetical List of Places Visited by Touring D'Oyly Carte Opera Companies during the Period 1878 to 1962* (1994). The
train-spotting mentality evident in the collection and recording of this kind of
obsessive trivia is not wholly confined to the United Kingdom, but it is noticeable that whereas in the United States Gilbert and Sullivan attracts serious study
from professional academics in learned journals, in Britain it is much more the
province of amateurs, either beavering away on their privately published lists
and compilations of statistics or else indulging in more speculative flights of
fancy in the popular press. A wonderful example of this latter aspect of the
British amateur approach was the article in the *Daily Telegraph* in 1978 in which
Kenneth Baker, a leading Conservative politician and member of Margaret
Thatcher's shadow cabinet, speculated that the relationship between the Fairy
Queen and Private Willis in *Iolanthe* was modeled on that between Queen Victoria and John Brown and that Strephon was based on the figure of Lord Ran-
dolph Churchill.

There is another key difference in approach on the two sides of the Atlantic.
In the United States the focus of interest has tended to be on Gilbert whereas in
Britain it has been on Sullivan. It is no coincidence that the major recent biography of Gilbert should have been written by an American, Jane Stedman (who
is almost unique among those who have written about G & S in being female,
although she does conform to an important Savoyard archetype in also being
an ardent Methodist, described by one of her friends as 'straitlaced, proper, and
never without her hat and gloves'), and the comparable work on Sullivan by a
British scholar, Arthur Jacobs. Indeed, it is really interest in Gilbert rather than
in Gilbert and Sullivan which accounts for most of the G & S—related academic
literature in the United States. I have met several North American professors of
English and theatre studies who rate him as second only to Shakespeare in the
pantheon of English dramatists. John Bush Jones speaks for many when he says
that 'if indeed Gilbert was a serious satirist, the 'Victorian Aristophanes', as
some have liked to call him, then his works deserve serious scrutiny and
scholarship'.[2] I have never encountered a British academic with anything ap-
proaching this level of admiration for Gilbert. Sullivan, however, has had a
clutch of scholarly devotees in Britain, notably Arthur Jacobs, Nigel Burton, and
David Russell Hulme.

There has, in fact, been a fiercely partisan engagement between the (mostly
American) protagonists of Gilbert and (mostly British) protagonists of Sullivan. The first significant shot was fired by David Eden, chairman of the Sullivan
Society, in his book *Gilbert and Sullivan: The Creative Conflict* (1986), which,
significantly, had a U.S. publisher. He launched a devastating attack on Gilbert,

which he has recently continued in his book *W. S. Gilbert—Appearance and Reality* (2003), concluding that 'he had a highly abnormal personality, was capable of hysterical anger, sustained vindictiveness, bullying, mental cruelty and total selfishness'. Subjecting Gilbert to Freudian analysis, Eden finds him to be 'a sadomasochist at the infantile level' and lists the key components of his character as 'orderliness, parsimony, obstinacy, aggression, anger, cruelty, egocentricity and omnipotence'.[3]

Most of the efforts to rehabilitate Gilbert from the effects of this tirade have come from the other side of the Atlantic. In *Modified Rapture* (1991) Alan Fischler, professor of English at Le Moyne College, Syracuse, New York, undertook the first serious analysis of Gilbert's use of comedy. He suggested that it fitted in with the Victorian crisis of faith, replacing divine providence by human law and ingenuity, detaching conscience from God and providing a new kind of comedy for the Victorian middle classes in which law and authority lost the malignity traditionally ascribed to them in the theatre and became the prime agencies of salvation in the post-Darwinian world. Although Jane Stedman's *W. S. Gilbert: A Classic Victorian and His Theatre* largely steers clear of assessments of Gilbert's personality and achievements in favour of narrative and description, it is a broadly sympathetic portrait and pointedly does not even allude to Eden's work. More recently, there has been a significant single-handed effort by a young Englishman, Andrew Crowther, to rescue and promote Gilbert's reputation. Like American scholars, he speaks about Gilbert in the same breath as Oscar Wilde and argues that several of his non–G & S plays are classics which deserve revival. This has, indeed, begun to happen: *Engaged* has been performed at the National Theatre in 1975, in the West End in 1981, at Perth Theatre in 1998, and in Richmond, Surrey, in 2002–3; the BBC broadcast five plays on Radio 4 in 2003 under the title 'Gilbert without Sullivan'. Crowther maintains a website entitled 'Babliophile: An internet magazine for the seriously deranged W.S. Gilbert Enthusiast'. His important book *Contradiction Contradicted: The Plays of W. S. Gilbert* (2000), yet another title to come out under an American rather than a British academic imprint, presents Gilbert as a complex figure, fascinated by the absurdity and ridiculous quality of human existence, looking at life honestly, and mixing irony with sincerity and realism with fantasy. For Crowther, he is a writer who deals above all in contradictions—both a satirist of and an apologist for bourgeois values, who ridicules society while upholding its values but who also sees a spark of divine flame in humans and begets a kind of benign tolerance.

Until Crowther's recent efforts to redress the balance, it has been Sullivan who has had the lion's share of attention in Britain with full-scale biographies by Percy Young in 1971 and Arthur Jacobs in 1984. Ardent and effective advocacy

FIGURE 9.1 Set of stamps issued on 21 July 1992 to commemorate the 150th anniversary of Sullivan's birth *(Royal Mail Philatelic Bureau)*

by the Sullivan Society has also helped the composer's cause. While the 150th anniversary of Gilbert's birth in 1986 passed with very little in the way of celebration or recognition in Britain (in the United States, by contrast, there was a major sesquicentennial conference at Massachusetts Institute of Technology), the anniversary of Sullivan's six years later had a much higher national profile and was, indeed, the occasion for the issue of a set of stamps to celebrate the Savoy operas. It is significant that Sullivan rather than Gilbert should trigger this kind of tribute to their joint work. Broadly speaking, the last forty years in Britain has seen the composer's stock steadily rising as the reputation of his librettist has steadily fallen. A good indication of their changing fortunes in terms of popular perception is the very different treatment given to them in the 1953 film *The Story of Gilbert and Sullivan* and the 1999 film *Topsy-Turvy*. Although in both films, Sullivan comes over as the more human, vulnerable, and likeable of the duo, *Topsy-Turvy* portrays Gilbert not so much as an amiable if irascible buffoon but as a decidedly cold fish whose relationship with his wife borders on the cruel and unfeeling. The extent to which *Topsy-Turvy* has confirmed a growing disillusionment with Gilbert on both sides of the Atlantic is interestingly brought out in Max Keith Sutton's 'Confessions of a Lapsed Fanatic'. The author, a professor in the English Department at Kansas University, first came to G & S as a boy in backwoods Arkansas when he pressed his ear to the radio to try and hear 'Tit Willow' through the static—'no song had ever sounded lovelier, and the world it came from could not have seemed more strange'. Gradually, though, disillusionment set in, not just because of academic colleagues suggesting that 'G & S fanatics suffered from arrested development' but also because of a growing unease about Gilbert, considerably influenced by David Eden's work and reinforced by *Topsy-Turvy*. For Sutton, who admits that as an English teacher he can quote thirty lines of Gilbert to a half-line of Shakespeare, it is Sullivan who is closer to the Bard in all senses:

> Sullivan's artistic instincts drew him to Shakespeare; *The Tempest* inspired the nineteen-year-old composer, but it left Gilbert cold. Shakespeare embraced life, and Sullivan wanted to express it; Gilbert embraced the absurdities but not the full joy and pain and mystery of it.[4]

The increasing respect for and attention given to Sullivan has expressed itself partly in the production of new scholarly performing editions of the Savoy operas based on his autograph scores. Three different publishers have been involved in this enterprise. Broude Brothers, based in Williamstown, Massachusetts, were first off the mark with a critical edition of *Trial by Jury*, published in 1994 after more than a decade of preparation by an editorial team led by Dr. Percy Young and containing many of the great and the good among G & S scholars. A two-volume edition of *Pinafore* followed in 2003, and Broude is committed to publishing scholarly editions of each of the remaining Savoy operas in the form of a full score, piano/vocal score, and a full set of instrumental parts. Meanwhile Dover Publications have produced full scores, vocal scores, and libretti of *Mikado* (1999), *Pirates* (2001), and *Pinafore* (2002) edited by Carl Simpson and Ephraim Hammett Jones, and Oxford University Press has produced a full score, vocal score, and orchestral parts for *Ruddigore* (2000) edited by David Russell Hulme. In addition to these scholarly editions, much work has been done on Sullivan's orchestrations by John Owen Edwards, David Mackie, and David Steadman. James Newby has hugely helped amateur societies by arranging the entire G & S repertoire for a fifteen-piece orchestra.

As a result of all this work, both amateur and professional performing groups no longer have to use the D'Oyly Carte band parts and much 'lost' material is now readily available for performance. The recovery of discarded songs and dialogue has been a major activity of G & S scholars and enthusiasts over recent decades. My own *Annotated Gilbert and Sullivan*, first published by Penguin in two volumes in 1982 and 1984 and subsequently in one volume by Oxford University Press, attempted to include all material which had ever been written or performed and subsequently dropped. *Sing with Sullivan*, a collection of songs edited by Terence Rees and Roderick Spencer and published in 1977, contained such long-neglected gems as 'A Laughing Boy but Yesterday' from *Yeomen* and 'Fold Your Flapping Wings' from *Iolanthe*. These and other lost numbers were included in recordings made by the new D'Oyly Carte and New Sadler's Wells companies in the 1980s and 1990s (see pages 61, 80). In 2003, on the initiative of Ray Walker, Cramer brought out a freshly typeset edition of the original score of *Sorcerer* containing forty pages of material cut in the 1884 revised version, including the chorus 'Happy Are We in Our Loving Frivolity' and the lengthy scene with Ahrimanes in act 2.

Painstaking detective work has brought some even more obscure and long-buried material out of the woodwork. 'Though Men of Rank May Useless Seem', the aria for the Duke of Dunstable originally written for act 1 of *Patience* but discarded before the opera's premiere, was given its first performance by the pupils of Banbury Grammar School in 1967, the original lyrics and orchestral accompaniment having been tracked down by the school's senior English master, Kenneth Cardus, in different sources in the British Library. More than thirty years later the chance discovery of manuscript orchestral parts copied for the D'Oyly Carte enabled Helga Perry, a postgraduate music student at Birmingham University, and Bruce Miller, professor of music at the College of the Holy Cross, Worcester, Massachusetts, to reconstruct the vocal line of 'Reflect, My Child', a song written to be sung by Captain Corcoran to his daughter to dissuade her from marrying Ralph but dropped before the premiere of *Pinafore*. The song was given its first performance at the 1999 Buxton Festival and its reconstruction was described in a scholarly paper given at the tenth annual conference of the Society for Textual Scholarship at the City University in New York. In 2000, on the basis of a further discovery of D'Oyly Carte band parts, Miller and Perry produced a reconstructed version of the lost song from act 2 of *Iolanthe* 'De Belville Was Regarded as the Crichton of His Age'.

Perhaps the most spectacular recovery of lost material has been achieved in the case of *Thespis*, Gilbert and Sullivan's first collaboration, which has always tantalized aficionados by the lack of any surviving music for more than a couple of its songs. Terence Rees's *Thespis—A Gilbert and Sullivan Enigma*, published in 1964 to coincide with a performance of the work at the University of London with music selected and arranged by Garth Morton from lesser-known Sullivan operettas, provided a sound edition of the libretto and much useful background information. Since then at least fifteen different versions of *Thespis* have been produced and performed, eight with newly written music and seven using tunes by Sullivan. In 1990 Selwyn Tillett, chairman of the Sullivan Society (and as a Church of England vicar another example of devotion to G & S among the clergy), and Roderick Spencer discovered the long-lost *Thespis* ballet music as a result of impressive detective work among the manuscripts in the Pierpoint Morgan Library. They have subsequently collaborated to produce what is almost certainly the most painstakingly reconstructed and plausible version of the opera, using tunes from other Sullivan works. It was performed at the Sullivan Society Festival in Cirencester in 2002.[5]

It is significant that much of this activity has been undertaken by amateurs and supported by one of the appreciation societies which have played a considerable role in keeping G & S alive and spearheading the revival of interest which has taken place in the last thirty years or so. While not quite as venerable nor anything like as numerous as the amateur performing societies, the appreciation societies have a long and distinguished pedigree. The oldest established, the Gilbert and Sullivan Society, was founded in 1924 and currently has around 400 members although a very much smaller number come to its meetings, which are held monthly through the winter in central London. Known as the parent society, it has nineteen branches or affiliated societies, eleven of which are in the United Kingdom. The longest established of these is the Manchester Society, founded in 1932 and now with around 100 members, and there are also flourishing branches in Norwich, founded in 1978, and Sussex. The parent society has a strongly patriotic and royalist flavour—its patron was Princess Alice, Duchess of Gloucester, and its anthem, sung at the end of dinners and conventions, is 'He Is an Englishman'. There is also a strong emphasis on the magic word 'tradition'—the Manchester Society describes its objective as being 'to maintain intact the traditions of the Gilbert and Sullivan operas'. Church connections are once again strong—the chairman of the Manchester branch, David Walton, is an active Methodist and the Norwich Society meets in and has close connections with a United Reformed Church. There is a biennial convention which alternates between Manchester and London. Since 1925 the Gilbert and Sullivan Society has published a journal, which since 1982 has been entitled *Gilbert and Sullivan News*. Substantially revamped by Kevin Chapple in the mid-1990s, it is now edited by a team led by Jenny Butlin and provides an interesting commentary on new productions, old favourites, and general G & S news.

Outside the United Kingdom there are G & S appreciation societies in Western Australia and Jerusalem and a substantial clutch in North America, with a particular concentration in Canada and the northeastern United States. The titles of their newsletters indicate yet another use for phrases from the Savoy operas: *Precious Nonsense* (the Midwestern society), *The Trumpet Bray* (New England), *The Titipu Times* (Winnipeg and Western Australia), and *To-Ron-To-Ra* (Toronto). Membership of these societies is dwindling. Marc Shepherd, a leading light in the New York G & S Society and editor of its journal, *The Palace Peeper*, reports that 'the society is, alas, now tottering on the brink of extinction.

Meeting attendance is dwindling and the average age of attendees is around sixty-five. While I am quite optimistic for the future of G & S, I am not so sanguine for the future of this type of society'.[6] The picture is broadly similar in the United Kingdom, with appreciation societies mirroring the general decline in participation in voluntary activities brought about by social trends and the rise of home-based entertainment.

If the long-term future of societies dedicated to appreciating G & S seems somewhat uncertain, the state of those that are more specifically and individually focused on just one member of the partnership seems much healthier. Perhaps a little partisanship and rivalry is good for business. Both the W. S. Gilbert Society and the Sir Arthur Sullivan Society have sponsored and undertaken important scholarly work, and although they naturally feel the urge to promote their respective hero's non-Savoy work they have both also done their bit towards the general revival of interest in G & S. The Gilbert Society is the younger and smaller of the two, being founded in 1984. Under the editorship of Brian Jones, its journal has published important scholarly articles advancing Gilbert's cause, such as 'Gilbert the Brechtian', by Andrew Crowther. Another publication produced independently by a leading member of the society, Michael Walters's *Gilbertian Gossip*, has provided lively and opinionated reviews of G & S productions.

The Sir Arthur Sullivan Society was founded in 1977 and now has around 500 members. Virtually from the beginning, its principal driving force has been Stephen Turnbull, secretary since 1979. The Society must take much of the credit for Sullivan's rehabilitation and steadily rising reputation over the last quarter century. To mark the 150th anniversary of the composer's birth in 1992, it ran a conference entitled 'Arthur Sullivan, the Unperson of British Music'. By the centenary year of his death, just eight years later, this epithet could no longer apply. Sullivan's music is heard increasingly in concert halls and on radio and television. Yet there is still lingering prejudice against his work in some sections of the musical establishment. When the *Yeomen of the Guard* overture was dropped from the last night of the 2002 Promenade Concerts despite being in the programme, Sullivan enthusiasts detected evidence of the usual élitist conspiracy and fumed that the work of the British composer had been cut yet room found for Rodgers and Hammerstein songs. They were not wholly convinced by an assurance from Nicolas Kenyon, director of the Proms, that the overture had been dropped purely for reasons of time and that he himself had nothing against Sullivan, one of his earliest musical experiences being singing in the *Yeomen of the Guard*. While much of the society's energies have been taken up in securing and promoting performances, CD recordings, and new editions of Sullivan's oratorios, orchestral, chamber, and church music and his non–G & S operas, it has also published detailed and scholarly booklets on most of the Savoy operas and its excellent magazine and newsletter regularly carry G & S–related articles and news items. It has also done much to preserve and make more widely available vintage recordings of Gilbert and Sullivan. Both Stephen Turnbull and Roger Wild, a community pharmacist from Dorset, have extensive collections of early recordings on wax cylinders and shellac discs, and annual society conferences and festivals have often been enlivened by the crackling sound of early D'Oyly Carte artistes and foreign language performances. The Sullivan Society has also played a key role in transferring vintage recordings of G & S onto CD, supporting the efforts of specialist practitioners like Chris Webster.

The small but growing market for remastered (and original) vintage recordings is part of a trade in G & S merchandise and memorabilia which has grown up on the back of the passion for collecting among the more committed of the inner brotherhood of fans. There are at least four professional dealers who trade almost exclusively in G & S memorabilia—mostly books, old photographs and programmes, sheet music, and early recordings. One of them, Chris Browne, tells me that his clients are almost exclusively male, mostly middle-aged, more numerous (and more prepared to spend big money) in the United States than in the United Kingdom, and increasingly also to be found in Continental Europe. There are regular get-togethers of G & S collectors, particularly in North America. A gathering in Purchase, New York, in 1994 attracted collectors from both sides of the Atlantic to show one another their original *Mikado* fans, Little Buttercup toy clothes pegs, and luncheon menus from early D'Oyly Carte days out on the River Thames. Sullivan Society weekends, which always include a Sunday morning church service, often feature an auction of memorabilia in which items such as music boxes that play 'Little Buttercup', biographies of veteran D'Oyly Carte artistes, and LPs containing arrangements of the peers' chorus for brass band or male voice choir change hands often for relatively little money. The middle weekend of the Buxton G & S Festival has become another important date in the collector's diary, with a memorabilia fair held on the Saturday.

In addition to the continuing trade in vintage artifacts, there is now a thriving cottage industry producing new collectable items with a G & S theme. One of the spin-offs of the Buxton Festival is the 'Musical Collectables' business which manufactures and sells figurines based on D'Oyly Carte performers—Donald Adams as the Mikado and the Pirate King, John Reed as Sir Joseph Porter, and Alistair Donkin as John Wellington Wells. It also sells reproductions of the John Player cigarette cards first issued in the 1920s and spoons, mugs, glasses, key rings, aprons, table mats, bookmarks, and numerous sweatshirts

FIGURE 9.2 Donald Adams posing for Music Collectables figurine of the Pirate King shortly before his death in 1996 (*Music Collectables*)

decorated with G & S characters or insignia. One of the more recent North American entrants into the booming G & S collectables business, Tyson Vick, an illustrator from Sunburst, Montana, has designed and marketed a set of forty-eight greeting cards illustrated with scenes from twelve Savoy operas. A G & S fan since the age of thirteen, he initially did the illustrations for his father and came to see their commercial potential.

Although fascination with G & S in all its aspects and ramifications remains a predominantly British, North American and, to a slightly lesser extent, Australasian phenomenon, the last few years have seen a significant rise in scholarly interest, as well as in performances outside the English-speaking world and in particular in Continental Europe. In 1993 Meinhard Saremba published *Arthur Sullivan—Ein Komponistenleben im Viktorianischen England,* the first full-length book on Sullivan not written in English. Paolo Panico, an adjunct professor of economics, international banker, and opera fan, is currently writing the first book in Italian on Gilbert and Sullivan. First introduced to the songs as a child by an English teacher, he became an avid collector of LPs of old D'Oyly Carte performances and his interest was rekindled when he recently came across a *Mikado* piano score in a Vienna music shop. He now feels a mission to promote

G & S in Italy, where it has never had the appeal of Offenbach or Lehar. Another Italian academic, Marco Sonzogni, is currently engaged in making two Italian translations of *Pinafore*, one for reading and one for singing. Henrik Eriksson, professor of mathematics at the Royal Institute of Technology in Stockholm, has translated *Pirates* and *Iolanthe* into Swedish and started an opera society in his university which he hopes will stage semi-professional productions of the Savoy operas. He discovered G & S quite by accident in 1996 when he was on holiday with his family in London and saw an advert for the Buxton G & S Festival describing it as 'fun'. They travelled up for a performance of *Pirates* and were absolutely hooked. Eriksson now comes over to Buxton every year, usually bringing his two sons and daughter with their families. He finds the operas incredibly difficult to translate: 'It is Gilbert's fault that it isn't translated more and performed in other countries. You take the first song and you give up! I have spent all my spare time this year translating *Iolanthe* and I could sit up all night just to get two lines perfect'.[7]

The globalisation of G & S has been enormously helped by the internet, which allows G & S addicts to chat away across the ether regardless of geographical considerations. If G & S appreciation societies are suffering dwindling numbers, G & S on the web is booming. Among the thousands of websites devoted to them, the best is almost certainly the G & S Archive, which was established in 1993. It encompasses David Stone's complete Who's Who of anyone who sang with the D'Oyly Carte between 1875 and 1982, over 1,000 MIDI files, libretti and play scripts, lists of and links to G & S performing and appreciation societies throughout the world, and a wonderful G & S Discography compiled by Marc Shepherd, which lists just about every known recording of every G & S opera ever made and receives around 1,000 hits a day.

For those who want to chat with their fellow enthusiasts there is Savoynet, an unmoderated electronic mailing list dedicated to discussion of G & S and related matters. Set up in 1992 by Bill Venman with 20 or so fellow enthusiasts and initially hosted by the University of Massachusetts, it is now hosted by Bridgewater College, Virginia, courtesy of Ralph MacPhail, who served as listowner until 1998 when Marc Shepherd took over. Savoynet now has around 650 subscribers, who can expect to receive at least fifty e-mails a day ranging from reports of G & S references in television soaps, films, and novels to debates over dream casts and the merits of recent productions. Much of what is discussed tends towards the arcane and obsessional and it is very much for the committed inner brotherhood rather than for the only mildly interested—I once switched on my computer on a Monday morning to find that 392 Savoynet messages had arrived in the space of one weekend.

The success of Savoynet, and more generally the ever-burgeoning spread of G & S sites on the web, shows, yet again, their extraordinary survival powers and ability to adapt and thrive in successive new media and changing cultural climates. Indeed, in many ways G & S fandom, with its obsession with lists and precise records of artistes, performances, textual emendations and so on, is tailor-made for the internet. Thankfully, however, Savoynetters do not just exist in an etherized limbo. Several regularly meet face-to-face, recognizable through their distinctive T-shirts. Their main rendezvous, and that for all G & S aficionados, is every summer at Buxton. Since 1997 Savoynet has put on an annual performance at the festival there, planned and cast over the internet with the participants gathering as a group just a week before the show. It is a nice illustration of the way that new technology is helping the survival and revival of Gilbert and Sullivan and an indicator of the central role that this Derbyshire market town has in securing its future.

TEN

PEEP WITH SECURITY
INTO FUTURITY: BUXTON IT IS!

In *Ruddigore* the word 'Basingstoke' is used by Sir Despard Murgatroyd to calm Mad Margaret during her wild fantasies. So it is that this rather nondescript Hampshire town becomes 'a word that teems with hidden meaning'. For G & S fans around the world today the name of a more picturesque town in the heart of England's Peak District has taken on even greater iconic status—Buxton is the mecca where over 20,000 fans and 2,000 performers gather every summer in what has become the most visible expression of Gilbert and Sullivan's extraordinary powers of survival.

The Buxton International Gilbert and Sullivan Festival began in 1994 and has grown steadily ever since. There have been several attempts to extend it to other venues—Philadelphia in 1996, Philadelphia and Berkeley, California, in 1997, and Eastbourne on England's south coast in 2002—but these ventures further afield did not really work and the festival has now settled in the Derbyshire spa town for three weeks in August, with over thirty full-scale productions in the Edwardian Opera House and more than eighty 'fringe' events.

The content and atmosphere of the festival say much about the G & S world today. There is a strong vein of nostalgia focused on the 'golden days' of the old D'Oyly Carte Opera Company, whose ageing stars from the 1960s and 1970s are brought out year after year for master classes, reminiscence sessions, 'Together Again' gala concerts, and ever more tearful and emotional tributes. Commenting on the very first evening of the first festival, 'A Nostalgic Walk Down Memory Lane' with stalwarts of the old company, Marc Shepherd noted:

> It is perhaps indicative of the spirit of the evening that nearly half the jokes were about the participants' age. To be sure, these stars were among the best of their generation, and they mostly are able to turn the clock back

and remind us of their prime. But the applause that evening was as much a collective 'thank you' for nearly fifty years' worth of magical performances as it was for the imperfect recreation of that magic that these stars actually presented to the festival audience.[1]

This strange obsession with an institution now dead and gone for more than twenty years remains a central feature of the festival. In 2003 a gala evening for Tom Round, John Reed, and Kenneth Sandford ended with a stageful of former D'Oyly Carte artistes, several well on in their eighties, singing 'I hear the soft note of an echoing voice of an old, old love long dead' and then turning to face a logo of the old company as the lights were dimmed and the festival organizer, Ian Smith, intoned in a funereal voice: 'The D'Oyly Carte Opera Company, 1875 to 1982—there will never be anything like it again'.

Alongside these lingering last rites for the much-beloved and still deeply lamented guardian of G & S tradition, the Buxton festival also celebrates the dynamism of the current amateur performance scene. Each weekday evening there is a competitive adjudicated performance in the Opera House by an amateur company. Societies from both sides of the Atlantic send in videos of past productions in the audition process for the coveted honour of appearing in the festival competition. Those who are lucky enough to be selected have to cover the cost of coming to Buxton, although they are given the services of a professional orchestra and stage crew. They also have to work to an incredibly tight schedule, being given access to the Opera House at nine in the morning on the day of performance with just eight hours for set building and dress and technical rehearsals. As soon as the show is over, they then have to strike the set and get out. All this makes for a frenetic atmosphere—a classic Buxton moment which I treasure is the emergence from the stage door of a harassed-looking lady in a *Phantom of the Opera* T-shirt crying 'I've got four broken policemen's helmets and no time to mend them'. Amateur performers can also take part in the annual festival production, normally directed by Alistair Donkin, which is auditioned and rehearsed during one week of the three weeks festival.

If the old D'Oyly Carte and amateur traditions of G & S are at the heart of the Buxton festival, it also reaches out to embrace more modern professional and youth productions. Although the festival organizers shunned the new D'Oyly Carte company, they have welcomed Carl Rosa and Opera della Luna for weekend performances. They have also created the Gilbert and Sullivan Opera Company, composed of former old D'Oyly Carte stalwarts like Gareth Jones, Gillian Knight, Jill Pert, and Michael Rayner together with young professional singers, to mount two or three productions during each festival. An annual youth production, cast largely from local groups and schools and directed by Pamela Leighton-Bilik, provides performance opportunities for those aged between nine and eighteen. In 2004 an additional production was introduced specifically for young artistes aged between eighteen and thirty. St. Mary's Catholic High School has taken many of its innovative productions to Buxton, regularly winning major awards, and the Oxford University G & S Society has appeared twice at the festival.

Alongside the performances in the Opera House, a 'fringe' programme provides virtually nonstop G & S–related activity throughout the three weeks of each festival. Films, talks, seminars, workshops, selections of vintage recordings, and quizzes attract a predominantly male and middle-aged audience. A Saturday memorabilia fair caters to collectors who are also lured regularly into the festival portakabin to buy T-shirts, posters, figurines, and videos of the previous evening's show. A Sunday morning service in the elegant Georgian parish church across the road from the Opera House reinforces the G & S–churchgoing connection and allows a large and enthusiastic congregation to bellow out 'Onward, Christian Soldiers' to Sullivan's tune *St. Gertrude*. There are opportunities for equally hearty if slightly more raucous singing at the late-night festival club and cabaret, the frequent scratch performances, and the 'singing from the gallery' sessions which precede each Saturday evening performance in the Opera House. The fringe has increasingly expanded to take in performances of Gilbert's plays, Sullivan's choral works, and other non–G & S works such as *The Batsman's Bride*.

Buxton has become a mecca for serious G & S fans. The Savoynetters are there in force, recognisable by their distinctive T-shirts. Seminars and symposia have brought together many of the leading G & S scholars and academics, including Shani d'Cruz, Ralph MacPhail, Bruce Miller, David Mackie, and David Russell Hulme. But above all, the festival is fun. One North American participant described it to me as being 'as near as humanly possible to a G & S Theme Park' and another sent an e-mail to the organizers saying 'I thought I had died and was in heaven'. Perhaps the most telling tribute of all is from the woman who enthused 'I have had more pleasure from the Gilbert and Sullivan Festival than from either of my husbands'. An infectious atmosphere of both innocent and incessant merriment pervades Buxton throughout the weeks of the festival. Every church hall, hotel, and public room in the centre of town resounds to the strains of soloists and choruses rehearsing. The opening costume parade brings a procession of major-generals, policemen, village maidens, and bridesmaids wending its way through the elegant Pavilion Gardens. The Victorian bandstand regularly echoes to the sound of brass-band arrangements of *The Mikado* or *The Gondoliers*. Banners with the silhouetted busts of Gilbert and Sullivan hang from pubs and public buildings, and local shopkeepers join in the fun by

FIGURE 10.1 The G & S Theme Park. The costume parade at the 1995 Buxton Festival
(*Beryl Cooper/Chris Wain*)

participating in a G & S treasure hunt and decorating their windows with appropriate pictures and artefacts.

It is all wonderfully eccentric and wonderfully British and it is not surprising that the Buxton festival has provided the inspiration and the main location for the two major explorations on television of the world of G & S in the last ten years. The BBC broadcast its flagship religious programme *Songs of Praise* from the Pavilion Gardens in 1997, with a brass band and a 450-strong costumed 'congregation' performing 'Dance a Cachucha' and 'Poor Wandering One' alongside Sullivan's hymns and his sacred ballad 'The Lost Chord' and John Reed in full costume singing 'I Am the Monarch of the Sea'. The programme was as much an act of homage to the great Victorian duo as a service of Christian worship. The following year the BBC's arts programme *Omnibus* explored the religion of G & S and the bizarre cultlike behaviour of its devotees in a programme shot largely in Buxton but also featuring some of the more colourful episodes during the California and Philadelphia legs of the 1997 festival, including a party of middle-aged men creeping round Alcatraz singing 'Carefully on Tiptoe Stealing'.

The festival is the brainchild of father and son Ian and Neil Smith. Steeped in the amateur G & S tradition, they have both long been stalwarts of the West Yorkshire Savoyards and between them played all the principal patter roles. Ian came into G & S through the familiar northern Nonconformist route, starting out with the Shipley Wesleyan Reform Amateur Operatic Society as a ten-year-old in the early 1950s. Both his grandparents and his parents had performed with the society. His mother, who played the contralto roles, said 'you WILL be in, Ian'. He duly obeyed 'and that was the start of my love affair with G & S.' Perhaps even more formative were his boyhood visits to D'Oyly Carte performances: 'I went to see them every time they came to Manchester or Leeds. I took copious notes even when John Reed blinked and I wanted to scream if Isidore Godfrey ever cut a matinée encore'. Later, singing the patter roles with several West Yorkshire amateur societies, he was often being directed by former D'Oyly Carte artistes.[2]

Neil Smith was marked down from birth to follow in the G & S tradition and even named in accordance with it, as his father recalls:

> I was playing Bunthorne in Bradford when he was born. The cast thought it was essential he should be named after one of the central characters. So we had the choice of Archibald or Reginald and poor child I didn't really think that either would be suitable, but then there's that beautiful line 'Kneel, kneel, all kneel' and that is where his name originated.[3]

FIGURE 10.2 'Bless my heart, my son!' Neil and Ian Smith outside the Opera House, Buxton *(Author's collection)*

Unlike some children who have rebelled against a too early and too enthusiastic dose of G & S being shoved down their throats, Neil Smith shares his father's passion. In pride of place on the wall of his office a framed newspaper cutting records a typical piece of G & S lunacy by the West Yorkshire Savoyards, the society founded by Ian, in which all thirteen Savoy operas were performed back-to-back in twenty-nine hours and eleven minutes in thirteen different venues around the area, including the top of a bus for *The Grand Duke*, a Morison's supermarket for *Ida*, a municipal swimming pool for *Pirates*, a motorway service station for *Utopia*, and a variety of pubs, theatres, schools, and community halls for the other works.

The Smiths' motivation for establishing the festival sprang directly from the demise of the old D'Oyly Carte company. In Ian's words:

> If we go back to the late '70s and early '80s I had a burning anger inside that the original D'Oyly Carte Opera Company was allowed to close. What an absolute tragedy that here is yet another 'Best of British' that is just allowed to fade away and potentially die. As the years passed, the concept of doing something to ensure that the tradition and heritage was maintained became more and more acute and I think as the original stars from the D'Oyly Carte grew older, something had to be done.

Ian Smith feels a burning passion and evangelical zeal to preserve the old D'Oyly Carte tradition and pass it on to future generations. This is why he has summoned up the company's former principals to demonstrate through master classes the subtleties of the roles that they played and developed for so many years and to record their performances on video 'so that they will be there for our grandchildren and great-grandchildren'. When pressed as to what it is that distinguished these representatives of what he sees as a golden age of G & S performance, he identifies 'the wonderful training, discipline, and drilling they had in the old D'Oyly Carte company which has prepared them for anything.'

The idea of the competition for amateur societies came from the Waterford Festival in Ireland, where the Smiths were regular visitors with the West Yorkshire Savoyards throughout the 1970s and 1980s. In the words of Neil, 'We wanted to organise a festival which was purely Gilbert and Sullivan, not with G & S sandwiched between *La Cage Aux Folles* and *My Fair Lady*'. In fact, the Smiths did once try to put on a festival of musicals in Buxton immediately after the G & S Festival but it attracted very little support. The G & S theme provides a more focused and targeted attraction ideally suited to the nostalgic and old-fashioned charm of Buxton, which was chosen as the festival venue only after the initial choices of Harrogate and York had been ruled out.

The Smiths run the festival from a rambling Victorian vicarage in Halifax that also serves as the headquarters of their international marketing business, which specializes in publishing industry magazines, providing a secretariat for trade associations, and organizing conferences and exhibitions. Most of the ground floor rooms and the attic are stuffed with racks of costumes which are hired out to amateur companies, and the old garage is filled with the props lovingly assembled by Ben and Margaret Chamley (see page 133). In another room, figurines, T-shirts, and other G & S memorabilia are stacked waiting to be sent out around the world. From the start the festival has been very much a transatlantic affair. The overall winners in the first festival in 1994 were the G & S Society from Hancock County, Maine, and over subsequent years the Seattle, Houston, and Philadelphia societies and the Lamplighters from San Francisco have come to perform and compete along with smaller groups from Brussels, Jerusalem, and Estonia. A significant number of North American fans regularly come to Buxton. Indeed, Ralph MacPhail believes that the festival's success has effectively meant the end of major G & S gatherings in the United States.

The festival epitomizes the ambivalent position that Gilbert and Sullivan still occupies in British culture and perception. It has neither the kudos nor the prestige of the classical music and literary festival that precedes it every year in Buxton and draws national newspaper critics to the town. Yet the Gilbert and Sullivan Festival attracts more people who undoubtedly have more fun, even if they have more modest tastes than the classical music buffs and do not spend as much at the Opera House bars. A sense of indignation at the way G & S is treated by the cultural establishment often surfaces in Ian Smith's pre-show speeches. There are frequent digs at the BBC for running down 'the best of British', at the National Theatre and the Royal Opera House for putting on American musicals but no Savoy operas and at the government for promoting minority ethnic cultural interests but ignoring these 'English jewels'. An atmosphere of proud if slightly beleaguered and embarrassed patriotism pervades the festival. It is there in the singing of the national anthem which precedes several performances in the Opera House and the waving of Union flags at the last night of the festival proms. At the end of the emotional tribute to the old D'Oyly Carte Company which opened the 2003 festival, Gareth Jones led a salute to portraits of Gilbert and Sullivan by singing 'They Are Two Englishmen'.

Has Gilbert and Sullivan survived partly because it allows the British, and especially the self-conscious and tongue-tied English, to express their patriotic sentiment and sense of national identity in a relatively gentle and harmless way? Certainly my own annual immersions in the Buxton experience, which like others I can only describe as a kind of divine emollient with a distinctly heavenly quality, have confirmed my sense that G & S is still an important vehicle for the expression of a certain kind of British, as much as English, self-identity. If it is an identity that seems in many ways dated, rooted in a vanished age of elegance, innocence, charm and good manners, then this in itself seems to me to be a key factor in the continuing and future appeal of Gilbert and Sullivan. Buxton, with its elegant, if somewhat faded, Georgian crescents and Victorian villas, its duck ponds and model railway, is to that extent the perfect venue for a G & S festival. It breathes a sense of heritage, tradition, nostalgia, and continuity between a gentle and gracious past and a turbulent and troubled present.

In the United States as much as in Britain the future for G & S, at least in terms of securing funding, perhaps lies partly in exploiting its traditional and nostalgic appeal and playing up its 'heritage' aspects. In the words of Andi Stryker-Rodda, a pianist with NYGASP, 'Unfortunately for formal funding purposes, G & S falls into a no-man's-land. It's not American, it's not "ethnic", it's not a natural disaster or a disease, it's not even "experimental" theatre. Our best bet would be to position it as an "endangered species" or "historic landmark" or perhaps an "addiction"!!'[4] There are clearly dangers in emphasizing these aspects too much and making G & S seem even more of an eccentric and bizarre phenomenon than it already is. It is already being presented and packaged as part of the booming British heritage industry. This is being done very successfully at Gilbert's old home, Grim's Dyke near Harrow in North London, which is now an upmarket hotel. Over the last few years it has developed a number of G & S–themed events—professional performances of the Savoy operas interspersed with dinner in the old music room, summer concerts and performances in the gardens, and cream teas accompanied by extracts from the operas sung by members of the Grim's Dyke Opera Company. Real aficionados with the money can stay in either the Gilbert Suite or the Lady Gilbert suite—if they have seen *Topsy-Turvy*, it will come as no surprise to them that husband and wife slept in different rooms. Visitors can also make their way through the dank woodland that surrounds the formal gardens to inspect the site of the lake where Gilbert drowned, now drained and rather overgrown. Grim's Dyke, a faintly oppressive Arts and Crafts house full of mock-Tudor beams and exposed panelling formerly used as a location for Hammer horror films, provides an opportunity for modern Savoyards to connect in a tangible way with the lingering legacy of Gilbert's ambivalent and complex presence. Sadly, there is no comparable place where one can commune in the same way with the spirit of Sullivan, although visitors to the Museum of London can gaze on the front door of the house where he was born, thanks to the perspicacity of the comedian Spike Milligan, who rescued it when the house was being demolished in 1965.

At a time when heritage centres and historic theme parks are springing up all over Britain, it is surprising that there is not yet one dedicated to Gilbert and

Sullivan. Perhaps the nearest is the permanent exhibition of G & S memorabilia assembled by Melvyn Tarran at Oak Hall Manor, Sheffield Park Gardens in East Sussex, which is occasionally open to the public. There have already been two attempts to create G & S–themed pubs. The first, opened by Whitbreads in John Adam Street near the Savoy Hotel in 1962, housed a splendid collection of memorabilia and model sets for all the operas but was closed after a fire. Whitbreads subsequently converted 'The Old Bull' in Covent Garden to be 'The Gilbert and Sullivan' but, in the words of Andrew Goodman, 'the change was resisted by staff and customers alike and the items on display were pushed aside for gaming machines. The transplant did not take. Perhaps regulars resented the imposition of middle-class entertainment and the values it represents'.[5] This cautionary tale will perhaps spare us the indignity of G & S–themed bars and restaurants.

There is, however, a very strong case for a museum/heritage centre devoted to Gilbert and Sullivan. Buxton would surely be the ideal location for such a centre—it is already established as the mecca of the G & S world, it is a leading tourist destination, and it has a number of vacant properties in close proximity to the Opera House which would provide the ideal setting for a museum/ archive.

Now is a propitious time to launch this project. Several significant collectors of G & S memorabilia who are now in their late middle age are beginning to wonder what to do with their collections and are looking for a permanent home to which they could bequeath them. At the same time, the High Peak Borough Council has announced significant plans to redevelop the central area of Buxton, and the University of Derby is about to assume a major presence in the town. Here surely is a unique opportunity to create a living G & S museum in Buxton which would not simply display and store historic memorabilia but also function as a resource centre and archive for researchers, performers, and students of music, history, and performing arts. It could even be linked with the foundation of a Gilbert and Sullivan Academy which would offer courses and modules on aspects of both performance and appreciation. The Smiths have recently launched a Festival School to provide amateur stage and musical directors with the opportunity to work alongside and receive coaching from professionals. How wonderful if this could be extended to provide a permanent academy, perhaps under the auspices of the University of Derby, and linked to a national museum and archive devoted to Gilbert and Sullivan.

If Buxton points to the future for G & S lying partly in developing the 'heritage' aspect, it also suggests that the audience for G & S is an increasingly greying and ageing one. Research undertaken in the festival's early years confirms what is clearly evident to those of us who attend performances of the Savoy operas—that the audience is largely made up of those over fifty-five. The Smiths take some pride in the fact that a three-day package holiday to Buxton during the G & S festival holds the record for the fastest-selling short break offered by the British company SAGA, which specializes in holidays for senior citizens. Fewer people are being introduced to the delights of G & S at school or when they are young. But perhaps, like Katisha, it is now more of an acquired taste which people are coming to in middle age. If this is the case, it is by no means bad news for its future. The over-fifties are set to make up an ever-increasing proportion of the population—they also command considerable spending power and are going to be ever-more active. In these days of targeted and niche marketing, those staging G & S productions could do a lot worse than pitch for the more mature audience. When the British Conservative politician and novelist Edwina Currie remarried in 2001, she organised three theatre trips for the wedding guests: children were dispatched to *The Lion King*, those in their twenties and thirties to *Chicago*, and her own contemporaries to *The Pirates of Penzance*.

Buxton offers several pointers to the future style of G & S performance, as well as the future composition of its audience. It shows that there are now a number of amateur societies on both sides of the Atlantic which are virtually professional in both their musical and production standards. The gap between these groups and the smaller and less professional societies is likely to increase. So, more generally, is the responsibility that will fall on amateur performers to keep alive the lesser known Savoy operas as professional theatre and opera companies become ever more commercial and focused on sure-fire hits. As we have already noted, despite the perceived decline in performances over the last five decades, the amateur scene on both sides of the Atlantic is still, in fact, very buoyant and does, indeed, seem to have undergone something of a revival in the last few years.

The professional scene is also buoyant, and there seems every reason to suppose that opera companies on both sides of the Atlantic will continue to perform the more popular Savoy operas for the foreseeable future. It is also safe to predict that we are going to see G & S performed professionally in an increasing variety of styles. The success of the Essgee productions in Australia shows that there is a strong market and bright future for good updated productions in the style of Papp's *Pirates* which treat the Savoy operas like twentieth-century musicals. By contrast, the huge appreciation for Carl Rosa's recent performances in Britain, Australia, and North America show that there is also still a strong demand for traditional productions with sumptuous costumes and scenery and a large-scale chorus and orchestra. Perhaps most indicative of all in terms of future trends may be the scaled-down minimalist productions of

Opera della Luna which reinterpret the operas by concentrating on their more intimate aspects while preserving high musical standards. Compared to the blockbuster musicals which have so dominated the theatrical world of the last thirty years, Gilbert and Sullivan is intimate and minimalist. There are signs that the reign of the larger-than-life, in-your-face, gloomy-doomy mega-musical is coming to an end, not least for economic reasons. In the less extravagant and more straitened times in which we are now living, G & S in its modest and understated way may well come into its own again and appeal to producers and impresarios as a rather more attractive and less expensive option than a tour of *Miss Saigon* or *Sunset Boulevard*.

This is one of the reasons why I am basically optimistic about the future survival of Gilbert and Sullivan in a cultural climate which in many ways seems highly unpropitious and hostile. Do they really have a place in our relativist, postmodern, dumbed-down world where Big Brother and Jerry Springer rule the airwaves and where rudeness, political correctness, and celebrity status are the key cultural values? Do they have any relevance in today's Cool Britannia where the hereditary peers have been banished from the House of Lords, the office of Lord Chancellor abolished, and the accent is on the hip and the relentlessly modern? Several commentators are pessimistic about their chances of survival. The journalist Stephen Pile feels that they have 'undergone a popularity crisis' because 'Englishness has changed its nature in the past 25 years. The taste now is for tougher, coarser quips than G & S's gentlemanly humour'.[6] Andrew Crowther, for whom G & S are irredeemably tied up with a middle-class morality and intellectuality, sees little room for them now that a new dominant class has emerged with no morality or interest in matters intellectual:

> I see that these people are the future and that they threaten everything which we hold dear—civilization, money, Gilbert and Sullivan. What have they in common with the genteel witticisms which Gilbert has to offer? Not much. Can we make the Savoy operas 'relevant' to them? Can we relocate *The Mikado* among the drug users of California? Can we recast *HMS Pinafore* as a parable of promiscuous sex? Or, rather than defacing these works of art in an attempt to pander to a generation we do not understand, maybe we should accept with good grace the extinction of our way of thinking and allow the Savoy operas not to die, but to go into hibernation until some strange future tribe of savages picks among the dust and rediscovers them.[7]

I do not subscribe to this counsel of despair. The fact is that *Pinafore* has virtually been recast as a parable of promiscuous sex in the highly successful gay version. Those of us who are purists and traditionalists may not much like it, any more than we may like the fact that Steven Dexter, director of Raymond Gubbay's new production of *Pirates* which opened at the Savoy Theatre in January 2004, proclaims his main aim as being 'to bring out the sexiness in G & S's ideas'.[8] But the fact is that both these productions, aimed at a twenty-first-century mass audience, acknowledge the vitality of Gilbert and Sullivan and treat the Savoy operas as a living organism rather than a corpse. Like the other updated and reworked versions, they also point to their huge resilience and indestructibility. There will almost certainly be many more gay, self-consciously sexy, and ever-more camp productions of G & S in the future, but I suspect that there will also be many simpler, more straightforward, and, dare one say, innocent treatments, not least because they will provide a very welcome antidote to so much in our current culture. We come back to that quality of divine emollient and that indefinable but unmistakably spiritual essence which are at the heart of Gilbert and Sullivan's work and which mean, I am convinced, that they will be appreciated more than ever in the dark and uncertain times through which we are now living and which seem to lie ahead.

It would be all too easy to end this book, as so many Savoyards are wont to do, in praise of the old days which have long since passed away. It has been written from the perspective of a middle-aged man who has his full share of nostalgic memories of the glory days of the old D'Oyly Carte and the wonder and excitement of discovering Gilbert and Sullivan as a child. I want to give the last word to an eighteen-year-old girl who e-mailed me when my work was nearing completion and whose personal story confounds just about everything I have written about the gender and age bias in the appeal of G & S—and confounds it in a way which fills me with delight and hope for the future. Sarah-Jane Read saw her first Savoy opera when she was taken at the age of six to see a performance of *Pinafore* by the East Norfolk Operatic Society. She had already been introduced to the music by her mother and her grandmother, who were both keen Savoyards. She joined the Ipswich Gilbert and Sullivan Society at fifteen, becoming its youngest member, and has taken part in all its productions since. She is also a member of the Norwich G & S Appreciation Society. For her eighteenth birthday she chose to go to the Savoy Theatre to see the D'Oyly Carte *Pinafore* in preference to a party. Accompanied by her mother and grandparents, she attended the Buxton Festival in 2002 and 'we thoroughly bathed ourselves in what was on offer'.[9] As a result of the festival, she joined the Savoynet and is now an enthusiastic member.

Sarah-Jane Read lists her hobbies as 'singing G & S, playing G & S on my flute, performing G & S, scouring the charity shops for G & S memorabilia and records and searching second-hand book stores for G & S books'. Although none of her schools performed G & S, she did an arrangement of 'Three Little Maids' for three flutes and three clarinets for her GCSE music exam and for AS Level composed a tune to a poem about *The Gondoliers*. She admits that none of her school friends could be classed as G & S enthusiasts but says that 'having introduced them to G & S I have found that most of them accept it and even those that avoid classical music normally will listen to my tapes and come along to, and say they enjoy, concerts and shows that I am in—I even found one friend with my stereo listening to the Cachucha on repeat!' When trying to get friends along to a G & S show, she describes it as 'a West End musical with operatic touches'. She believes that Opera della Luna's 'fast-paced, colourful and hilariously funny productions' and Papp-style updated versions are both good ways of introducing young people to G & S.

When I asked this youthful enthusiast how she would describe G & S and its particular appeal, she had no hesitation: '100% pure fun and entertainment. G & S seem to have a song for all moods. Many is the time I have cried along to "Love Is a Plaintive Song" or "Tit Willow" or happily rejoiced with "O Happy the Lily" etc.'

I don't think anything more needs to be said. As long as people feel that life needs a touch of poetry in it, Gilbert and Sullivan will not just survive but thrive. Oh joy, oh rapture!

NOTES

APOLOGIA AND ACKNOWLEDGEMENTS

1. E-mail from J.G. Ballard to Nicholas Hopton. Quoted by permission

1. SOMETHING LINGERING

1. J. Bush Jones, *Our Musicals, Ourselves* (Brandeis University Press, Lebanon, NH, 2003), p. 11.

2. S. Morley, *Spread a Little Happiness* (Thames & Hudson, London, 1987), p. 9.

3. D. Cannadine, 'Gilbert and Sullivan' in R. Porter (ed.), *Myths of the English* (Polity, Cambridge, 1992), p. 18.

4. A. J. Lerner, *The Musical Theatre: A Celebration* (McGraw-Hill, New York, 1986), p. 26.

5. P. G. Wodehouse, *Author! Author!* (Simon and Schuster, New York, 1962), p. 15.

6. W. McBrian, *Cole Porter: A Biography* (Knopf, New York, 1998), p. 363.

7. P. Furia, *Ira Gershwin* (Oxford University Press, New York, 1996), p. 81.

8. Ibid., pp. 16–17.

9. G. Wren, *A Most Ingenious Paradox* (Oxford University Press, New York, 2001), pp. 299–300.

10. T. Rice, *Oh, What A Circus* (Hodder & Stoughton, London, 1999), p. 26.

11. Wren, *Ingenious Paradox*, p. 311.

12. Ibid., pp. 298, 304.

13. Ibid., p. 303.

14. Ibid., p. 303.

15. D. Mitchell, *Britten and Auden in the Thirties* (Faber & Faber, London, 1981), p. 170.

16. G. Wren, *Ingenious Paradox*, p. 294.

17. *Sunday Telegraph*, 22 June 2003.

18. Programme notes for Opera Australia's *Iolanthe*, 2002.

19. *Independent*, 8 February 1994.

20. *Independent*, 28 February 2000.

21. *Guardian Guide*, 28 June 2003.

22. *Daily Telegraph*, 28 February 2000.

23. *Daily Telegraph*, 29 January 2000.

24. *Sunday Times*, 27 December 1981.

25. *The Times*, 26 December 1990.

26. Letter to author, 11 June 2003.

27. D. Cannadine, 'Gilbert and Sullivan', pp. 19, 20, 22,25. An amended version of this

article is published under the title 'Tradition: Gilbert and Sullivan as a "National Institution" ' in D. Cannadine, *In Churchill's Shadow: Confronting the Past in Modern Britain* (Allen Lane, London, 2002).

28. Article in *Punch* reproduced in *Savoyard*, September 1973, pp. 18–19.
29. *Scotland on Sunday*, 19 March 2000.
30. *Savoyard*, January 1968, p. 12.
31. D. Cannadine, 'Gilbert and Sullivan' (2002 version), pp. 221–22.
32. E-mail, 3 October 2003.
33. *Gilbert & Sullivan News*, Vol. 3, No. 3 (Autumn 2001), p. 5.
34. Ibid., Vol. 3, No. 7, p. 7.
35. Ibid., p. 5.
36. Ibid., Vol. 3, No. 3, p. 11

2. A THING OF SHREDS AND PATCHES

1. *Savoyard*, January 1968, pp. 11–12.
2. *Gilbert and Sullivan Journal*, Vol. 8, No. 4 (January 1961), p. 43.
3. Report by Voice and Vision, D'Oyly Carte Archives.
4. *Savoyard*, April 1962, p. 3.
5. C. Morey, *Inclined to Dance and Sing* (Prospero Books, Chichester, 1998), p. 71.
6. Valerie Masterson in conversation with Ian Smith, Buxton, 31 July 2003.
7. D'Oyly Carte Archives.
8. Interview in 1981. The quotation is from Dodie Smith's play 'Dear Octopus'.
9. C. Morey, *Inclined to Dance*, pp. 21–22.
10. *W. S. Gilbert Society Journal*, Vol. 1, No. 2 (Autumn 1995), p. 44.
11. D'Oyly Carte Archives.
12. C. Morey, *Inclined to Dance*, p. 27; Beti Lloyd Jones interview with the author, December 1981; John Reed in conversation with Ian Smith, Buxton, 3 August 2003.
13. D'Oyly Carte Archives.
14. R. Morrell, *Kenneth Sandford* (K. Sandford, Shropshire, 1999), pp. 33–34; Kenneth Sandford in conversation with Ian Smith, Buxton, 2 August 2001.
15. 'Comes a train of D'Oyly Carte Reminiscences', Buxton, 30 July 2000.
16. John Reed in conversation with Ian Smith, Buxton, 3 August 2003.
17. Interview, December 1981.
18. *Chicago Daily News*, 22 December 1962; *Toronto Daily Star*, 29 December 1962.
19. *Gilbert and Sullivan Journal*, Vol. 9, No. 2, p. 31.
20. R. Morrell, *Kenneth Sandford*, p. 128.
21. Interview, December 1981.
22. *Savoyard*, May 1968, p. 16.
23. Interview, December 1981.
24. D'Oyly Carte Archives.
25. D'Oyly Carte Archives.
26. Conversation with Ian Smith, Buxton, 3 August 2003.
27. Light Opera Enquiry (Arts Council of Great Britain, 1981), p. 2.
28. Ibid., p. 10.
29. Ibid., p. 11.
30. Ibid., p. 11.
31. Ibid., p. 11.

32. Ibid., p. 12.

33. Ibid., p. 12.

34. Ibid., p. 13.

35. Ibid., p. 13.

36. Ibid., p. 13.

37. Arts Council Press Release, 9 February 1981.

38. *The Times*, 2 January 1981.

39. Letter from Edward Higgins, 15 February 1982.

40. P. Ziegler, *Wilson: The Authorised Life* (Weidenfeld & Nicolson, London, 1993), p. 474.

41. Interviews, December 1981; D'Oyly Carte Archives.

42. D'Oyly Carte Archives.

43. *Daily Express*, 5 March 1981.

44. Memo, August 1981, D'Oyly Carte Archives.

45. D'Oyly Carte Archives.

46. *BBC Music Magazine*, June 2003, p. 71.

47. C. Morey, *Inclined to Dance*, pp. 126–27.

3. UNFRIENDED, UNPROTECTED, AND ALONE

1. *Carte Blanche*, Vol. 1, No. 6 (May 2001), p. 2.

2. Press launch, 1 March 1988.

3. D'Oyly Carte Archives: Letter from Lord Wilson, 3 July 1987.

4. W. S. Gilbert Society Journal, Vol. 1, No. 5 (1987/88), p. 132.

5. *D'Oyly Carte News*, October 1990, p. 2.

6. Ibid., p. 4.

7. *The Times*, 10 April 1991.

8. *Sullivan Society Magazine*, Spring 1991, p. 18.

9. *DC*, No. 5 (Christmas 1992), p. 4.

10. *The Times*, 19 March 1993.

11. *Daily Telegraph*, 19 March 1993.

12. *The Stage*, 8 April 1993.

13. T. Joseph, *The D'Oyly Carte Opera Company 1875–1982* (Bunthorne Books, Bristol, 1994), p. 361.

14. G & S Archive: A Buxton Travelogue, 31 July 1994.

15. *Daily Telegraph*, 21 March 1995.

16. *Parliamentary Debates* (Commons), Vol. 282, 24 July 1996, col. 292.

17. *The Times*, 19 December 1996.

18. *Parliamentary Debates* (Commons), Vol. 309, 1 April 1998, col. 1196.

19. Ibid., col. 1198.

20. Ibid., col. 1203.

21. Ibid., col. 1212.

22. Ibid., cols. 1207, 1210.

23. Ibid., col. 1214.

24. Hilary Tange, *Gilbert and Sullivan News*, Vol. 2, No. 13 (Autumn 1998), p. 9.

25. Letter from James Lewis, *Daily Telegraph*, 18 May 2001.

26. *The Times*, 23 February 2002.

27. Irene Salter, *Carte Blanche*, Vol. 1, No. 10 (September 2002), p. 4.

28. Interview with author, 2 September 2003.

29. *Metro* (Scottish edition), 31 October 2000, p. 17.

30. Peter Parker, *Gilbert and Sullivan News*, Vol. 3, No. 5 (Summer 2002), p. 17.

31. *Sunday Telegraph*, 12 January 2003.

32. Interview with author, 2 September 2003.

4. VIRTUE IS TRIUMPHANT ONLY IN THEATRICAL PERFORMANCES

1. *Gilbert and Sullivan News*, Vol. 11, No. 17 (Spring 2000), p. 10; *Gilbert and Sullivan Journal*, Vol. V3, No. 7 (January 1962), p. 94; Vol. V3, No. 8 (May 1962), p. 105.

2. Interview with Albert Bergeret, Scranton, Pennsylvania, 14 November 2003.

3. Quoted in *Gilbert and Sullivan News*, Vol. 11, No. 8 (March 1997), p. 4.

4. Quoted in *The Times*, 23 December 1981.

5. Interview with George Walker, May 1981.

6. *The Mikado* (Sir Arthur Sullivan Society, 1985), p. 4.

7. *The Times, Daily Telegraph, Financial Times*, 16 November 1992.

8. *Gilbert and Sullivan News*, November 1992, p. 13; *Sullivan Society Magazine*, No. 37 (Spring 1993), p. 15.

9. *Toronto Globe and Mail*, 6 March 1994.

10. This and subsequent remarks by Jeff Clarke and members of the Opera della Luna company are from a conversation with the author in Buxton on 28 July 2003. The comments by audience members are from letters and e-mails sent to Jeff Clarke.

11. Peter Mulloy's remarks are from a conversation with the author in Buxton on 2 August 2003.

12. Flyer, September 2003

5. MASCULINE INSECTS WITH THE MORALS OF A METHODIST

1. 'Naughty Victorians', *New York Times Book Review*, 12 August 1996.

2. Interview in Buxton, 28 July 2003.

3. 'Gilbert's sour note spoils the hum factor', *Daily Telegraph*, 28 February 2000.

4. Conversation in Buxton, 28 July 2003.

5. D'Oyly Carte Opera Company Press Release, 1 March 1988.

6. Andrew Nicklin in conversation with Ian Smith, Buxton, 29 August 2003.

7. T. Joseph, *The D'Oyly Carte Opera Company, 1875–1982*, p. 325.

8. Ibid., p. 325.

9. Ibid., p. 314, and conversation with author, 14 November 2003.

10. Mel Moratti's website (http://homepages.ihug.co.nz/~melbear/home.htm).

11. Conversation at Buxton, 28 July 2003.

12. G. Gordon, *Aren't We Due A Royalty Statement?* (Chatto & Windus, London, 1993), p. 11.

13. P. Medawar, *Memoir of a Thinking Radish* (Oxford University Press, Oxford, 1986), pp. 29–30.

14. Text of lecture at symposium, Buxton Festival, 1999.

15. *Church Times*, 17 November 1995.

16. Ibid., 12 July 2002.

17. Quoted in D'Oyly Carte programme for 1979–80 season.

18. J. Bush Jones, *Our Musicals, Ourselves*, p. 220.

19. *Daily Telegraph*, 15 May 2001.

20. Article in *Punch* reproduced in *Savoyard*, September 1973, pp. 18–19.

21. Foreword to R. Wilson and F. Lloyd, *Gilbert & Sullivan: The D'Oyly Carte Years* (Weidenfeld & Nicolson, London, 1984), p. 7.

22. P. Ziegler, *Wilson*, pp. 7, 47. *The Times*, 25 May 1995.

23. C. Reid, *Malcolm Sargent—A Biography* (Hodder & Stoughton, London, 1968), p. 43.

24. Ibid., p. 58.

25. Ibid., p. 94.

26. Ibid., p. 25.

27. M. Seabrook, *Max* (Victor Gollancz, London, 1994), p. 16.

28. *Savoyard*, January 1968, p. 10.

29. www.westhollywood.com, 23 September 2001.

30. *The Times*, 20 May 1964.

6. AMATEUR TENORS SING CHORUSES IN PUBLIC

1. 'Dainty Little Fairies: Women, Gender, and the Savoy Operas', *Women's History Review*, Vol. 9, No. 2, 2000, p. 345.

2. Ibid., p. 362.

3. J. A. Young, *A Century of Service—The National Operatic and Dramatic Association* (NODA, London, 1997), p. 3.

4. Typescript account of the conception and birth of the G & S Fellowship by H. W. Bickle.

5. Ibid. This was made available to me by Pauline Smith, the fellowship's archivist.

6. *History of Rose Hill Methodist Church* (privately printed, 1972), p. 37.

7. Letter to the author, 2 September 1997.

8. *Church Times*, December 1999.

9. *Scotsman*, 24 March 2001.

10. VLOG Notes, Vol. 4, No.12 (June 1999).

11. *New York Times*, 13 August 2000.

12. Interview in Buxton, August 1996.

13. Interview in Buxton, 8 August 2003.

14. 'Dainty Little Fairies', p. 351.

15. Interview in Buxton, August 1996.

16. V. Allan, 'We are the crew of the Pinafore', *Scotland on Sunday*, 19 March 2000.

17. Programme notes for Opera Australia's *Gondoliers*, 2002.

18. Programme notes, North Toronto Players *Mikado*, 1991.

19. Interview in Buxton, August 2003.

20. Information from David Packman.

21. D. Dew, *On Song and Story* (1998), privately published, Oundle, p. 16.

22. Letter to author, 26 February 2003.

23. *Scotland on Sunday*, 19 March 2000.

24. P. Bathurst, *Here's a Pretty Mess* (Romansmead Publications, Chichester, 1998), pp. 10, 105, 198, 239.

25. Conversations in Buxton, August 2003.

26. *W. S. Gilbert Society Journal*, Vol. 1, No. 9 (Summer 1997), p. 271.

27. Interview in Buxton, August 1996.

28. Interview in Buxton, August 1996.

29. I. Taylor, 'Whither G & S?—A Centenary Appraisal', *NODA Bulletin*, Vol. 34, No. 2 (February 1975), pp. 23–25.

30. R. Morrell, *Kenneth Sandford*, p. 49.

31. E-mail, 24 February 2004.

32. Conversation in Philadelphia, November 2003.

33. Conversation in Buxton, August 2003.

34. Interview in Buxton, August 1996.

35. E-mail, 30 November 2003

7. IN THIS COLLEGE, USEFUL KNOWLEDGE

1. *Savoyard*, May 1966, p. 8.

2. Ibid., p. 9.

3. Ibid., p. 12.

4. Ibid., p. 13.

5. NODA Bulletin, October 1973.

6. These and subsequent quotations are from 'A Source of Innocent Merriment', talk given at Buxton Festival, August 1999.

7. 'Victorian Values', *Music Teacher*, September 1999, p. 29. See also Susan Elkin's article 'Oh for a song to sing O!' in *The Times*, 23 November 1992 and 'Operetta's better', *The Stage*, 22 October 1998.

8. *The Stage*, 10 October 1996.

9. Programme notes for production of *HMS Pinafore*, Buxton Festival 2001.

10. E-mail from Andrea Atherton, 9 November 2003.

11. Interview, Bridgewater College, 18 November 2003.

12. Interview, Buxton, August 1996.

13. Interviews, Buxton, August 1996.

14. Interview, Scranton, 14 November 2003.

15. Interview, Buxton, August 1996.

16. *Varsity*, 18 February 2001.

17. Interview, Yale, 11 November 2003.

18. Interview, Buxton, 8 August 2003.

19. Interview, Buxton, 10 August 2003.

20. Interview, Buxton, 8 August 2003.

8. THINGS ARE SELDOM WHAT THEY SEEM

1. *Sunday Times*, 28 February 1993.

2. I owe this reference to Robert Wardell.

3. *Gilbert and Sullivan News*, Vol. 2, No. 18 (Summer 2000), p. 15.

4. *The Tablet*, September 1993.

5. *Daily Telegraph*, 31 March 2001.

6. *Financial Times*, 13 May 1985.

7. *Guardian*, 11 October 1996.

8. Quoted in *Precious Nonsense*, December 1991.

9. The hymn 'A Man Set Out to Build Himself a Tower' was first published by Stainer & Bell in *Hymns and Congregational Songs*, Vol. 2, No. 3 (December 1991), pp. 22–24.

10. *Washington Post*, 25 March 1986.

11. *Richmond Times-Dispatch*, 24 January 1993.

12. *Financial Times, Daily Telegraph,* 9 April 2001.

13. *South Florida Sun-Sentinel,* 18 January 2003.

14. Quoted by permission of the Flanders and Swann Estates.

15. *The Anna Russell Song Book* (Elek Books, London, 1960), pp. 18–37 .

16. I owe this reference to Stephen Turnbull.

9. MAINTAINING WITH NO LITTLE HEAT THEIR VARIOUS OPINIONS

1. *Gilbert & Sullivan Journal,* vol. 9, No. 21 (September 1972), p. 436.

2. E-mail, 16 December 2003.

3. D. Eden, *Gilbert & Sullivan: The Creative Conflict* (Associated University Presses, Cranbury, NJ, 1986), pp. 53, 71.

4. *W. S. Gilbert Society Journal,* Vol. 2, No. 12 (Spring 2001), p. 359.

5. The discovery of the Thespis ballet music is discussed in an article in the *Sullivan Society Magazine,* No. 30 (Summer 1990), pp. 5–15 and 'Forty years of *Thespis* scholarship' in an article in the same journal, No. 55 (Autumn 2002), pp. 12–43 .

6. E-mail, 4 December 2003.

7. Interview in Buxton, August 2003.

10. PEEP WITH SECURITY INTO FUTURITY

1. G & S Archive, 31 July 1994.

2. These and subsequent remarks by Ian Smith are from conversations with the author at various occasions in Buxton in 1996, 2001, and 2003.

3. These and subsequent remarks by Neil Smith are from a conversation with the author in Halifax, 5 December 2003.

4. Contribution to Savoynet, 21 February 2004.

5. A. Goodman, *Gilbert and Sullivan's London* (Parapress, London, 1988), p. 49.

6. 'G & S in good company', *Daily Telegraph,* 21 March 1995.

7. 'We are going to abolish it in England'—typescript of talk delivered in Buxton, August 2003.

8. *Guardian,* 10 January 2004.

9. These and the following quotations are from e-mail to the author, 12 October 2003.

INDEX